James Fraser

University and Other Sermons

James Fraser

University and Other Sermons

ISBN/EAN: 9783337087388

Printed in Europe, USA, Canada, Australia, Japan

Cover: Foto ©Lupo / pixelio.de

More available books at **www.hansebooks.com**

UNIVERSITY AND OTHER SERMONS

AND OTHER

SERMONS

BY THE
RIGHT REV. JAMES FRASER, D.D.
Second Bishop of Manchester

EDITED BY
JOHN W. DIGGLE, M.A.
VICAR OF MOSSLEY HILL, LIVERPOOL
AUTHOR OF "GODLINESS AND MANLINESS," ETC.

ΑΠΟΘΑΝΩΝ ΕΤΙ ΛΑΛΕΙΤΑΙ

London
MACMILLAN AND CO.
AND NEW YORK
1887

The Right of Translation and Reproduction is Reserved.

RICHARD CLAY AND SONS,
LONDON AND BUNGAY.

PREFACE

The Sermons in this volume divide themselves into two separate portions; each portion being arranged with a view to chronological order. The first portion consists of seventeen Sermons preached, upon various occasions, during the term of Bishop Fraser's Episcopate. Ten of the seventeen were preached before the University of Oxford; one before the Nottingham Church Congress; one at the re-opening of Chester Cathedral; one in Manchester Cathedral, before the British Medical Association; one in York Minster, before the British Association; one at St. Andrew's Church, Holborn; two in Westminster Abbey. Moreover, of the ten Sermons preached before the University of Oxford, five were also preached in Westminster Abbey, and one before the University of Cambridge.

The second portion of the volume consists of five Sermons preached in Bishop Fraser's earlier days; although the last of the five—Christ the Healer—was preached upon several occasions after his call to the Episcopate. The Bishop's sympathies were doubtless enriched, and his way of thinking, as well as of expressing his thoughts, wonderfully ennobled by his contact with the masses of toiling humanity in Lancashire; yet the deep, broad, lofty, practical utterances which signalized his conspicuous episcopal ministry, had signalized also his secluded parochial ministry. His entire teaching, from its commencement to its close, flowed from the fountains of intense communion with God and intense fellowship with his brother men.

THE VICARAGE, MOSSLEY HILL, LIVERPOOL,
St. Matthew's Day, September 21st, 1887.

CONTENTS.

I.
ABRAHAM 1

II.
CHRIST, THE TRUE JOSEPH 18

III.
MYSTERIES 29

IV.
SOME CHURCH PROBLEMS IN THE NINETEENTH CENTURY . 41

V.
RESPONSIBILITY 55

VI.
THE EVIDENTIAL VALUE OF MIRACLES 67

VII.
CATHEDRALS: THEIR USE AND ABUSE 83

VIII.
THINGS HARD TO BE UNDERSTOOD 97

IX.
PAUL BEFORE FELIX; OR, THE MORAL BASIS OF CHRISTIANITY 118

CONTENTS.

X.
DEBORAH 137

XI.
THE WORD OF LIFE 154

XII.
IMMORTALITY 167

XIII.
RIGHTEOUSNESS 183

XIV.
INFLUENCE OF CHARACTER ON INTELLECTUAL PROGRESS . 204

XV.
RELIGION AND SCIENCE 213

XVI.
THE GIFT OF PROPHECY THE SUPREME NEED OF OUR AGE 225

XVII.
THE GOSPEL AND THE MASSES 236

XVIII.
THE MIGHTINESS OF REDEMPTION 248

XIX.
ST. ANDREW 263

XX.
THE DIVINE CALL AND THE HUMAN CALLING 275

XXI.
THE REVELATION OF GOD'S LOVE THE DISTINCTIVE CHARACTERISTIC OF THE GOSPEL 288

XXII.
CHRIST, THE HEALER 300

UNIVERSITY SERMONS.

I.

THE TYPICAL PERSONS OF THE PENTATEUCH: THEIR MESSAGE TO THE CHURCH IN ALL AGES.

I.—ABRAHAM.

"Know ye therefore that they which are of faith, the same are the children of Abraham. And the scripture, foreseeing that God would justify the heathen through faith, preached before the gospel unto Abraham, saying, In thee shall all nations be blessed. So then they which be of faith are blessed with faithful Abraham."—GALATIANS iii. 7—9.

THE principle of typology, it must be confessed, stands in need of justification; and the adoption of this mode of interpreting Scripture has been, by some theologians, so profuse, so indiscriminate, and so extravagant as to throw a slur upon the principle itself, and to indispose minds of a critical and philosophic order to the reception of any teaching based upon what they consider to be such illusive ground. Even a pious purpose cannot be allowed to justify an unsound deduction.

"What mean you," we are scornfully asked, "by these *typical men*; men made, so to speak, to order; cut out and shaped after a pattern; stereotyped in every thought and action down to the most insignificant; set, as it were, immovably in the block; mere painted pictures; automata, moving only at another's will; their whole life, therefore, a *mechanical* result; and so capable of meaning whatever the artist who designed it might choose that it *should* mean: but a result, judging by the processes we experience in ourselves and believe to take place in others, utterly impossible under the conditions of moral existence: at variance too, with all that common sense, and science, and Scripture unitedly attest to be the normal phenomenon of humanity?"

Such a theory, if it were what were really held, of the typical relationship between one human being and another, whether human or divine, or between a human being and a dispensation, would be incredible and therefore untenable. If Adam, Noah, Abraham, were living historical men, they were not, they could not be, types in the *mechanical* sense—as a mere external act or ceremony might be, the sprinkling of the blood of the Paschal Lamb on the doorposts, or the propitiatory rites of the Great Day of Atonement—nor even in the *etymological* sense, as impressions struck off with hard, defined outlines from a fixed die or mould. They must have been "types" in a higher, freer, diviner, idealised meaning of the word.

They were "types" in the region of mind, not of matter; of moral and spiritual laws and workings, not of physical; "types" of the law of liberty which, operate in what matter it will, is still a law of uniformity. It is the Pauline sense of the word, as when he tells the Romans that Adam was a "type" of Him that was to come; or, philosophising history to the Corinthians, teaches them that all that happened to Israel in the wilderness were "types" written for our admonition: or bids the Philippians walk as they had him for a "type"; or exhorts Timothy to be a "type" to the believers; or praises the integrity of the faith of the Thessalonians, that they were "types" to all that believed in Macedonia and Achaia. A type that is sought, not in a single isolated act, but in the whole career of a living human being, making him a *pattern* to after generations of the power of divine grace and the possibilities of human nature, must be a type governed by human, that is, moral or spiritual laws, and cannot consist in mere symbolism—mere literal, physical conformity.

There is a phrase of St. Paul which appears to me to imply these ideas. It was God the Father's purpose, says the Apostle, in the dispensation of the fulness of time " to gather together in one all things in Christ, both things in heaven and things on earth," that so, as he teaches the Colossians, He might be not only the "image of the invisible God," but the "first born of every creature."

The force of the Greek word ἀνακεφαλαιώσασθαι is very inadequately rendered by the expression "to gather together in one." That is a vague phrase, and the Greek word is a most precise one, meaning "to bring to a head," "to collect as in a focus," "to sum up in an organic whole" what has before been dispersed, disjointed, dismembered, spread over a wide surface; "to recapitulate," as the Latins call it; to reproduce to the eye, or ear, or understanding, in a compact, complete, living way, that which before had been fragmentary, partial, disconnected, apparently incongruous, or separated in its parts by long intervals of place or time. Thus the Gospel was the ἀνακεφαλαίωσις of all previous revelations—" the dispensation of the fulness of time;" and Christ was the ἀνακεφαλαίωσις of all previous manifestations of the power of grace in the soul of man.

In Him they were reproduced, summed up, harmonised, developed, culminated. He was "the first-born of every creature." "Things," says Aristotle, "which are philosophically, and in the order of ideas, first; naturally, and in the order of time, are last." Jesus Christ, in the perfection of His human nature, and not Adam, was the archetypical idea of man. Adam was conformed to Him, not He to Adam. He was the type, the mould, the pattern-form. They that were saints and heroes did but take off the impression of His saintliness and heroism, as clearly as the coarser clay of which they were fashioned allowed its outlines to be seen. And so they were as shadows in the morning, projected before the body which generated them, whose outline they represent, and whose approach they herald, but which contract themselves more and more, and are finally absorbed, when the sun reaches his noonday height, and pours down in a direct ray his glory upon the earth.

Thus the principle of typology, even when applied to the whole life of a human being, is relieved from all just exceptions, and the simplest justification of it is also the truest. For it stands upon the relationship which may be claimed to exist between Christ the Head of the Church, and those who have belonged to His mystical body in every age. This relationship, issuing as it does from the verity of His human nature, rests upon the great philosophical dogma of the immutability of the laws—that is, of the will and purposes—of God.

These laws, which are simply the expression of His will, determined by the essential attributes of His character, are as unchanged and unchangeable in the moral and spiritual, as in the physical, world. The phenomenon which complicates the question here, and renders it philosophically inexplicable under our present conditions of thought, is that, in the moral world you have free agents, exercising their freedom, and by that exercise fashioning their character and their destiny, under a system of necessary and immutable laws.

So, when we speak of typical men, we mean those whom the conscience, the divine instinct within, recognises as the ideals of humanity, illustrating the capacities of the race, showing in what infinite variety both of ways and of degree the natural man may become spiritual, and the heirs of a fallen nature may once again become partakers of the divine.

"The types of the Book of Genesis," says an ingenious and pious writer, "exhibit God's great dispensational purposes and the course appointed for man's development." By the phrase "dispensational purposes," he means "the mode in which God, at various periods since the Fall, has dealt with man, in different degrees of intimacy, and in a certain sense, also on different principles." "Throughout all He has had one purpose in view—to reveal what He is, and to show what man is; but this one end has been brought about in different ways and under various repeated trials."

I demur, however, to the statement that in the course of this development the Creator has dealt with the creature even "in a certain sense," on different principles. The outward manifestation of the principle may have been different, but the inward power and energy of it have been the same. The God of the Old Testament is the God also of the New. The proclamation of the name of the Lord to Moses on Mount Sinai—"the Lord, the Lord God, merciful and gracious, long-suffering and abundant in goodness and truth, keeping mercy for thousands, forgiving iniquity, transgression, and sin; yet that will by no means clear the guilty, visiting the iniquity of the fathers upon the children and upon the children's children unto the third and fourth generation"—is as true now as it was then.

The God of the Jews, says St. Paul, is also the God of the Gentiles. Faith is the condition of justification to 'the circumcision' and 'the uncircumcision.' "The righteousness of God manifested without the law;" rather perhaps should it have been translated, "manifested without an accompanying code of rules," embodied in a Divine Person, was yet "witnessed by the law and the prophets" (Romans iii. 21).

"God," says the text, "preached the Gospel to Abraham." The very oath sworn to him by his Maker was, according to the Epistle to the Hebrews, designed to show to the heirs of promise, down the whole stream of time, the immutability of God's counsels. God forbid, cries St. Paul, that any one should think that the law—the schoolmaster who was to bring us to Christ—was against the promises of God. Though the sanctions of the two covenants might be different—a circumstance which does not in the least affect the moral obligation—the terms on which they dealt with man were the same. This development may be more complete, more uniform, more equable, more progressive, under the Gospel than under the law, but the direction of that development was ever, if not consciously towards Christ, at least towards Christianity. "Your father Abraham rejoiced to see My day," said Christ, "and he saw it and was glad."

And so these men, living under what we sometimes call "another dispensation," and certainly surrounded by very different circumstances, may yet be regarded as typical. They have their message for us "on whom the ends of the world are come." "They sought a country," a brighter, better land than any which their feet had ever trod, or on which their eye had ever rested. "They died in faith," "confessing themselves strangers and pilgrims," "persuaded of the promises" and embracing them, though they never actually received them—indeed, they seemed ever to retreat from their yearning gaze. Even now they are waiting with us for their perfection. Even now their impatience, perchance, has to be quelled, like that of the souls seen beneath the altar, who cried with a loud voice, "How long?" They must rest yet for a little season until the number of their fellow-servants is fulfilled, and the better thing revealed, which God is providing for both us and them.

And of this patient, saintly, faithful band, who being dead yet seem to speak—the cloud of witnesses by whom we are compassed about as we run our Christian race—Abraham is the foremost figure. It is with him that we shall sit down to eat meat in the kingdom of God. In his bosom they that sleep in Jesus find a resting-place. In the steps of his faith we are to walk. The Israel of God are "the seed of Abraham, His friend."

This man's life-story must have something in it that it concerns Christians of every age to know. Three chief features strike me as prominent and characteristic—the way, namely, in which it illustrates

(1) What faith is.

(2) What it is to walk by faith.

(3) What it is, with the eye of such faith, to see Christ's day.

(1) It was evidently *the faith* of Abraham that so attracted and riveted the interest of St. Paul. To the Apostle of the Gentiles, the Hebrew pilgrim, dwelling even in the land of promise as in a strange country, is the great type of what it is to believe in God, to possess a faith which shall be counted for righteousness, not "*instead* of righteousness" (as though it had been ἀντὶ δικαιοσύνης): but εἰς δικαιοσύνην, as that which con-

stituted, or was put to the account of, his righteousness (Romans iv. 5).

And so Abraham, to the eye of St. Paul, before and above any other saint in the annals of his race, is the representative of the *nature* of faith, and of its *power*: faith, not as opposed to reason—for faith must be rational, or it degenerates into fanaticism or credulity—but as opposed to sight. Faith, not so much a function or faculty of the intellect, as a posture or condition of the will: moral in its nature rather than intellectual; "casting down imaginations and every high thing that exalteth itself against the knowledge of God, and bringing into captivity every thought to the obedience of Christ."

Never, perhaps, was there a time in the history of the Church of Christ in which there was greater need to ascertain carefully what this typical faith of our father Abraham was. It was not the acceptance of a highly-developed, articulated creed. It was not the investiture of the act of worship with an elaborate ceremonial symbolism. It was not a fanatical conception of the media through which the spirit of man seeks, and finds, communion with the Spirit of God. The simple Bible record of it is, "Abraham *believed God;*" and "it was counted to him for righteousness," because his whole life was the continued evidence of the reality of his faith. It was not *perfect*, but it was *real*. It rested on the simplest verities—on the providence of God and His sovereignty, His rewarding those that diligently seek Him, the efficacy of prayer, the reasonableness and the comfort of worship—these, and little more than these truths and practices, made up Abraham's creed, his religion.

Some have thought that revelations were made to Abraham which would have enabled him to see as far into the purposes of God as did St. John or St. Paul; and particularly that after the averted sacrifice on Mount Moriah the whole mystery of Calvary was unrolled before his eyes—that this is the sense in which 'he saw Christ's day.' We will try to discover presently whether there may not be a more congruous interpretation of our Lord's word than this. Suffice it to say now that all this is mere assumption, foisted into the Scripture record, not only gratuitously, but utterly marring the proportions, and structure, and development of the revelation of God's purposes to man. It is not only a vain invention; it is an anachronism.

No; the merit of Abraham's faith lay not so much in the *breadth* as in the intensity of its view; not so much in its comprehensive grasp of the whole scheme of God, as in its deep persuasion of the duty of man. It was the faith of a saint rather than of a theologian. So was it also in the older and better days of Christendom. The faith that could remove mountains—and there was a grace even higher than that—was simply the intense energy of a soul throwing the whole force of its being upon the promises of God. The condition of the Saviour's putting forth His healing power was, "Believe only and thou shalt be made whole." When the Ethiopian eunuch asked his Heaven-sent Teacher whether, through the mystic instrument of the new birth he might enter into the "better covenant" with God, Philip said, "If thou believest with all thine heart thou mayest;" and he answered and said, "I believe that Jesus Christ is the Son of God." When St. Paul proclaims the word of faith which he preached, it is simply this: "If thou shalt confess with thy mouth the Lord Jesus, and shalt believe in thine heart that God hath raised Him from the dead, thou shalt be saved." The Gospel that he delivered to the Corinthians, wherein they stood, by which also they were saved, contained expressly only three grand articles—"how that Christ died for our sins according to the Scriptures, and that He was buried, and that He rose again the third day" (1 Cor. xv. 1—4).

I know, of course, what is *involved* in these grand, simple utterances of primitive faith, but I am dealing only with what is *expressed*. The implicated truths are not formulated: the inferential dogmas are not authoritatively imposed. It seems to have been the purpose of the Church in her earliest and best days to make men religious rather than theological; to limit, rather than to extend, the field of authoritative dogma: to discourage speculative, gnostic tendencies; and to win her way against those that opposed themselves rather by the power of living convictions and saintly graces, than by the canons of councils, and the elaboration of creeds.

A simple, earnest faith in the mission and work of Christ; a deep profound consciousness of the sinfulness of man, and of his need of something beyond himself to lift him out of the mire; a strong conviction that God is ever to be found by those that seek Him, and that He will, "with every temptation make a way of escape," that He is the believer's "shield and exceeding great reward"; and a consistent endeavour to walk before Him in perfectness, as One to whom we owe the best service of our lives—this, or something like this, would be the faith of Abraham illuminated by the light of the Gospel; adapted to the phenomena of the revelation which has thrown a fresh tint over the life that "now is as well as on that which is to come." Sure I feel that it is faith enough to be "counted" to us "for righteousness"; faith enough to fix our hopes "on the city which hath foundations"; faith enough to sustain us under earthly trials and disappointments, "as seeing Him who is invisible."

(2) A consistent endeavour to frame the life so as to be in accordance with these convictions, so that what we *are* should be an expression to others of what we *believe*—avoiding the greatest of moral contradictions, the spiritual state which has the "form of godliness" but is dead to its power—this is what the Apostle means by "walking by faith and not by sight"; being "saved by hope"; living with the eye fixed, not on the things which are "seen and temporal," but on the things which are "unseen, and eternal."

The faith of Abraham is the sufficient account of all the moral phenomena of his character: of his obedience, his unselfishness, his courage, his generosity, his placableness, his patience, his power of self-surrender. He seems never to have needed to sit down first and count the cost of what he was about to do. The divine instinct of his faith in God superseded the necessity of all such laborious calculations. To him, the Almighty God—the Lord who had provided and would still provide, the God who had listened to his intercessory prayer, and remembered him when He destroyed the cities of the plain and spared Lot for his sake, the Great Being with whom he had entered into covenant —was not a mere name, had not been petrified into a conventionalism, nor become a metaphysical abstraction. He was *his* God; a constant source of strength and energy; the God before whom he lived and who was with him in all that he did.

It was a faith almost evangelical in its nature. It stretched far beyond the horizon of this present world. It never looked back; it was always looking forward. His whole life declared plainly, as the author of the Epistle to the Hebrews testifies, that "he sought not the country from which he came out," to which he might have returned, but that "he desired a better country—that is, an heavenly"; "wherefore God was not ashamed to be called his God, for He prepared for him a city."

(3) Seeking God's blessing, not as his children were taught by Moses to seek it, in the fruit of his body, nor in the fruit of his cattle, nor in the fruit of his ground, but "in the joy and peace of believing"; in the precious gift of a "conscience void of offence towards God and towards men"; realising the higher life of the Spirit, and leaving it to others to quarrel about pasture-lands and flocks and herds, do we find the evangelical temper of his faith. Not in any fancied anticipatory

revelation of the great mystery of godliness, afterwards to be wrought out by Him who, when He came to deliver man, "took not on Him the nature of angels, but the seed of Abraham"; but in this higher and more natural sense, I conceive we are to understand that this great saint of God "rejoiced to see the day of Christ, and saw it, and was glad." He saw it, not at one particular place, nor at one particular time; not only on Mount Moriah, when "in a figure" he had received his only-begotten son from the dead, but all his life through—wherever he pitched his tent, and built his altar, and waited patiently for the promise, and found himself strong from his trust in God.

For what is "Christ's day" but that measure of knowledge of the will of God which it is our privilege to enjoy, and those opportunities of access to Him which all have, though all may not use? Even to us who live in the middle of that day, the light can be called neither clear nor dark. The knowledge is partial and fragmentary; the view is "through a glass" and full of riddles ($\dot{\epsilon}\nu$ $\alpha\dot{\iota}\nu\dot{\iota}\gamma\mu\alpha\tau\iota$): the hopes, but not the eyes, enter into that which is within the veil. And just so, with less precise knowledge perhaps, but perhaps also with even intenser insight, fared Abraham.

What does Christ do for those who consciously live in the light of this day? He lifts them up from earth to heaven; "sets their affections on things above"; helps them to understand what that meaneth—"Ye are dead, and your life is hid with Christ in God."

It must have been the same influence, the same divine light, which guided the steps of Abraham when he left house, and substance, and friends, at what he believed to be the bidding of God, and went out a homeless wanderer, "not knowing whither he went": that let Lot have the best of the land, instead of going to a judge and saying, "Bid my brother divide the inheritance with me": that waited those five and twenty years "because he knew Him faithful that had promised": and, clearest instance of all, that taught him on Mount Moriah that sublime lesson of self-sacrifice which can cheerfully surrender everything to the even suspected will of God.

And so when the blessed Jesus would reprove the eye-service and hypocrisy of those "who honoured God with their lips, while their heart was far from Him," He can find no more effective contrast by which to set forth the hollowness of such service than the faithful Abraham "rejoicing to see His day." They might be Abraham's natural seed, these hypocritical worshippers, but they were not Abraham's spiritual children. They might call Abraham their father, but they did not the works of Abraham. They thought it impossible that they could ever lose their spiritual prerogatives; but they were told that God, if He pleased, could even of the stones of the highway "raise up children unto Abraham."

The Psalmist's account of the forfeiture by the Israelites of their spiritual privileges, and their gradual degeneration as a people, is "that their heart was not whole with God"; and so "they continued not steadfast in His covenant." Abraham was a marked contrast to his posterity in this respect. If ever there was a man whose heart might be called *whole* with God, it was he: more so certainly than David: more so perhaps even than Moses. It was the special characteristic quality of his faith: its entirety, its roundness, its complete submission to the will of God. Do not dwell on its few specks and flaws, on its equivocation in the courts of Pharaoh and Abimelech, on its impatience evidenced by the marriage with Hagar: reckon its triumphs, its achievements. The Bible, with its rare truthfulnesss, portrays the whole man for us, in his strength and in his weakness, and, as ever, that "strength made perfect in weakness."

No character drawn in Holy Writ seems to be the property of all time more than he. There is nothing Jewish about him; nothing local; nothing essential that can be called the product of his age, the result of his peculiar circumstances. He is a grand, statuesque type of the grace of faith: faith in its essence rather than in its development: faith in the power, the providence, the sovereignty of God. Alas! how much more truly did he see Christ's day than we see it! How much nearer did he reach the measure of the stature of Christ's fulness than we can! How far beyond our poor attainments was he penetrated with that transcendent Christian grace which "believeth all things, hopeth all things, endureth all things, and finally, never fails."

In the inquisitive temper of a realistic age, an interest has been re-awakened in the Hebrew patriarch's grave. To have visited the mausoleum at Hebron is one of the achievements of Eastern travel. There, in their sepulchres, though in outward form strangely different from that natural cave "in the end of Ephron's field" where first their bones were laid—cave and field and trees having long since disappeared—there still lies the dust of Abraham, and Sarah, and Isaac, and Jacob, "the heirs with him of the same promise." It hardly needs a visit to the tomb to realise the lesson it conveys. "Of illustrious men," said the great Athenian statesman, "every land is the sepulchre." The grave of Abraham is dear even to those who count not their descent from him. Standing in imagination, reverently before either the memory of his life or the sepulchre of his dust, our hearts are kindled with the single thought of the conquering might of true and living faith. "The victory," cries one who himself had proved its power, "the victory that overcometh the world is faith" (1 St. John v. 4).

Preached—St. Mary's, Oxford, March 18, 1870.

II.

THE TYPICAL PERSONS OF THE PENTATEUCH: THEIR MESSAGE TO THE CHURCH IN ALL AGES.

II.—CHRIST, THE TRUE JOSEPH.

"The good of all the land of Egypt is yours."—GENESIS xlv. 20.

THE questions to which I invite your attention are, (1) What is the true principle of interpretation to be applied to a particular class of so-called "types;" and (2) What is the relation in which Christ's people have a right to consider themselves as standing to that outer world, which in some schools of theology is described as "their spiritual enemy"; and in all schools is allowed to be the sphere of their trial.

(1) In what sense do we use the words, when caught by, and gazing on, some old saintly or heroic character, whose deeds are chronicled in the history of the people of God, we say instinctively, "Here is a plain type of the Lord Jesus Christ?" He Who first by His bodily presence and counsel, and afterwards, and still, by the Spirit Whom He sent, "comforted His Church;" He, the Preacher of an evangelical righteousness, is the *true*

Noah. He, Who from the post of glory on His throne in heaven, is "not ashamed to call us brethren;" Who feeds us with His hidden sustenance through years of drought and famine; Who makes our homes glad for us in the days of our pilgrimage, is the *true Joseph*. He Who is the Mediator of the New Covenant is the *true Moses*: the Apostle and High Priest of our profession, the true *Aaron*: the Captain of our salvation, the true *Joshua*: in Whom are hid, and not hid only, but to Whom are imparted, all the treasures of wisdom and knowledge, the true *Solomon*: out of whose loins, as it were, springs renewed, restored, regenerated humanity, the Second *Adam*. What do we mean by this manner of speaking? What sort of relation between type and antitype do our words imply?

For, mark you, it is quite a different thing from saying that the Paschal Lamb, or the Scape Goat, or the High Priest's "going once a year into the Holiest of all to make Atonement for the sins of the people," were types of Christ, or of corresponding acts of Christ. That a ceremony, an institution, or even a prescribed and formal human act, in which freewill is not concerned, and which therefore could be moulded and fashioned after any rule, or (in the hands of Omniscience) for any purpose—that things like these should be typical and prefigurative, and should shadow out the outlines of a coming and better dispensation, is possible enough and intelligible enough. But the fact is placed under altogether different conditions—is removed, indeed, into another department of thought, and as it seems to me, has to be interpreted by a different principle, when we take such a wonderfully complex organism as a living, thinking, free-acting man, and set him up and say, " Mark that man, and read his history well ; for he is a sign of things that shall be hereafter."

" Whatsoever things are true," says the Gospel's most renowned preacher, "whatsoever things are honest, whatsoever things are just, whatsoever things are pure, whatsoever things are lovely, whatsoever things are of good report ; if there be any virtue, if there be any praise—think on these things." Think of them as exhibited one by one—by each man according to the measure of his gift—in the saints of old. Think of them as the diadem of grace that crowned the head of Him to whom the Father "gave not the Spirit by measure;" "Who was made flesh and dwelt among us" that we might behold what is indeed "the glory of the only-begotten of the Father;" Who made for Himself one glorious crown of all these precious jewels, and set it upon His head that all men might behold its beauty, and Who now weareth it on His throne in the heavenly place for evermore.

Was compassion ever shown by man to man? No pity, we are told was like *His* pity. Were words of wisdom ever uttered by human tongue? *He* spake, we are told, with a power and constrainingness such as never fell to the lot of orator or philosopher before. Did men ever go forth with brave calm hearts of heroism on missions of peril and to battle-fields? None ever went with so cheerful, so calm a heart as *He*, to that tremendous blood-weltering agony, where Sin, and Death, and Satan combined and intensified their power to distract and rend His soul. Have there been saints who have drawn draughts from the cup of suffering? *He* drained it to the very dregs, when every ingredient had been poured into it that could enhance its bitterness, without one quivering nerve, one angry, or self-justifying, or reproachful word.

So *He* was the perfect man; the "recapitulation" of humanity, the incarnation—the prototype, rather than the antitype—of all that men had ever seen, or dreamed of, or pictured to themselves in fancy of the heroic, the pure, the altogether lovely and spotless, the godlike in man. "*He* was full of grace and truth:" and men have but received in divers and unequal measures, " of *His* fulness."

If the patriarchs were "*types*" of Christ—as no doubt they were—it was in this sense only, that the Spirit of God, which dwelt in Him in its fulness bodily, struck out from their natures too, from time to time, sparks of fire and gleams of light, which men's consciences and spiritual intuitions recognised and canonised as Divine; and which kept alive faintly but not altogether vainly, the true conception of goodness, and beauty, and saintliness, in a world upon which a murky darkness was fast settling down—conceptions that should revive, and once more become impersonate when the epoch of the new creation, "the time of refreshment," "the manifestation" of the archetypal Son of Man, should dawn.

No one type is adequate to set forth the image of "the King in His beauty." He exhausts, and more than exhausts, the significance of them all. He realises and gathers into one, all that men had ever admired, loved, honoured, well-nigh worshipped, in what they rightly saw were the perfectible capacities of man. In Him dwelt "all the fulness" not only of Godhead, but of manhood, bodily. These old saints were not dumb, incomprehensible signs, but living, manifest interpreters of the purposes of God. They taught men incompletely, but approximately, to discern the lineaments of that form of perfected humanity which the Son of God should wear when, in the dispensation of the fulness of time, He should leave His Father's glory to visit and redeem a perishing world.

(2) "The good of all the land of Egypt is yours." So spake Joseph to his kindred; so speaks Christ to us who are members of His body. We are in Egypt, or at least on the edge of it, in Goshen—the "land of approaching"—and though our trade and calling be an abomination to its people, yet because we claim kinship with the True Joseph, they shall not, dare not, harm us. We can dwell safely there, ay! increase and multiply. There is a wonderful parallel in those twin histories: of the little family of Israel, three score and ten, multiplying in scarce 200 years, and in spite of scorn and tyranny, oppression and bloody edict, into a nation of 600,000 that were grown men alone; and the history of the little stone, as King Nebuchadnezzar saw it, smiting the bright and terrible image, and becoming a great mountain that filled the whole earth. Both speak of powers at work in the world greater than are ofttimes dreamt of in our philosophy.

We dwell in Egypt, and all its good things are ours.

We are not taken *out* of the world; but by providences and graces, inscrutable in their processes, palpable only in their results, are kept from its evil, and suffered, bidden to enjoy its good.

"Good in Egypt?" asks one sharply and scornfully. "*Good* in a world lying dead in trespasses and sins! As well good in a charnel-house of festering corpses and mouldering bones."

Ay, "good"! and plenty of it: "good" to the outward eye and to the inward: "good" to the senses and to the fancy: fair visions of beauty and noble objects of aspiration: "good" wherewith to sublime the intellect, and "good" wherewith to enlarge and enrich the soul. For is not ours the New Creation—the initial epoch of the restitution of all things? As St. Paul says, "All things are yours—Paul, Apollos, Cephas"—might we not add, Raffaelle, Shakespeare, Dante, a hundred more—"the *world*, life, death, *things present*, things to come, all are yours; for ye are Christ's, and Christ is God's."

Oh! What glorious scope this gives to the idea of Redemption! How worthy the end thus contemplated—the restitution of all things: not the mere salvation of a few picked and chosen souls—though that were more to be desired than rubies—but *the Redemption of the Universe*, of "the whole creation that groaneth and travaileth in pain together." How worthy the end seems of the means by which it was accomplished—the personal manifestation, the humiliation even to the death of the cross of the only-begotten Son of God!

"The eye sees nothing," says the poet, "but what it brings with it." And so the change of which we speak is not in the world, but in us who have to use the world. It was a problem that puzzled the, as yet, half-taught mind of St. Jude—"Lord, how is it that Thou wilt manifest Thyself unto us, and not unto the world?" It is still a puzzle to the mere reason. What charm do the heirs of glory bear about with them that disinfects for them this living lazar-house; that keeps them scathless from moral plague and pestilence; that enables them to walk loose in the midst of the furnace even at its whitest heat, and when they come forth, as they assuredly will, men mark with wonder that upon them "the fire hath had no power, neither is a hair of their head singed, nor has so much as the smell of fire passed upon them"?

For it is possible "to use the world as not abusing it;" and not only so, but to use it *and be the better for the use*. A Christian man may come in contact with what is loathsomest and foulest, and instead of being defiled he shall be the purer, the saintlier, the nearer and the liker God. We do not necessarily become clean and chaste by immuring ourselves in a convent, or leading the lives of anchorites. A Greek legend taught men that foul lusts and passions could break through even a brazen wall. With a pure conscience and a Christ-like purpose, a man may touch anything—go anywhere. Our Blessed Lord did not shrink from the contact even of the woman that had been a sinner. "To the pure all things are pure."

Men have no right to come to their neighbours with

their "Touch not, taste not, handle not;" to set up their arbitrary conventionalities as though they were God's eternal laws; to dogmatise about proprieties and improprieties; to sanction this and condemn that; to lay down tyrannous laws how far the world may be used in this direction, how far in that. There are no two human souls, perhaps, so identical in their constitution that they can use it with equal safety in all directions. In the true, but homely, proverb, "What is one man's meat is another man's poison." The echoes of that voice which was heard by St. Peter on the housetop at Joppa still teach each regenerated man, "What God hath cleansed, that call not thou common."

"Let every man be fully persuaded in his own mind." "All things indeed are pure; but it is evil for that man who eateth with offence." These are two of the very grandest principles of the Gospel. They will cut sheer in twain, with their keen trenchant edge, a hundred thousand knots that the most delicate manipulation of the subtlest casuistry would never be able to untie.

We are made so unwisely scrupulous, so needlessly austere, by the narrow views we take of the Redemption—its scope and purpose. We do not believe, or else we do not know, how to handle the truth that "all the good things of Egypt are ours." We think that everything that savours of Egypt—that grows there or has even passed through it—must be contaminated. We are slow and niggard to realise the great fact that a Christian may be in the world—may mix in its concerns and even share its pleasures—and yet not be worldly; may dwell in Goshen, yet with his heart and all his best affections not merely travelling back by an act of memory, or onward from time to time by an effort of hope, but fixed abidingly, and habitually, upon the hills and valleys and babbling brooks of Canaan. I defy any one to prove that it is God's purpose that I should embitter, and in fact disutilise, my life on earth by crying out ever and anon, "Wo is me," like David when he was constrained to abide among the tents of Kedar. We may claim our inheritance in the New Creation with a bolder, hopefuller heart than this.

I do not mean to ignore the evil and corruption that are in the world. Egypt is Egypt still: a land lying under a curse: visited ofttimes with plagues: where idols are worshipped with more zeal than God. But if I am Christ's this Egypt is mine. Its curse shall not scathe me. Its plague-spots shall not infect me. When the "darkness that could be felt" was spread like a funeral pall over it "all the children of Israel had light in their dwellings."

But although I may use the world freely and lawfully, and though its evil cannot harm me if I am of Christ's kin, yet the very existence of this evil imposes upon me certain cautions and limitations. "All things are lawful for me, but all things are not expedient." "Happy is he that condemneth not himself in that thing which he alloweth." "The kingdom of God is not meat and drink; but righteousness and peace and joy in the Holy Ghost." What noble, disenthralling doctrines! How they make me feel at once that it is only when I am serving God that I am really free:

only when I am following conscience that I am truly pure.

While, then, I assert unfalteringly my claim to all the good things of Egypt, I shall limit myself in the use of them by three main considerations:—

(1) By my neighbour's good.
(2) By the possibility of misconstruction.
(3) By a wholesome fear of becoming secularised.

I know not that we need any other safeguards; and I do not find that the Gospel has multiplied restraints. A few great guiding principles are better than many subtle, fine-drawn rules. "All is yours." Do not let go your hold of this. Godliness, remember! has "the promise of this life as well as of that which is to come." God placed us in this world not to be miserable, but happy. The purest happiness is the truest, the most permanent. Egypt is not Israel's home. They are but tarrying there. The "good land" is far away. The fulness of the Divine blessing cannot be tasted even in Goshen. Joseph will not have even his bones to lie there. His faith desired a better country, which he knew God would give His people in His own good time.

And so though we live and die in Egypt, we hope to rest in Canaan. As the True Joseph has placed us in Goshen, so we trust the New Moses will guide us through our pilgrimage in the wilderness; and that under the True Joshua we shall be able to pass, with brave, calm hearts, through the swelling waters of Jordan. Then may the New Jerusalem open to us her gates of pearl, and our good angel bring us to the footsteps of the throne of God and of the Lamb, there to serve Him, and see His face, "and have His name written on our foreheads, and reign with Him for ever and ever."

Preached—St. Edmund's, Salisbury, December 7, 1859. St. Mary's, Oxford, November, 9, 1862.

III.

MYSTERIES.

(*With allusions to the Death of Charles Dickens.*)

"Great is the mystery of Godliness."—1 TIMOTHY iii. 16.

IT ought to be no valid objection to Christianity that it concerns itself with mysteries.

If Revelation had *undertaken* to clear up all doubts and difficulties that might beset or cross the path of a man travelling from earth to heaven, *then*, that anything were left dark, that all were not so plain that even he that ran might read, would naturally, and might fairly, be occupied as a vantage-ground by gainsayers.

But such notoriously is not the case with that revelation which we Christians believe to have come from God. Over the mind of the Jew, as he tried to fathom the meaning of the Old Testament, we are distinctly told by St. Paul, there was spread "a veil." "Verily thou art a God that hidest thyself," was almost a complaint of the evangelical prophet—and though that veil is done away in Christ, and much that before was dark is now made clear, still we see only "as through a glass darkly"—as men interpreting a riddle. Even the Apostle, who had been caught up to the third heaven, and there beheld visions and revelations of the Lord, found it impossible, when he returned to the conditions of terrestrial life, to utter what he had seen.

If any one were asked beforehand what he would expect a revelation, given by such a Being as God to such a being as man, to contain; he would answer, if a person of reflection, that such a revelation might be anticipated to reveal nothing more of the nature of God than it concerned the recipient, for the purposes of his probation to know, that it would be intended *not to gratify curiosity*, but *to establish faith*.

It seems to me that the mysteries of what is called "Nature" are every whit as inscrutable as the mysteries of what is called 'Grace.' The student of science, as well as the student of theology, must halt again and again on the verge of the unknown, and find himself confronted by barriers which he cannot pass. Of all natural phenomena, the phenomena of *life* are the most mysterious. What marvel, therefore, if the phenomena of spiritual life are governed by a parallel law, and are found too subtle for analysis, and hide themselves from the mere speculative inquirer?

I shall not attempt to explain the great revealed mystery of the Triune Godhead, which we believe simply because it has been revealed. No doubt it is an exceeding mystery. It has been put into words, but still, in a certain sense, it remains unutterable. The mind attempts to grasp it, yet it eludes the grasp. Even the Creed, which has attempted to adjust the doctrine to the proportions of our finite intellect, recoils, as it were, baffled from the task, and confesses that the Father is "immeasurable," the Son "immeasurable," and the Holy Ghost "immeasurable."

But to live on the edge of mystery is the very condition of our being. "I seem like a boy," said Sir Isaac Newton, "playing on the seashore, and picking up a few pebbles here and there, but with the great ocean of truth undiscovered before me." "There are mysteries," said Leibnitz, "infinite in number, where moderate minds may find an explanation sufficient to enable them *to believe*, though inadequate to enable them *to comprehend*. The fact that *a thing is*, is enough for us to know; *how* it came to be is beyond our ken, and is not even necessary for us to know."

It is the mark, not of a philosophic, but of an unphilosophic mind, to ask for explanations of a phenomenon which, from the very conditions of its existence, or else from the limitation of the powers of the investigating mind, *must* of necessity be inexplicable.

The field of religious inquiry is one thing: the field of rigid mathematical demonstration is another. Each has its own proper methods, its own evidential cogency You cannot demonstrate the doctrine of the Trinity as you can the truth that two sides of a triangle are greater than the third; nor can it be called a self-approving axiom, as that two straight lines cannot inclose a space, or that the whole is greater than the part.

The Trinity is a matter of express revelation, and of Christian revelation. If the Jew knew it at all, which may justly be doubted, he saw it as he saw so much of the Divine purpose, through a glass darkly.

We cannot even presume to say that the doctrine of the Trinity is the utmost knowledge of the Divine nature to which man may ultimately attain. There are things concerning ourselves and our own future which St. John tells us "have not yet been revealed." If the precise character of our own future existence is not yet fully revealed, surely we may be prepared to admit that there may be further and fuller revelations in store for us of the nature of the Ancient of Days.

Some would bid us retain the *morality* of the Gospel and discard its *doctrines*. But it is impracticable counsel. Doctrines and precepts are woven into one tissue. The morality of the Gospel all depends on one fundamental axiom, that sin need not have dominion over those that are under Grace: that human nature can achieve any conquest over Satan through Christ strengthening it.

And in that same single axiom lies wrapped up the whole mystery of Redemption: the dogma of the Father's eternal counsel consummated by the administration of the Son, and applied to the sanctification of each individual soul by the operation of the Holy Ghost.

If we begin to discard doctrines from the Christian scheme because they are mysterious, it is hard to say where the process will end. Discard the Trinity: there remains the Incarnation. Discard the Incarnation: there remains the Atonement. Discard the Atonement: there remains the life of Christ—the miracles of Christ. Discard Christ Himself: there remains St. Paul—so mighty an evidence that one acute writer was not afraid to put the whole strain of the proof of Christianity to it alone. Discard St. Paul: there remains the Church. Discard the Church: there remains without adequate explanation the world's history for eighteen hundred years.

Attempt to analyse the phenomena of the world's present social life—the facts that make up the sum of human existence—the facts that are involved in the development of a single soul in what all instinctively acknowledge to be its noblest, highest form; and at the first step backwards you are brought face to face with mystery, with a sequence of causes and effects, or at least of phenomena that *look like* causes and effects, which certainly find their readiest reason for existence in the hypothesis that God, in the person of His Son, by the power of His Spirit, has taken possession of, and is redeeming, the world.

There is no attempt in the Bible to conceal the fact that the Revelation which it conveys is mysterious. St. Paul speaks of the "mystery of the faith," the "mystery of Godliness," the "mystery" of the relation between Christ and His Church, the "mystery" of the change which is to clothe this mortal with immortality, and to swallow up death in life. Without going the length of his paradox who said "I believe because it is impossible," it would argue an ignorance of the conditions under which alone the revelation of an Infinite God to a finite creature is conceivable were we to say, " I refuse to believe because it is mysterious."

It is not unnatural that the human mind, in its pride of conquest and of power, should chafe impatiently under limitations which make it conscious of its feebleness. But it is not for us to fix the conditions of the Divine gifts. The brightest things are ever the most dazzling. We cannot gaze full in the face of the noonday sun; and the darkness in which God hides Himself is simply, we are told, "light unapproachable."

Our Blessed Lord once spake certain "hard words" which so offended some of His disciples that they walked no more with Him. Simon Peter's temper was cast in a better mould, or had been more wisely trained. He would not forsake One who, he felt, had "the words of eternal life;" because there dropped from His lips other words past his comprehension. The poor fisherman, besides, was not too wise to be conscious of his needs: he knew not where else to go.

If Christianity is no better than a cunningly devised fable, will philosophy condescend to listen to human nature's deepest, most agonising cries; help it out of its darkness and unrest; answer Pilate's question, whether proceeding from cynicism or despair, and tell the world "what is truth?"

A wise writer, dealing with the subtle problem of the union of the Divine foreknowledge with the freedom of the will of man, recommends him who would approach the subject with any hope of a satisfactory result, to begin his inquiry from below—with the experienced fact that his own individual will is free. It is the maxim of Aristotle over again that in all speculations in the field of moral inquiry, the best beginning is from the facts that lie closest to ourselves. And so in approaching the contemplation of all mysteries, it is safest to start from the phenomena of our own experience. When the whole of Asia was turning away from him, and counting him nothing better than a fanatical dreamer of dreams, nothing could shake the stedfastness of the faith of St. Paul. "I know," he cries, "in Whom I have believed, and I am persuaded that He is able to keep that which I have committed to Him against that day."

All minds, it must be admitted, have not passed through the same discipline, nor can build their hopes on the same foundation. To some, one truth has proved more precious than another—more full of light, or strength, or comfort. Saul might feel safe in the battle in his armour of proof, David when trusting to nothing better than his shepherd's sling and stone.

But any truth, *that is held as truth*, is a help towards attaining further truth. It is the posture of *the will* before the Divine message that is the condition of knowing the doctrine. The temper in which we believe is much more important than the greater or less articulation of our creed. A stout ship, ere now, has rode out the wildest gale on a single cable. It is a *dragging* anchor—an unstable mind—that tells of the coming wreck of faith.

Says the poet of his friend:—

> "He fought his doubts and gathered strength:
> He would not make his judgment blind:
> He faced the spectres of the mind,
> And laid them: thus he came at length

> "To find a stronger faith his own;
> And Power was with him in the night,
> Which makes the *darkness* and the light,
> And dwells not in the light alone."

Yes: God hath said, "I dwell in the thick darkness;" and what we see and know of Him are but, as it were, the outskirts of His march of Majesty. "To see Him as He is," is the beatific vision reserved as the crowning glory of that day when "we shall know even as also we are known."

Admitting this principle, we must not shrink from accepting its legitimate and necessary conclusions. If this be the condition of all knowledge of things Divine, we may well tolerate differences of opinion where "the foundation standeth sure," and we have no reason to suspect insincerity, or that any dishonour is intended to the Name of our God.

The wisdom and tenderness—some would say the happy fortune of the early Church—is shown in the simplicity of her creeds: and even they are more developed, or to borrow a word of Jeremy Taylor's, more "articulated," than that Gospel which St. Paul preached to the Corinthians, which he says "they received, wherein they stood, by which they were saved," and of which the three corner stones were the Death, the Burial, and the Resurrection of our Lord.

From the multiplication of dogmas, or at least from the growth of the spirit of dogmatism, which is always more or less imperious and tyrannical, sprang the schism of the Eastern Church from the Western; the rupture between Catholics and Protestants, the "varieties of Protestantism." The issue may have been inevitable under the circumstances, but it certainly has not been an issue favourable to the propagation of truth. "Varieties of judgments and opinions," says sober Richard Hooker, "argueth obscurity in those things whereabout they differ." "What has been held by all Churches, in all places, at all times," is the remarkable test of a great Doctor for discerning catholic truth.

To fulfil these conditions we must reduce our dogmas, Bishop Jeremy Taylor thinks, to the grand, simple outline of the Apostles' Creed. There you find the doctrine stated, not as a dry theological abstraction, but in its direct relation to man's spiritual needs. The creed called after St. Athanasius (though none of his) more abstract in form, and cumbered with that invention of a later age, when councils and doctors thought that the traditionary deposit of faith must be guarded by anathemas, is yet simple *in substance;* while the Nicene Creed, though more explicit and detailed in statement, can hardly be considered as a development of *ideas.* If the maxim, *Quod semper, quod ubique, quod ab omnibus*" can be applied to any body of truth at all, it surely can be applied to the truths summed up in the Christian creeds.

On other points, we must agree to differ: or if not

that, we must at least convince, not by appeals to authority, but to reason, and proof, and argument. I never can be brought to admit that the principle of reason is contrary to the principle of faith; or that a measure of procedure which would be proper in any other field of cognate science is improper in Theology, which aspires to be the Queen-science of all.

And even if we fail to persuade, we can still respect those who differ from us conscientiously, however wide the divergence, and however erroneous we deem the views, if only we see proof of sincerity in steadfast purpose and loftiness of aim. If the hope of a re-united Christendom be nothing better than a soothing dream, let us not disturb it needlessly by misrepresentations, suspicions, rivalries, jealousies, heart-burnings.

There may be unity of purpose beneath divergence of thought, and in spite of apparent differences of aim. St. Paul, earnest as any for what he believed to be the truth, still bore with those who were "otherwise minded;" still could pray that God's grace might be with all those that loved the Lord Jesus Christ in sincerity. Even though the tongue pronounce "shibboleth" with a perceptible dissonance, earnest hearts still beat, if not in unison, at least in harmony. Because she has lost the note of *Unity*, there is no need that the Church should lose—there is all the greater need that she should cherish—the higher and more blessed note of *Love*.

It will not be out of harmony with the line of thought we have been pursuing, suggested by the contemplation of the great mystery of to-day, certainly it will be in keeping with the associations of this place,[1] dear to Englishmen, not only as one of the proudest Christian temples, but as containing the memorials of so many who, by their genius in arts, or arms, or statesmanship, or literature, have made England what she is; if in the simplest, briefest words I allude to that sad and unexpected death which has robbed English literature of one of its brightest ornaments: and the news of which, two mornings ago, must have made every household in England feel as though it had lost a personal friend. He has been called in a notice that I have read of him "an apostle of the people." I suppose this means that he had a mission from God to man. He preached not in a church nor from a pulpit, but in a style and fashion of his own—a gospel, a cheery, joyous, gladsome message, which the people understood, and by which they could hardly help being bettered.

It was the gospel of kindliness, of brotherly love, of sympathy in the widest sense of the word, of humanity. I am sure that I have felt in myself the healthful influence of his teaching. Probably we might not have been able to subscribe the same creed in relation to God, but I think we should have subscribed the same creed in relation to man.

And he who has taught us our duty towards our fellowmen better than we knew it before; who knew so well how to weep with them that weep, and to rejoice with them that rejoice; who has shown, with all his knowledge of the dark places of the earth, how much sunshine may rest upon the lowliest lot; who

---

[1] Westminster Abbey.

had such evident sympathy with suffering, such a love of innocence, such a natural instinct of purity that there is scarce a page of the thousands he has written which might not be put into the hands of a little child, may be regarded by those who recognise the diversity of the gifts of the Spirit as a "teacher sent from God." Surely he would have been welcomed as a fellow-labourer in the common interests of humanity by him who has asked the question—"If a man love not his brother whom he hath seen, how can he love God whom he hath not seen?"

Preached—Westminster Abbey, Trinity Sunday, 1870. St. Luke's, Cheetham Hill, Manchester, Trinity Sunday, 1872.

IV.

SOME CHURCH PROBLEMS IN THE NINETEENTH CENTURY.

"I say unto all 'Watch.'"—St. Mark xiii. 37.

THE picture of the latter days, which the Divine Master unfolded to the gaze of His four Apostles, as they sat together that quiet eventide upon the Mount of Olives over against the Temple, was by no means one to reassure men whose hearts were already not free from apprehension at the prospect of the work which lay before them. The walls of the holy city of which He was the architect, and they the master builders, were indeed doomed to rise in troublous times. There would be enemies without — deceivers and traitors within. The hindrances would be many; their mundane supports but few. The signs of the times should be so portentous, so perplexing, as to shake, if that were possible, the faith even of the elect. No doubt there were lights, here and there, streaming across this dark canvas. There was the promise of the assisting presence of the Holy Ghost; the promise of safety to him that endured to the end; the promise for the elects' sake of a shortening of the days, that the burden of them might not be simply insupportable; the promise of the final revelation of the Son of Man in the plenitude of His sovereign power and glory, when it might be hoped the same voice which once calmed the raging waters of Gennesaret would again say to a yet more furious storm, "Peace, be still."

But these promises, besides the indefiniteness of some and the remoteness of others, were too few and far between to lighten up with any appreciable effect the depth and awfulness of the surrounding gloom. So, at least, might have murmured a feeble or a desponding soul; and to such a one the words must have sounded almost like bitter irony, which bade men "not be troubled," for whom even the "beginnings of such sorrows" were in store. But they were not feeble nor desponding souls that were listening then. They were men who had given up all to follow Him. And though one of them, with a not unnatural impulse, had once asked the question—"What shall we have therefore?" neither he that asked the question, nor they that heard the answer—that they should have their reward, but "with persecutions," $\mu\epsilon\tau\grave{\alpha}\ \delta\iota\omega\gamma\mu\hat{\omega}\nu$—repented of their choice, or turned back again.

Not only did the simplicity of their *love* revolt from the idea of seeking another master, but the simplicity of their *faith* too felt—deeply, strongly, over-masteringly —that amid all the dark riddles and hard sayings that dropped occasionally from His lips—the Master, Whom they were following with such an indefinite sense of awe and wonder, had, as none other had, "the words of eternal life." He had touched their faith at its very root—in the moral basis of their being : and the anchor on which their ship rode was strong enough to keep her to her moorings, even though all these waves and storms beat over them. One—not, it is true, of these four, but who had either heard or read their tale—has pictured to us the condition of his soul—"troubled on every side, yet not distressed : perplexed, but not in despair : persecuted, but not forsaken : cast down, but not destroyed." It was the very text of the first Evangelists as they travelled to and fro, publishing the Gospel, and confirming the souls of the disciples, that spiritual conquests are not won by carnal weapons; that the Cross, both in time and in the order of the Divine Counsels, precedes the Crown ; that "we must through much tribulation enter into the kingdom of God."

I shall not occupy your time with any detailed examination of the times and seasons—real or supposed—in which the various parts of this Divine prophecy may reasonably be thought to have been fulfilled. Expositions and interpretations of prophecy, after the manner of Bishop Newton, are, to my mind, singularly unsatisfactory, and are apt to generate a self-sufficiency and spiritual pride on the one hand, or an uncharitableness and polemical rancour on the other, which are as far removed as possible from that temper of simple religious dependence upon God—that confidence that the cause of truth and righteousness will, against all appearances, ultimately prevail—which I conceive to have been the chief educational purpose of that light, "shining in a dark place," to which, we are told, "we do well when we take heed." The main function of prophecy is not to tempt us prematurely to draw aside the veil that hides the future, but to enable us to interpret on true principles the phenomena of "this present time."

But this, I may take for granted, will be generally allowed to have been the Church's career—a career, however, not peculiar to herself, but shared in common with many another great and good cause, whether working apart from the influences of the Gospel, or in conscious union with them, for all alike are governed by one apparently irreversible and universal law—"out of weakness she has become strong." She has made her port not with favouring gales, but "against winds that are contrary:" she holds the moral conscience of the world in subjection, not because the world loves her rule, but because it cannot gainsay her claims: she has wrestled with principalities and powers, and has prevailed. Even with shrunk sinew and halting upon her thigh, she has had power with men: and her King, though He does not reign everywhere with equally undisputed sway, is yet the King of all that is noblest, best, purest, loveliest, upon the earth.

I know that unfriendly minds have given, and will give, a different philosophy of the Church's history. They will say she has won her way by unholy secular alliances—by superstitions, and wily priestcraft—by understanding only too keenly how to redeem the time—ἐξαγοράζεσθαι τὸν καιρὸν—and turn it to marketable account—by compliance with the vices and follies either of monarchs or of the age—in a word by serpent-like wisdom, rather than by dove-like innocence. And no doubt there have been passages in her history which give only too true a colour to these taunts: but they have been passages of the Church's shame, not of her glory: moments when she *seemed* to be gaining strength, but was really losing it: apparent victories, bitterly rued by subsequent defeats. No: the Church's course has been chequered, but on the whole it has been triumphant. And it has been, not by the help, but in spite of, this soil and taint of evil, in spite of men— Princes, Popes, Bishops, Statesmen—who have used her holy name, and blessed offices, for purposes most alien, most unholy, that her progress has been achieved. Even Gibbon confesses the "victory" to have been " remarkable ;" and endeavouring to discover the "secondary causes" which led to its rapid accomplishment, allows that the four prominent causes (for though he enumerates a fifth — the assumption of miraculous powers—he only mentions it to scoff at it), —allows, I say, that the four prominent causes which he considers to have brought about this indisputable success were all of them causes operating in the moral sphere, — the union and discipline of the Christian republic, the inflexible zeal of the Christians, their pure and even austere lives, and that doctrine of a future state, without the support of which, as Paul testifies, they would have been of all men the most pitiable (*Decline and Fall of the Roman Empire*, ch. xv.).

One word of explanation before I proceed. I have been using the word "Church" in a way that would be utterly unreal, if I limited it to the senses that are often imposed upon it by this, or that, narrow ecclesiastical school. I am not thinking of the primitive Church merely, nor of the Eastern Church, nor of the Western, nor of the Anglican Episcopal Church, nor of Protestant non-Episcopal Churches. My conception was generalised from all these concrete, individual bodies (under none of whose forms is the perfection of the typical idea adequately realised), and was meant to express the aggregate of those spiritual forces radiating from Christ; which, even under the limitations of flesh and blood—of earthly passions and human alloy—have done so much for man, and, " if they had free course and were glorified," would seem to be capable of the entire regeneration of the world. We all remember Bishop Butler's description of a perfectly virtuous kingdom, when he argues for the future triumph of good over evil from present apparent tendencies in the nature of things. The dream might have been long since realised, if, according to the measure and scope of the divine purposes, the kingdoms of the world had become, in any true and sufficient sense, " the kingdoms of the Lord and of His Christ." Of these regenerating spiritual forces, the visible organisation to which we belong may fairly be allowed to claim her full share. But she has no exclusive proprietorship of them: and though I am preaching to a Congress of Churchmen, I should be defeating my own purpose if I tried to fortify them in what would be a superstitious, rather than a rational, belief; that the Church, to which we are justly and loyally attached, and whose power of influence we desire to strengthen and extend by every means at our command, enjoys any monopoly of divine grace, or can presume to invite members of other communions, certainly not destitute of tokens of the Divine Presence, to seek refuge within her pale, on the ground that their salvation is impossible, or at best precarious, where they are. Untenable pretensions react in honest minds on those who make them. To those who appreciate the value of a solid basis for unity—of a primitive, apostolic form of government—of the security that is given by law to freedom—of a ritual at once sober and reverent —of a Liturgy breathing the very spirit of a devout and chastened piety—of a parochial system which, if truly carried out, would be the perfection of an ecclesiastical organisation—the Church of England can commend herself on solid and sufficient grounds. We shall not strengthen our cause, but the reverse, by associating with it preposterous or unsubstantial claims.

But to pass on.

It seems natural to the human mind to exaggerate the importance both of the achievements, and of the failures, of its own day. And there are those who think the Church, and the great cause she holds, are passing now through a trial-fire, seven times hotter than any she has passed through before. Perhaps, as those whom we deem enemies have not fully disclosed themselves —are still uncertain about the positions they will eventually occupy, we are not in a condition to measure the force or the direction of the attack—cannot, perhaps, be sure that the attack will ever come, or that those who show so menacing a front are, in fact, or at heart, enemies at all. I utterly refuse to recognise as enemies those who, in the field of scientific inquiry, are trying patiently, laboriously, honestly, to solve some of the problems of nature—"questioning God," as one of the most eminent of them calls it (Huxley), in a spirit of loyal allegiance to truth, and to truth alone. I cautiously distinguish true sons of science from those aggressive sciolists, who, in that wantonness which seems to cleave to all half-knowledge, thrust their puny spear in the face of beliefs which they forsooth have discarded, but which the better and wiser part of mankind still entertain with reverent regard. The true labourers in this field, by whom it is being really cultivated and bringing forth fruit, frame their hypotheses, it is true, sometimes, we may think, with a somewhat perilous rashness; but they are careful to tell us that they offer them only as hypotheses, as a provisional and possible explanation of phenomena, and they are content to wait patiently and hopefully till the truth, upon which they can plant their feet as upon solid ground, shall be revealed. "For the Darwinian hypothesis," said Professor Huxley three days ago at Manchester, "I do not think there has been, and I do not suppose there will be, obtained, for a century yet, anything more than probable evidence." "I can wait 200 years," said Kepler, "for my views to be believed, if the Almighty has waited 6,000 years to publish them." And when, if ever, the time comes, if the evidence prove irresistible, the human mind, from its very constitution, *must* receive it. Meanwhile, it is not ill for the Church to have before her eyes the spectacle of men who are seeking truth, in any field of inquiry, for the truth's sake; and not claiming men's acceptance of anything which they cannot prove.

In the programme of our discussions which has been sketched out, and which I may presume is in the hands of most of you, we are attempting to define with some precision—or at any rate to examine—the existing relations of the Church to the various powers and forces with which she is surrounded, and by which she cannot but be affected either for good or harm. You will attempt to ascertain the relations of the Church (1) to Education—*i.e.*, to the intellectual forces of the age; (2) to the State—*i.e.*, to the political phenomena; (3) to other Christian, and even non-Christian bodies—*i.e.*, to the religious developments; and (4) to that complex system which we call Society—*i.e.*, to the moral tone and tendencies of the age. Difficult, perhaps insoluble, problems! problems, too, some of them, the solution of which, if attempted, is not likely to be that which we, as Churchmen, should desire: but problems which we shall certainly do well to approach without the bias of prejudice or prepossession—with an earnest desire, above all things, to be guided into truth, and with an honest wish to realise the position of others who may not look at these phenomena as we ourselves have been taught to do. One of the features of the Jewish mind in our Lord's day was an inability to discern the signs of their time—that they applied different measurements to phenomena which seemed to touch their traditional faith, from those which they applied to other phenomena,

E

or would have applied to the same phenomena under other circumstances: as our Lord asked them, "Why even of your own selves"—by your ordinary standards of right and wrong, truth and falsehood—"Why, even of your own selves, judge ye not what is right?" (Luke xii. 58.) Let us try to get rid from our deliberations of all "idols" (as Lord Bacon calls them), whether of the tribe, or of the cave, or of the market, or of the theatre. We have two special dangers, those of us at least who are clergymen. We are a tribe, and many of us live in caves, more or less secluded from the busy walks in life, outside the stream of active thought. And so we sometimes dream our distempered dreams in solitude, and never attempt to check them by experiment: or we follow blindly those who set up to be our leaders, without reckoning whither *they* are leading, or *we* following.

And so our teaching is weak and aimless, and effects no lodgment in men's souls; or we have no sense of the relative value of the great issues that are being tried in the world of thought outside our own, and to men who are craving bread, we have nothing better to offer than a stone.

"In our day," says a modern French preacher, "in all classes of society (strange phenomenon!), what piety there is seems confined almost exclusively to women. Just as a family consisting only of brothers would be found lacking in grace, in sweetness, in modesty, so the piety of the nineteenth century lacks force, vigour, robustness. Need I paint its weakness? Need I say that it consists in a sensibility either morbid or affected? Need I tell its mincing manners? or reproduce its languid, methodised utterances? In our meetings, in our books, in our works, one breathes a sort of insipid perfume, which sickens and disgusts masculine and sober minds. Ah! let enter in here the fresh air, keen and free, such as God made it in His wisdom."—(*Colani's Sermons*, i. 313.)

And so let us scatter our dreams and visions, and confront the actual situation manfully, trustfully. We are not living in the fourth century, nor the tenth, nor the sixteenth, but in the nineteenth—

> "The old order changeth, giving place to new;
> And God repeats Himself in many ways,
> Lest one good custom should corrupt the world."

Let us try to recognise and appreciate the permanent principles underlying all these changes. The foundation of God standeth as sure as it ever did. It is the only thing really worth earnestly contending for. The technical and conventional language of theological schools is fast disappearing, even from sermons; but all earnest men's hold on the vital truth's of Christianity is tightening, rather than relaxing. But the age will not be kept in leading-strings. It does not turn a deaf ear to teachers; but when it has listened, it claims a right to judge. Who shall deny it that right? or deny that it has the faculties proper for the safe exercise of it? Would he, think you, "who would have every man fully persuaded in his own mind"? Or he, again, who writes to a Christian community in this strain, "Ye have an unction from the Holy One, and ye know all things"? At any rate, whether there ever was a time or not when it was desirable, in the interests of religion, that a caste or order of men should be considered exclusive authorities of divine truth, or exclusive depositaries of divine grace, that time has passed away, and from all present appearances is little likely to return. But I do not think we are living in an age that is unfavourable to the calm and dispassionate consideration of solemn questions. There is a restlessness of inquiry, no doubt; but that very restlessness betokens, not the triumph of doubt, but rather an anxious search for truth—

> "There lives more faith in honest doubt,
> Believe me, than in half the creeds."

And our wisdom is to direct this spirit of inquiry, not to spend strength in vain, endeavouring to stifle it. Men are yearning for certainty—for something, like Noah's dove, to rest the soles of their feet upon. But they are quick to catch the ring of unreality—they will not be put off with phrases or conventionalisms. They want a religion that will help them in the battle fray. Have you, my brethren of the clergy, got such to offer them? Do you believe, and therefore speak? Are the counsels that drop so glibly from your tongues counsels borrowed at second-hand, or counsels that you can recommend from an experimental conviction of their worth?

Never, as it seems to me, was there a nobler opportunity of usefulness spread out before any Church than is now spread out before the Church of England; and yet it is just possible, that either from some unhappy conjuncture of circumstances, or from want of faith, or want of wisdom, we may miss it. It is with us, as it once was with Paul at Ephesus—"A great door and effectual is opened; but there are many adversaries." But we have just grounds for hoping for the ultimate success of any cause in which we are conscious of labouring with single aims, with directness and earnestness of purpose. "All things are possible to him that believeth"; and where there is true faith there is certain to be no obliquity of conduct. The worst evil that could befall us would be that our people should suspect our loyalty, our truthfulness, our honesty.

"We shall all gradually advance," wrote Goethe to Eckermann, "from a Christianity of words and faiths to a Christianity of feeling and action." It may be questioned whether the two can really be separated: but there can be no doubt that what men are seeking in Christianity is, not a technical system, but a vital power: something not taught in catechisms or formulated in creeds, but entering into their souls and quickening them with the conviction that, in Christ, the dead can be made alive. Catechisms and creeds will still have their scientific or theological value: cannot be dispensed with in thorough Christian training: but their power over the heart is small; their worth as motives to right conduct is insignificant. The spiritual lever that has moved the world has been the simple revelation of the love of God in Christ; the fulcrum on which it has acted has been the sense of the need of such love in the human soul. Bring these forces together, either through the medium of holy discourse, or reverent worship, or Blessed Sacrament, and you have done all that man can do for the regeneration of his fellow-man. The rest we leave, in faith and hope, to the free and sovereign action of the Spirit of our God.

Inaugural Sermon, preached before the Church Congress at Nottingham, October 11, 1871.

V.

RESPONSIBILITY.

"And as they heard these things, he added and spake a parable, because he was nigh to Jerusalem, and because they thought that the kingdom of God should immediately appear. He said therefore, A certain nobleman went into a far country to receive for himself a kingdom, and to return. And he called his ten servants, and delivered them ten pounds, and said unto them, Occupy till I come."—St. Luke xix. 11—13.

I suppose it would be true to say that it is the Parables of its Divine Author, rather than any more formal and dogmatic exposition of its principles, which have impregnated the world with the genius of Christianity. In those divine discourses—now a simple tale, now an exquisite allegory, now a glorious vision—we see mirrored, as on the bosom of a deep lake, the very "mind of Christ." "Without a parable spake He not unto them:" and with that perfect adaptation of means to ends, which marked all His conduct as a Prophet, or Teacher of men, we may be sure He chose the aptest vehicle for conveying into the soul, at least of ordinary hearers, the great truths He willed to dwell there. If a systematic course of theology would have accomplished the same purpose more effectively, we cannot doubt that He would have taught as a theologian teaches, as Augustine, or Aquinas, or Calvin, or Bishop Pearson taught. That He taught otherwise is sufficient proof, if proof were needed, that theology, however valuable in its place and for its proper purpose—and *in* its place it is *in*valuable—is not the fittest instrument for kindling in the soul of man that intense yearning for an insight into the things of God, which is the true correlative of the manifested and revealed love of God to man.

If we would know those secrets of the kingdom of heaven, which it most vitally and intimately concerns us to know, which not only enlighten the understanding, but supply an adequate spring to the will, let us place ourselves in imagination among those who gathered round Him, now as He taught out of a boat on the Galilean lake; now as He sat at meat in the Pharisee's house on the Sabbath day; now as He turned to the multitudes who followed Him on His journeys; now as He spake to the publicans and sinners who found in Him what they could not find elsewhere, One who sympathised with them, and Whom they could understand; now, as sitting on the Mount of Olives, over against the temple, He expounded to the chosen four, far more plainly in parable than he had before expounded in prophecy, the signs of His second coming, "and of the end of the world."

It is true there is one dark, mysterious reason why He spake to them in parables: "Because they seeing, saw not; and hearing, they heard not, neither did they understand." But the wilfully blind never can see;

the wilfully deaf never can hear. It needs a will—a purpose—to do the will of God, in order to understand the doctrine. The foolishness of preaching—ἡ μωρία τοῦ κηρύγματος—has ever proved a stumbling block to those who "seek after wisdom, or require a sign." The difficulties of Christianity, at the present day, are felt by those who demand a complete theological or scientifically developed system: not by those who are satisfied if they find a "testimony of the Lord giving wisdom unto the simple"—"an undefiled law, converting the soul." The *metaphysical* bases of belief have, at times, been rudely shaken: the *moral* basis has stood like a rock, upon which a man may build the structure of his spiritual life without fear.

It may be assumed that one of the reasons for the variety in our Lord's parabolic teaching was that different images were likely to exercise different degrees of influence upon different minds. Farm labourers would be caught by every allusion to the operations of nature or the processes of husbandry; fishermen would discern some of the purposes of His mission under the figure of the net cast into the sea and gathering of every kind; thrifty housewives would learn spiritual lessons from the parable of the leaven, or of the piece of silver diligently sought with broom and candle till it was found; speculators on the nature of the human soul would ponder the story of the unclean spirit driven out once by a potent spell, yet returning again, because the power of the charm was not maintained; speculators on the nature of the life of the world to come, and its relations to the life of this present time, would discover food for thought in the parable of the ten virgins, or the vision of the King seated upon His throne. It was hardly possible that any one who was really seeking light for his steps amid the darkness of the world—clearness of vision amid the uncertainties of doubt, and the perplexities of speculative inquiry—should fail to find it, in one or other of these gracious words, in which the grandeur of the thought stood in such marked apparent contrast to the simplicity of the form.

Of all these wondrous parables there is none, perhaps, that touches the soul with a profounder sense of solemnity and awe, than that from which I have taken, what I may call, the opening scene, for my text. It meets us in the sacred narrative in two forms. There is no irreverence, I hope, in supposing that our Blessed Lord repeated from time to time these figurative illustrations of the laws of His kingdom, and did not always care to repeat them in precisely the same form. And so we meet this parable once in the form of an unequal distribution of talents, and again in the form of an equal distribution of pounds. Both forms have their expression in the actual phenomena of life. There are those who make a disproportionate use of equal opportunities; and there are those who make a proportionate use of unequal opportunities. One man with his five talents makes them other five; another who has received but two, gains other two. Here one intrusted with a pound, gains ten; there another, with the same trust, and possibly the same opportunities, gains but five. Under both forms of the teaching there is the same picture of the unprofitable servant, with the wretched, transparent, self-condemning excuse for his unprofitableness, spoiled of his hoarded, and therefore wasted, wealth, "cast into outer darkness," the appointed portion of unbelievers.

It is not necessary for my present purpose to discuss these differences of detail; they may have been accidental (as we speak of accidents), or they may have been essential to the aims of the teacher, governed, as these are likely to have been governed, by the circumstances of the place or time. I wish to confine your thoughts, and my own, simply to one feature in the tale, which constitutes its awfulness—its solemnity.

The Great Master is gone into "a far country," He tells us, "To receive for Himself a kingdom, and to return." Meanwhile, we see Him not, and hear no direct tidings of Him. "Yea, though we have known Christ after the flesh; yet now, henceforth, know we Him no more." There are no tokens of Him for many days and many years. All things stand, or seem to stand, as fast as they have stood from the beginning of the creation. Some, who speak as prophets, tell us "the whole creation groaneth and travaileth in pain together," and that they who have the first-fruits of the Spirit are waiting anxiously, with outstretched necks and yearning eyes, for a deliverance from "the bondage of corruption into the glorious liberty of the children of God." But the world calls such men dreamers, visionaries, enthusiasts; and hardly cares to tarry and listen to them as they tell, or else try to interpret, their dreams. With marriages to be made, and houses to be finished, and gardens to be laid out and planted, and contracts to be fulfilled, and great schemes of policy to be developed, practical men can't stay and lend an ear to the Noahs of the age; who, believing themselves warned of God, prepare an ark for the saving of their house, preaching the while of righteousness. The world "which is" has got to make very light of the faith in the world "which is to come." It is an old wives' fable to frighten children with, but of no avail with men "who are learned in all the wisdom of the Egyptians." The Master, however, tells us that He is gone; that the time of His absence is utterly uncertain; the very angels know it not; but that "in a day and hour when they think not;" in the very heart and midst of all the busy pre-occupations of the world, "He will come again and reckon with His servants."

Whatever interpretation we choose to place upon this figurative language—for it *is* figurative and not literal—whatever sense we choose to assign to the coming or to the reckoning—if there is any reality in the words at all, there is one inference (and that the only practically important one) from which we cannot escape, and that is, that we are all of us living in a state of *responsibility*. I do not think we could divest ourselves of that consciousness without breaking in upon the harmony of our spiritual being, even if the horizon of our hopes and fears were bounded by the limitations of this present scene; but if we believe in a hereafter, the consciousness of *responsibility* naturally becomes a motive to action, doubled in its constraining and controlling power. The variations in this consciousness of responsibility are probably determined by the variations of belief in this vital article of the Christian Creed. "If there be no resurrection of the dead," cries Paul, no change awaiting all, no life beyond the grave, "preaching is vain, and faith is vain." "Let us eat and drink, for to-morrow we die."

I do not know with sufficient accuracy what Oxford is now; but I know pretty well what the general world is now, and I remember what Oxford was thirty-five years ago. That great religious movement, which owes its origin to this place, and which with all its faults, its waverings, its extravagances, even with its disloyalties, quickened the pulse of the moral conscience in England, and taught men that they had other and higher duties than mere self-seeking, was accompanied by, if it did not spring from, a heightened sense of personal responsibility. The great leaders of that movement, and their more conspicuous followers, were men of lofty aims, severe self-control, simple habits, self-denying, almost mortified, ascetic lives. Oxford felt—I recollect the feeling myself as a young man—as she has hardly felt since, that there was a spirit moving within her, which could not be called even by those whom it did not touch, a spirit of this world. Men had convictions, and exhibited them in their lives. They believed, and their practice was according to their belief. That the movement took an unhappy turn I am ready to admit, but, in its best and brightest days, it was a movement governed by noble impulses, aiming at a lofty end. There were signs on every side of quickened consciences; not ostentatiously sensitive, nor morbidly restless, but alive, keenly alive, to the sense of duty; so that even careless lookers-on began to see a meaning in those deep dark words, "Ye are dead, and your life is hid with Christ in God" (Col. iii. 3). Much has changed since then, and we have reached "an age of light, light without love," in which subtle questionings, whether for good or evil, have displaced simple believing, and what was *faith* then is deemed *credulity* now. We live in an age of cold calculating cynicism, in which enthusiasm is ridiculed; earnestness deemed unfashionable; self-sacrifice reputed folly. An age when "knowledge is increased," but "wisdom lingers"; when passions are strong, wills weak; when high ambitions are tainted by self-seeking, and noble gifts sometimes prostituted to ignoble purposes. An age, in which boys and girls know as much of the world, in some of its least pleasant forms, as mature men and women used to do: an age of social chasms daily widening: of the various classes which constitute society becoming more and more separated from, more and more ignorant of, each the other; an age of yearnings, vast, but impotent because aimless; of sympathies waxing weaker and colder, because never suffered to develop into the activities of benevolence. On all sides one hears the uneasy cry of discontent; on all sides one discerns symptoms of that weary restlessness which is the proper retribution of desires fixed on objects which fail to content, even when they are realised. With aching heart, one beholds the spectacle of the rich in their luxury, "enlarging their desires as hell," yet still "unsatisfied"

(Hab. ii. 5); of the poor in their deep poverty, sinking into more and more hopeless brutality and degradation. And neither care to learn a parable from the fig-tree (Mark xiii. 28, 29) or look up and lift their heads, as though a "redemption" from a life, in which all the conditions of health are reversed, "were nigh," or even possible.

Yet here, from this place, speaking to the young heart of England, to those who will be the strength and stay both of the Church and of the Nation, both of Religion and of Society, when we, whose sun has passed its meridian height and is now sloping towards the west, shall be sleeping in our quiet or unquiet graves, one would fain try to rouse spirits that cannot yet be fully steeped in the narcotic, deadening influences of the world, to an adequate sense of what an apostle calls "their high calling of God in Christ Jesus."

"He went about doing good," is at once the simplest and truest description of the work which the Lord Jesus set Himself to do upon this earth. "To go about doing good," wherever his hand finds good to do,—and he will not need to look far for opportunities—is the surest token still of a man having the mind of Christ; of a man having his spirit touched by the Spirit of Christ. To wrap oneself up in an isolating selfishness, to stop our ears and close our eyes to everything likely to disturb the softness of our slumbers, the sweetness of our dreams,—to say to our soul (if such be our portion), "Soul, thou hast much goods laid up for many years; take thine ease, eat, drink, and be merry;" this, even men who have no spirit of faith, see to be a temper as alien from the proper temper of a Christian as anything can be conceived to be. Yet this is the temper which the luxurious, self-indulgent habits of the age have an almost irresistible tendency to form. You must exercise conscious efforts of watchfulness, and self-restraint, if you would struggle successfully against their slumberous, paralysing influence. "A useless life," said Goethe, " is but an early death." (*Ein unnutz Leben ist ein früher Tod.*) Many of your young hearts are leaping up with wild, and as yet unfixed, ambitions. You naturally and rightly desire to make your mark on your generation, to hand down your names to them that come after, as those who have been among the foremost men of their time. I know not whom you have selected from the page of history, by whose career to fashion your own. But if the ideal of Jesus Christ be deemed too high—and, of course, it is so far too high that no mortal man can hope to attain to it—you could not probably propose to yourselves a nobler example to be conformed to than that of Paul. I do not mean in what may be termed the *accidents* of his life (for you may be called to far other work than his): but in what constitutes the moral basis of his character, its chivalry, its generosity, its tenderness, its true refinement, its almost superhuman devotion to duty, its sustaining faith in the unseen. Souls of this stamp are what our diseased social condition emphatically demands; souls, willing to spend, and be spent for a noble cause; souls loving on, even though winning back scant love in return; souls steadfast though standing alone, firm where others waver, loyal where others betray, because "they know in whom they have believed, and are persuaded that He is able to keep that which they have committed unto Him against that day."

And so we are brought back to the thought with which we began. We need hopes "entering into that within the veil"—reaching beyond the confines of this lower world—to sustain, in a day when "our tokens are not so clearly to be seen" as once they were, fainting hearts and drooping hands. "If in this life only we had hopes in Christ, we should be of all men the most miserable." We shall hardly make the use of our five talents, or of our single pound (if that be all that has been intrusted to us), that we ought to do, unless we believe that the Master, Whom we serve, will one day "come and reckon" with us. No need to ask captiously or querulously, "What are the signs of His coming?" nor again, "Will His reward when He bestows it satisfy us for all the toil that we have borne?" The value of the reward will depend upon the expectations we are forming of it. If we are dreaming of places "at the right hand or the left," perhaps they never may be ours. If our hearts are set upon some gross, almost material and sensual payment in kind, that certainly never will be ours either. But if we have so longed to see Him "in His beauty" here, that hereafter to "see Him as He is" will suffice us, we shall have *that*. If it be enough to share His joy, though we know not of what sort it be, we shall have that for our portion too. If, by heaven, we mean a place where there shall be infinite scope for almost infinite development of all that is best, and purest, and noblest in our nature, that heaven shall

F

be ours. This much we are told plainly and without figure; and more than this we need not ask nor care to know. We must not elevate the reward into the rank of a primary motive; it is but a subsidiary support to a frail and wavering heart. The work itself carries with it the highest, the most abiding reward. No prize, either in earth or heaven, so rich as that which the conscience offers, unasked, unprompted, to him who simply strives to do his duty. "Thus," according to the beautiful thought of the *Christian Year* (Advent Sunday),

"Thus bad and good their several warnings give
 Of His approach, whom none may see and live;
  Faith's ear, with awful still delight,
  Counts them like minute bells at night,
 Keeping the heart awake till dawn of morn,
 While to her funeral pile this aged world is borne.

"But what are heaven's alarms to hearts that cower
 In wilful slumber, deepening every hour,
  That draw their curtains closer round,
  The nearer swells the trumpet sound?
 Lord, ere our trembling lamps sink down and die,
 Touch us with chastening hand, and make us feel Thee nigh."

Preached—St. Mary's, Oxford, October 29, 1871.

VI.

THE EVIDENTIAL VALUE OF MIRACLES.

(As a Motive Power in Spiritual Life.)

"Then certain of the Scribes and of the Pharisees answered, saying, Master we would see a sign from Thee."—ST. MATTHEW xii. 38.

ON examining the records of Holy Scripture which contain the story of miraculous events, I cannot help arriving at the conclusion, that the evidential value of miracles, as a basis of belief, is and always was, considerably less than is commonly assumed or supposed. Not only do we read the story, and dwell on the thought, of them now, less as *proofs of a revelation*, than as *illustrations of the character* of Him who partly by and partly with them, was revealing Himself to man: less as τέρατα or even δυνάμεις than as σημεῖα (the word by which they are most frequently designated); less as tokens of a *physical*, than of a *moral*, governor of the world—but it would seem to have been always so. When Jesus raised the widow's son at Nain, there came a fear—an awe-inspiring, reverent fear—upon all; and they glorified God, saying "that a great *prophet* is risen up amongst us," and "that God hath visited His people." (Luke vii. 16.)

Not but what the miracles are set, so to speak, in a stratum of historical facts, from which it is impossible to dislodge them, retaining the truth of the remaining history. As it has been well put by a distinguished French writer, "The whole Gospel is one tissue of supernatural events; is the birth of a Virgin's son; is the resurrection of one dead; begins and ends in miracle." And yet we do not build—not one of us, I suspect, has built—the foundation of our spiritual life, or even of our faith, on these things merely as "supernatural events." It is not in this aspect that they affect us. We do not consciously separate them from the system to which they appear to belong. The whole march of Christ was a march of mystery. We seem to see in it the outlines of a purpose, each step in which we cannot pretend to understand. And the miracles seem almost a necessary part of the process of the evolution of this purpose. We should be surprised if we did not find them. We are brought so very near to God or rather God is brought so very near to us, that we feel we must be, if not in the midst, yet on the edge, of marvels, which the keen eye of mere physical investigation, endeavouring to trace the footsteps of Law everywhere, cannot pretend to penetrate. A revelation of God to the world, supposing such a thing to have occurred, which should contain nothing transcending the ordinary limits of human knowledge and human power, and even of human method, would, in the very absence of those signs of its divine origin, furnish a presumption of improbability. I do not say, as some have said, that what we call "miracles" are *necessary* for a divine revelation; but at any rate they are *in place* in it, and strengthen rather than weaken the validity of its claims. There they are, and they are in harmony with their surroundings.

I admit that it is not a very easy thing to fix the proper place and just value of miracles among the evidences of Christianity. It is not very easy to define a miracle—to say with any philosophical accuracy what it is. It is utterly out of keeping with the whole train of scientific processes and scientific thought, to regard it, as it once was regarded, as a violation, or even as a suspension, of natural laws: rather, as Bishop Butler has taught us, is it the manifestation of a higher and as yet undiscovered law, such as that which governs the course of comets, or other extraordinary cosmical phenomena; which, however, no one supposes, because they are seemingly irregular and extraordinary, to be above or beyond the domain of law. "That part of the course of nature," says the philosophical bishop, "which is opened to our view, is but as a point, in comparison of the whole plan of Providence, reaching throughout eternity past and future; in comparison of what is even now going on in remote parts of the boundless universe; nay, in comparison of the whole scheme of the world."

Miracles do not seem to have had the evidential power that we are apt to attribute to them upon those who saw them with their eyes. It is true that in one case (John x. 41) the multitude contrasted Christ's thaumaturgic power with the absence of such credentials in John the Baptist (whom, however, they acknowledged to be a prophet, though he wrought no miracles (Matt. xiv. 5). In another instance we are told that "many believed in His Name when they saw the miracles which He did" (John ii. 23). But elsewhere it is said with equal distinctness that "though He had done so many miracles before them, yet they believed not on Him" (John xii. 37). The works to which, in John x. 37, 38, He so confidently appealed, as a token that He came forth from God, and that the Father was in Him, and He in the Father, saying, "If I do not the *works* of My Father, believe Me not; but if I do, though ye believe not Me, believe the *works*," were not necessarily miraculous:—it is the simple Greek word ἔργα, the things He was continually doing; and might have merely pointed to His ordinary march of benevolence, His going about doing good, His very words accompanied with grace and power. A few further Scriptural instances may be noticed in connection with this subject.

1. Reflect on the case of the dreamer of dreams, hypothetically stated in Deut. xiii. :—"If there arise among you a prophet or a dreamer of dreams, and giveth thee a sign or a wonder, and the sign or the wonder come to pass whereof he spake to thee"—what were men to do? to believe his message or his dream, because the sign with which he announced it had been fulfilled? By no means. They were to measure the value of the apparent proof of the message having come from God by the nature of its contents—" If the sign or

the wonder come to pass, whereof he spake unto thee, saying 'Let us go after other gods, which thou hast not known, and serve them,' thou shalt not hearken unto the word of that prophet or that dreamer of dreams; for the Lord your God proveth you to know whether you love the Lord your God with all your heart, and with all your soul, and that prophet or that dreamer of dreams shall be put to death, because he hath spoken to turn you away from the Lord your God." It is plain that the message itself remained to be tested by some other criterion of its truth or falsehood, its moral goodness or its moral evil, quite apart from the fulfilment of its sign: and indeed that this very fulfilment was one of the many modes in which God designed to prove His people's faith—whether "their heart was whole with him," and they were minded to "continue stedfast in His covenant."

2. Remember again that most remarkable phenomenon—I know not whether to call it moral or intellectual—of the staggering faith of John the Baptist, even after the epiphany on the banks of Jordan. It might be supposed that even the shadow of the shade of doubt could never have passed across the mind of him who, though once he "knew Him not," had seen the heavens opened (as he had been forewarned he should see them) and the Holy Ghost descending in bodily shape, like a dove, upon the Christ, and had heard that voice from heaven which said, "This is My beloved Son, in whom I am well pleased." Yet, in the space of eighteen months or so, the effects of this vision had passed away, and we read

of the Baptist from his prison cell at Machærus sending two of his disciples to Jesus with the strange question, "Art Thou He that should come, or do we look for another?" Plainly the most stupendous sign had not been a conclusive proof to him.

3. Remember yet again, that the Bible asserts that things hostile to God have the power of working miracles, and thereby deceiving the world. There are "the spirits of devils working miracles which go forth unto the kings of the earth to gather them to the battle of the great day of God Almighty," spoken of in the book of Revelation (xvi. 14): there is that Wicked One, the mystery of whose iniquity was already working when St. Paul wrote his second epistle to the Thessalonians, who, in his full manifestation, "shall be seen to come after the working of Satan with all power and signs, and lying wonders, and with all deceivableness of unrighteousness in those that perish, because they received not the love of the truth that they might be saved." (2 Thess. ii. 8—10).

Bishop Butler has shown, in his admirable way, that there is no peculiar presumption from the analogy of nature against miracles, so as to render them in any wise incredible; and that, on the contrary, our being able to discuss reasons for them gives a positive credibility to the history of them in cases where those reasons hold (*Analogy*, p. ii., ch. 2). You will understand, therefore, that I am not raising the question of the fact of miracles as recorded historical events, but simply trying to estimate their evidential value. The question of historical fact has to be determined by the criterion of historical evidence, and not on *a priori* grounds, as Hume dealt with it. "And to ascertain the degree of strength which belongs to the evidence for the Gospel miracles, we must go into the special case of that evidence; and what we maintain is that when we do go specially into the evidence for those miracles, we find this high degree of strength in it: that its foundation lies so deep in the wonderful character and extraordinary probation of the witnesses, and in the unique character and result of the revelation, that it sustains the weight which it is required to sustain." (Mozley's *Bampton Lectures*, p. 235.)

But the question of the credibility of miracles and the question of their evidential value, as a basis of Christian faith *and a motive power in spiritual life*, are distinct questions; and it is with the latter, not the former, that I am concerned.

And here again let me recall two or three Scriptural incidents to your recollection.

1. There is the case of those men of Sychar, among whom Jesus abode two days. Their curiosity had been stimulated by the strange story of their countrywoman, who, full of the excitement of the interview at Jacob's well, had rushed into the streets, bidding every one whom she met come and see the man who had "told her all things that ever she did." "Many of the Samaritans of the city," we are told, "believed on Him" from the woman's testimony; but "*many more* believed because of *His own word*," and said unto the woman, "Now we believe, not because of thy saying; for we have heard Him ourselves, and know that this is indeed the Christ, the Saviour of the world" (John iv. 41, 42). And from

analogous cases, we cannot doubt, if these two beliefs, based, one upon a sign or wonder, the other upon teaching which came home to the conscience or the understanding with power, had been subjected to any severe subsequent strain, which would have been the more likely to bear the strain unharmed—or if temporarily weakened, to recover the more rapidly its former strength.

2. A not dissimilar case occurs in the circumstances of the miracle on the impotent man, whom Peter healed at the Beautiful gate of the temple (Acts iii, iv.). A notable miracle was wrought; the Sanhedrim admitted it, did not attempt to deny it, or explain it away; and yet they seemed to feel that the effect which had been produced upon the people did not depend upon the wonder, but upon another and even mightier power. Peter had not merely bidden a man rise up and walk in Jesus' name, but he had preached this same Jesus to the wondering crowd. He had taught them their covenant relation to the God of their fathers, and the blessedness of the blotting out of sins, when the times of refreshing should come. "And many of them which *heard the word* believed; and the number of the men was about five thousand." There was more converting, spiritualising power in the apostle's spoken words than in his mighty deeds; and so to prevent the mischievous influence, as they deemed it, from spreading further among the people, the council called Peter and John before them, and commanded them—not to perform no more miracles, but—"not to speak at all, nor teach in the name of Jesus."

3. St. Paul, again, coveted those gifts most which

conduced most directly to edification (1 Cor. xiv.). He went about the world, emphatically as a preacher, not as a thaumaturge. Christ sent him, not even "to baptise," but "to preach the gospel" (1 Cor. i. 19). He tells the Corinthians that he had the capacity of "speaking with tongues more than they all, yet would he rather speak five words with his understanding, that by his voice he might teach others also, than ten thousand words in an unknown tongue." He wrought, it is true, "the signs of an apostle" among them "in all patience, in signs, and wonders, and mighty deeds" (2 Cor. xii. 12): "from Jerusalem round about unto Illyricum, through mighty signs and wonders, by the power of the Spirit of God, he fully preached the Gospel of Christ" (Rom. xv. 19): but it was apparently the preaching itself—not the *manner* of it, for that was feeble, but the *matter* of it, "in demonstration of the Spirit and of power"—that carried conviction to the hearers' souls. It was not as a philosophical system such as the Greek mind demanded, nor as a miraculous dispensation such as the Jews required, that the simple preaching of "Jesus Christ and Him crucified" first subdued the affections, and then satisfied the reason of the world. "An evil and adulterous generation" sought after a sign: and there was no sign given unto it; but they which were humble, teachable, and, in the truest sense, reasonable souls, recognised Christ as "the power of God and the wisdom of God" (1 Cor. i. 24).

4. The story of Philip preaching in Samaria points the same way (Acts viii.). Long before the evangelist came down thither, there had been a man in that city who had bewitched the people with his sorceries, "to

whom they all gave heed, from the least to the greatest, saying, "This man is the great power of God." It might be necessary under such circumstances that Philip should put forth the thaumaturgic power, with which he, like his fellow deacon Stephen, was endowed; and so we read that "unclean spirits, crying with loud voice, came out of many that were possessed with them; and many taken with palsies, and that were lame, were healed." But the purpose of these miracles is distinctly stated. Philip's mission to the Samaritans was to "preach Christ unto them." He did not wish these people to regard him as they regarded Simon Magus: as a man gifted with supernatural powers; but as a man charged with a Divine message, in which they were vitally interested. The miracles were not so much *proofs*, as *signs;* and so we read, "the people with one accord gave heed unto those things which Philip spake, hearing and seeing the miracles which he did."

This, I take it, is the proper *spiritual* function of signs, whether we call them miraculous, and out of the order of nature, or not. Their purpose is to draw— we may even say, to compel—attention to phenomena of a higher order than themselves: for I may assume that the moral order of the world is higher than the physical: the sphere of the spiritual higher than the sphere of the material. The example of Moses at Horeb is a typical and significant one in this regard. The shepherd, on whom, remember, all the wealth of Egyptian learning had been bestowed, sees a tall thorn bush in the desert, burning with fire, yet not consumed. The spirit of scientific inquiry is raised within him, and he says, "I will now turn aside, and see this great sight, why the bush is not burnt." He had little conception of the revelation which awaited him. It can hardly be said that the prodigy of the burning bush constrained that lingering, almost reluctant, faith. There is no reference to the portent again after that the voice of the Lord God had been heard. True, some further signs were given, but even they failed to nerve the timid heart—to convince the mistrustful mind; so that (as the tale is told) "the anger of the Lord was kindled against the man," whom no appeal seemed able to lift to a consciousness of his great destiny. So again, in after days, beneath the shadow of the self-same Horeb, another prophet, he too of a despondent and mistrustful mind—or at least, at that moment, in a despondent and mistrustful mood—traced the presence of God, not in the strong wind which rent the mountains; not in the earth quaking beneath his feet; not in the fiery flashes of the thunderstorm; but in "the still small voice," which bade him return to the deserted post of duty, and do his work with more courage and more faithfulness.

And so, universally, the faith of mankind has not rested on the miracles, though they have their place among the evidences of Christianity, but on the Incarnate Lord Himself, and the message from the Father which He, and those sent by Him, delivered to the world. We believe in the Gospel because we find in it a revelation answering to our *spiritual* needs; something satisfying our desire to pierce through the veil of sense; something helping us to read more clearly than we otherwise could, the riddle of this puzzling universe; something which, while assuring us that "all things work together for good to them that love God" here, tells us also of "the far more exceeding and eternal weight of glory" which shall reward all faithful service hereafter. If we do not feel our need of a Saviour; of some One sent from God "to bless us in turning us away from our iniquities;" of some One in whose strength we can be strong, and for whose sake we can be forgiven— if, with a stoical self-sufficiency we wrap ourselves up in our own virtue, or with a light cynic sneer consider virtue impossible, perhaps unnecessary, no amount of miracles, considered as so many thaumaturgic acts—as bare signs of supernatural power, will compel belief; or make us sit, like Mary of Bethany, at Jesus' feet to hear His word. As it is recorded in one striking passage, "Though He had done so many miracles before men, yet they believed not on Him, that the saying of Esaias the prophet might be fulfilled which he spake, Lord, who hath believed our report? and to whom is the arm of the Lord revealed?" (John xii. 37, 38). The truest, strongest, most stedfast, most rational faith is like that of the men of Sychar, who believed Jesus "because of His own word." I do not say that faith may not have been strengthened, or even produced, by miracles; but not the highest, noblest, most daring, most constant faith. "Thomas, because thou hast seen Me, thou hast believed; blessed are they that have not seen, and yet have believed" (John xx. 29).

If the position which has been taken up is a sound one, two inferences seem capable of being drawn from it.

1. First: we can see a reason why miracles are suspended, if they have not altogether ceased. The season for them is closed. There are other agencies more calculated to generate faith. The eye of the

world is sufficiently turned towards Christianity; and it, of itself, offers sufficient inducements for men to examine its credentials, without being obliged to have recourse to others which, in our day, would detract from, rather than add to, its power. For it is quite certain that in an age which prides itself upon its scientific methods, any pretension to miraculous or supernatural powers, would provoke incredulity instead of stimulating faith. As has been well remarked, "the general progress of science has been to introduce law and order into ideas in which at first they did not seem to prevail; and perhaps its most fundamental effect on the human mind has been to encourage the idea of law and order, although in some respects it has encouraged it erroneously—or rather has encouraged an erroneous idea of what law and order mean." Not that arbitrary and *à priori* limitations on the power of God are the necessary accompaniments of the spirit of scientific inquiry. "You never hear," says Professor Tyndall, at the conclusion of his brilliant essay on the scientific uses of the imagination—"you never hear the really philosophical defenders of the doctrine of uniformity, speaking of impossibilities in nature. They never say, what they are constantly charged with saying, that it is impossible for the Builder of the universe to alter His work. Their business is not with the possible, but with the actual; not with a world that might be, but with the world that is. This they explore with a courage not unmixed with reverence, and according to methods which, like the quality of a tree, are tested by their fruits. They have but one desire—to know the truth. They have but one fear—to believe a lie. And if they know the strength of science, and rely upon it with unswerving trust, they also know the limits beyond which science ceases to be strong. They best know that questions offer themselves to thought, which science, as now prosecuted, has not even the tendency to solve. . . . 'Two things,' said Immanuel Kant, 'fill me with awe—the starry heavens and the sense of moral responsibility in man.' And in his hours of strength and health and sanity, when the stroke of action has ceased, and the pause of reflection has set in, the scientific investigator finds himself overshadowed by the self-same awe. Breaking contact with the hampering details of earth, it associates him with a power which gives fulness and tone to his existence, but which he can neither analyse nor comprehend." We can hardly expect the physical inquirer to assist us with his methods in the field of religious speculation: it is enough that he allows that there is such a field in the sense of moral responsibility in man, and that he gives us leave to pursue it by our own methods, which are legitimate so long as they are rational.

2. The second and last point on which I wish to say a few words, is the supremacy of conscience over the mere understanding, in judging of the evidences of faith—the grounds of believing. Let us recall for one moment the case of that dreamer of false dreams in Deut. xiii. If the sign came to pass, how were men to be prevented from recognising him who foretold it as a heaven-sent prophet of the Lord? Simply by the intuitions of their conscience. So, too, the great Apostle Paul. When all seemed failing—when the cherished hopes of years were vanishing, and the things for which

he had laboured were crumbling into dust—when all men forsook him, and he seemed to stand in a crisis such as Christianity had never passed through before, and has hardly ever passed through since, almost alone, his faith never wavered. He "*knew* in Whom he had believed." The spiritual experience of a life was not to be shattered and falsified, because he could not read distinctly a few external signs. It is the spectacle of such a might in faith that has upheld the Church in all critical times; that must uphold her now. Never had those who fear the Lord more need of the strength that comes from quietness and confidence than now. Men are looking for the Kingdom of God to come with outward show; because they see not what they deem to be its proper signs, they doubt if it exists; they forget their Lord's warning words, that His Kingdom is not without us, but within. It needs the strength of a deep conviction to keep the feet steady, when the earth seems rocking beneath us, and the very foundations—principles, beliefs, institutions, that we have long clung to—are out of course. The false prophets—or at least those who prophesy the opposite of what we have always held for truth—have, or seem to have, their signs, able to deceive, if that were possible, even the elect. And we oft-times look in vain for tokens of the same mighty arm which, in the days of old, "cut Rahab and wounded the dragon." Nevertheless, as Paul told Timothy in a like perplexing time, a still small voice within whispers, when we have commanded a moment's hush amid the hubbub of the world, "the foundation standeth sure, having this seal, The Lord knoweth them that are His. And, Let every one that nameth the name of Christ depart from iniquity." (2 Timothy ii. 19.) Philosophers tell us that under the influence of new ideas, the world is rapidly casting off its old illusions. It is easy to call what has sustained the faith of saints, illusions; it is easy to say, as has lately been said, "*Insomnia vana, valete*," but we have a right to ask philosophy what has she to give us in place of what she is destroying, more real, more trustworthy, more satisfying, more abiding? Are the best products of Christianity inferior to the best products of philosophy? Does St. Paul stand on a lower moral level than Socrates? Does Platonism give a better foundation to society than the Gospel? As Arthur Clough sings, it is easy to say :—

> "'Old things need not be therefore true,'
> O brother men, nor yet the new;
> Ah! still a while the old thought retain,
> And yet consider it again!
>
> "The souls of now two thousand years
> Have laid up here their toils and fears,
> And all the earnings of their pain—
> Ah! yet consider it again!
>
> "We! what do we see! each a space
> Of some few yards before His face;
> Does that the whole wide plan explain
> Ah! yet consider it again!
>
> "Alas! the great world goes its way,
> And takes its truth from each new day;
> They do not quit, nor yet retain,
> Far less consider it again!"

Preached—St. Mary's, Oxford, January 28, 1872.

VII.

CATHEDRALS: THEIR USE AND ABUSE.

"The house that is to be builded for the Lord must be exceeding magnifical."—1 CHRONICLES xxii. 5.

THIS may be regarded as an utterance, not so much prompted by any direct inspiration, as of the instinct of the religious nature that is in man. Egyptians, Brahmins, Buddhists, Mahometans, as well as Jews and Christians, have striven to give expression to it. The most "magnifical" buildings in the world are those that are or have been connected with religion—pagodas, mosques, temples, minsters. You know to what extent this spirit pervades the whole—or almost the whole—of the Old Testament Scriptures. You remember the story of the tabernacle, which two men of constructive genius were specially inspired to build, and which women, skilled in various kinds of needlework and embroidery combined to adorn. You remember the splendours of that Temple which the Great King, in all his pride of wealth and empire, erected upon Mount Moriah. You remember how the poor and feeble remnant returning from their Babylonish captivity did their best to restore those splendours, and how the consciousness of inability to rival the glories of the first house drew tears from their eyes as they laid the foundations of the second. You remember Herod's costly expenditure of time and money on what was regarded not only as the holiest, but the grandest of their national monuments, by which he hoped to reconcile his reluctant subjects to his rule.

There was indeed one period—and, so far as I know, only one—in the religious history of the Jewish nation, a period not of lapse into idolatry, but of a decayed, an almost dead faith—when the instinct of which I have spoken seemed as though it had expired, and when a prophet was specially sent to revive it. I refer to the age of the prophet Malachi, when men who professed to be seeking God and desirous to serve Him, offered polluted bread upon His altars, and the blind and the lame and the sick for sacrifice; and though they knew that the satrap of an earthly monarch would have spurned such gifts, expected, or pretended to expect, that He who was "a Great King," and whose "Name was dreadful among the heathen," would have pleasure in them and accept these offerings at their hand. (Malachi i. 6-14.)

I may be told that Christianity has changed all this, and has made a sanctuary for the Lord of Hosts in the hearts of men, and that the conception of God dwelling any longer, if indeed He ever did dwell, in temples made with hands, is alien from the genius of the better covenant established on better promises. (See Heb. ix.-x.) This view is perhaps true in part, but not wholly. Doubtless it matters not now—as Christ told the woman with whom He held converse at Jacob's well—where we worship, whether on Gerizim or Moriah. A Catholic Church has taken the place of a localised religion. A high spiritual worship, of which every act is, or ought to be, significant, has liberated the human heart from bondage to the weak and beggarly elements of a ceremonial law. But still the first preachers of the Gospel seem to have never missed a chance, if I may say so, of inspiring those who listened to their message with a sense of that awe and reverence which certainly must always be in place when such a being as man falls down in worship before such a Being as God. Those glorious visions with which the Book of the Revelation of St. John the Divine is filled from end to end, certainly appeal more or less to the sensuous imagination, to that æsthetic faculty of the soul which feels elevated—and not only elevated but purified—by what is graceful, beautiful, solemn, stately, grand.

The first Christians—those of whom we read in the Acts of the Apostles and in the Epistles of St. Paul—with their surrounding difficulties of poverty or persecution, could not do much of a material kind to express this sense of divine awe. "Not many noble, not many great, not many rich were called" then. The Apostles did not teach—they were not so preposterous as to try and teach—their converts to set to work to build cathedrals, to raise solid towers on every hill side, or soaring spires on every plain, or humbler, but still graceful and picturesque churches in every nestling village. There is a time, says the wise man, "for every purpose under heaven" (Eccles. iii. 1): and the time for building stately minsters and cathedrals had not yet come. But those who preached the Gospel then with mighty signs and wonders, and demonstrations of the Spirit and of power, did try to impregnate the minds of believers with a sense of awe, without which our approaches to God in worship can hardly be otherwise than profane. (See Heb. xii. 18-29.)

A time came, and that before long, for greater things, and for a display of the majesty of external ritual to the eyes of the world; and the religious instincts of the heart, having first found satisfaction of their yearnings within, craved also an opportunity of expressing that satisfaction, in outward form. And as in Richard Hooker's words "Solemn duties of public service to be done unto God, must have their places set apart and prepared in such sort as beseemeth actions of that regard." Men felt with David that the house they built for God should be exceeding magnifical; and the basilicas of imperial days and the cathedrals of the middle ages sprang from the same heart's desire that poured itself out in so lavish an expenditure of costly material and artistic skill on the plateau of Mount Moriah. (See Hooker's *Eccl. Pol.* book v. ch. xi.)

The instinct—for, from its universality and uniformity, it would seem to have been an instinct rather than a mere formal or conscious effort of the mind—founded itself upon, or else was accompanied by, many ideas; but one was paramount, and that was the idea of a noble and (so far as human resources could make it) a commensurate worship of Almighty God: that nothing should be wanting to help the worshippers to feel that the service rendered to God is and ought to be the highest of all earthly services. Even materials, base in themselves, like wood and stone, when built (so to speak) upon that one foundation which God had laid—consecrated as instruments in the diffusion of the Gospel of the Lord Jesus Christ—acquired from that use a sort of sanctity, and stood as it were on holy ground.

The main idea—I have said—in the minds of the founders of our cathedrals, seems to have been the desire to exhibit in their services the highest and most perfect pattern of Christian worship. They wished to unite in one great purpose all that was at once most grand and graceful in architecture, most sublime and elevating in music, most solemn and reverent in ritual, most grave and touching in language. Beneath the vaulted roof of one of our old English minsters, typical in its very structure and ground-plan of the Cross of Christ, with its solid towers standing for half a thousand years firm and immutable, like the Church's creed; or its tall tapering spire soaring, as the soul would fain soar, into the calm blue ether which fancy dreams to be the dwelling-place of the Most High; with mellow light streaming across the inlaid marble floor:—

"From many a storied window
In richest colours dight;"

while the swelling organ and clear-voiced harmonious choir ring out triumphantly that glorious anthem which, if anything earthly can be, must be the echo of angels' songs in heaven—"Hallelujah! for the Lord God omnipotent reigneth;"—or again, when priests and people, with measured voice and low, with bended knees and faces buried in the hands, as if to shut out for one brief half-hour the disturbing thoughts of an evil world, beseech the good Lord " by the memory of His agony and Bloody Sweat, His Cross and Passion, His Burial, His Resurrection, His Ascension, to deliver them;" one has felt, when the heart has been rightly attuned, as it is seldom permitted to sinful man to feel in a sinful world, in a passionate ecstasy, or else in a deep solemn thrill of spiritual worship; almost like Paul, as though "caught up to the third heaven;" almost as able, though but for a moment, to realise what it must be to stand, like Gabriel, in the presence of God.

It is a natural, and when kept within bounds, a legitimate desire of the human heart, when it has been once touched by religious influences, to yearn after an elevated and beautiful type of worship. The tendency of a utilitarian age is to lose to a great extent the feeling—indeed almost the *conception* of worship—as, for instance, David conceived it. It is true we have not altogether "forsaken the assembling of ourselves together," but the motive by which we are influenced is too often the attraction of a popular preacher, or an elaborate and gorgeous ritual, or a highly-finished musical service, rather than any desire to realise, in the truest sense and highest measure, the blessedness of communion with God. The sentiment which prompted the 68th Psalm, written, as is probable, for the ceremonial of removing the ark from the house of Obed-Edom to the place which David had prepared for it in

Zion, would be unintelligible to many modern fashionable congregations.

Men perhaps will ask—nay, they do ask—the question: "How can you justify the vast expense of rebuilding or restoring those old cathedrals, which perhaps had their purpose in their day, but which you, when you have restored them, will certainly be unable to put to any adequate use?" Some eighteen months ago I attended a large meeting at Liverpool, held for the purpose of increasing the funds required for the restoration of this cathedral, and there I heard an elaborate justification of the large expenditure that has been incurred in the work, from the lips of a nobleman whose words always sink deep into the minds of those who listen to him, on the ground that the cathedrals of England are great historical monuments, linking the present with the past, which we, the generation who have received them, are bound to maintain. I think we ought to recognise this obligation, and it is an argument which may be fairly urged, by those who are engaged in such an enterprise as yours, in reply to the captious question which measures everything merely by the commercial standard of value, and asks "To what purpose is this (seeming) waste?" And even upon utilitarian principles—at least upon the principles of a generous and elevated utilitarianism— we cannot afford to part with one single evidence of a high and rightly-directed public spirit. The poet Horace marked it as a token of degeneracy in his age that his countrymen were lavishing all their wealth upon personal and selfish objects—their villas, their porticoes, their gardens: and we should regard it, and justly, as a proof that the heart of England was strangely changed for the worse, if, spending as we do, untold sums of money on our 'cieled houses,' we suffered our cathedrals—the memorials of the piety and patriotism of our forefathers—to lie waste.

But, I confess, I regard our cathedrals from another point of view than merely as so many national monuments. We may not be able to apply them to all the purposes contemplated by their original founders, but we can at least develop in them, as nowhere else besides, the highest and grandest form of worship, according to the sober and reverent mind of the Church of England. It cannot be said that, as a rule, in Church of England congregations the error is on the side of excessive ceremonialism. The movement in the direction of ritual development, which has assumed in some few instances extravagant and fantastic and even superstitious shapes, has been based partly, no doubt, on a desire to exhibit certain aspects of Christian doctrine; but quite as much perhaps upon a reaction from the slovenliness and irreverence of that listless form of service which seems sufficient to satisfy the spiritual yearnings of genteel and fashionable piety. We need, not fewer, but more types and patterns of that fervent yet chastened spirit of devotion which harmonises so well with the true spirit of the Church of England, and without which her glorious, inimitable Liturgy becomes the dreariest and most unedifying of forms. Any one who has seen those vast congregations gathered into the nave of Westminster Abbey or beneath the dome of St. Paul's Cathedral, must allow that in our cathedrals we have an opportunity, if only we will use it, of exercising that "gift of prophecy" to which St. Paul attributes so potent an influence both on those who believe not and on those who believe. (1 Cor. xiii. 2, xiv. 22—25.) At the same time, I entirely feel —and I do not wish you to forget, and therefore I do not pass it by without notice—that we may add to the pomp and external solemnity of religion, without thereby proportionately increasing its power. I take it that there can be no contrast so hateful in the eyes of Almighty God as that of a magnificent temple, such as the one in which we are now assembled, filled with worshippers " of the earth, earthy "—" having the form of godliness without the power." Christ's one act of severity was to drive out of the courts of the temple, with a scourge of knotted cords, those who, by their godless trafficking, carried on under pretext of religion, had made God's House of Prayer "a den of thieves."

But these grand cathedrals teach, moreover—or if they do not directly teach, they indirectly remind us of—some great moral, I may even call them some great national, lessons. They teach us a lesson which, in our pride of science and in our pride of strength, we have much need to learn. We of this nineteenth century are not in all respects better than our fathers, nor wiser. In some respects, it is obvious, we have more light, greater power, wider opportunities, larger capacity; but in many other respects we are but copyists, and copyists at a humble distance, of those who have gone before us. We could hardly build nowadays one of these cathedrals; nor, if we could find the money, could we perhaps find the architect to design Westminster Abbey, or Lincoln Minster, or Salisbury spire. And even the money, the lowest of all the elements contributing to the result, we should not find it very easy to raise. We have not got the faith, perhaps we have not got the piety; certainly we have not got the spirit of self-sacrifice. We boast of our far-sightedness, of our advance upon the knowledge and resources of the ages that are gone by; and we forget sometimes that we are but as children carried on the shoulders of a giant, and on that account alone are able to see a little further than our ancestors.

And yet another lesson may be learned from our cathedrals. A popular and influential writer complains that the civilisation of England is sadly lacking in the elements of "light and sweetness." But life, human life, needs something more than "light and sweetness": needs breadth, spaciousness, grandeur, elevation. We do not want merely to bask in the sun and eat sugar plums, like children on a holiday. What we need to have ever before us is a noble aim, an inspiring motive, a worthy end: and of all these we find a type in the cathedral.

I wish you working men—if, as I was led to expect, this congregation is composed mainly of working men —I wish you knew Greek. I would try to make you understand the full force of those words of St. Paul, who, in writing to the Christians of Philippi, tells them that if they saw "anything true, anything honest"—the

Greek word is σεμνά, and should have been translated
grand, majestic, stately—" anything just, anything pure,
anything of good report"—rather, perhaps, anything with
that indefinable character of solemnity about it which
casts a corresponding influence over the soul—they
should "think of these things." (Philip. iv. 8.) Putting
aside for the moment the idea of justice, all those other
ideas—truth, grandeur, purity, loveliness, and the awfulness that hushes the soul—all these are found in our
great cathedrals. They are, or ought to be, to us as a
type of true nobility of life. If you that I see before
me are indeed working men, there must be a contrast
obvious to your eyes, my friends, between this grand
and lofty and well-proportioned cathedral and your own
home—perhaps a home in a dark and cheerless court,
where the sun hardly ever shines, where sweet sounds
are seldom heard, where you can scarcely find a place
to rest and seek quiet communion with God. Well,
even that contrast, sharp and painful as it is, is typical;
for it portrays the contrast between this life and the
next. Yes, friends, there will be a change when the
lowest of the sons of toil shall shake off his earthly
tabernacle, and all the earthliness that has adhered to
it, and shall be clothed upon with that new house prepared for him of God, "eternal in the heavens." The
change we look for—the clearness of vision promised to
us—the rest after labour, the Sabbath-keeping, as the
writer of the Epistle to the Hebrews calls it (iv. 9)—
the glory—the life of the world to come, all stand in
the same startling contrast to the life that you and I
and all of us are spending now.

I admit that cathedrals have been desecrated. Go where you will—I do not know the traditions of this cathedral—but go to Lichfield, to Bristol, to Exeter, and you shall hear tales told you by the verger who takes you round to show you the sights of his cathedral, of the doings of Cromwell and his troopers, or other iconoclasts of that fanatical time, how they dashed the statues from their niches, how they broke into fragments the stained windows, how they mutilated the curiously-carved stalls or screens, how they stabled their horses in the cloisters. No doubt those men, filled with a wild, unreasoning piety—for though they did profane acts, they were not at heart profane men—did do such things: but, in my judgment, there have been worse desecrations than ever were perpetrated by Cromwell and his soldiery. Cathedrals have been desecrated by those who, having received them as an inheritance, wasted that inheritance; those who dozed out sleepy useless lives under the very shadow of influences which should have had a tendency to inspire every action with a noble motive; those who built a fortune or founded a family out of what was intrusted to them for far other than personal or selfish ends; those who made the very name of a cathedral a synonym for formalism and spiritual death. Happily for us, before it was too late, a higher sense of duty has taken possession of the nation now. Acts that were tolerated, if not applauded, fifty years since, would be impossible to-day. Not only are cathedrals being restored on every side, and there is hardly a cathedral city in England where you will not find that much has been done, or is being done, of the same kind as that which you are doing here—not only, I say, are cathedrals being restored by the patriotic spirit of a generous people, but deans and chapters are awakening, or have awoke, to a sense of the use of them.

We cannot afford to spare these purifying, ennobling and (in a secondary sense) sanctifying influences. We must not let cathedrals just yet pass into the rank of "national monuments," like Stonehenge; and become the objects of a mere historical interest or antiquarian curiosity. We have a use for them—a need of them. We have a right to make a complaint of that scepticism —too often atheism in disguise—which, under the pretence of exalting human nature, really degrades it by making man, with his heavy downward-gravitating tendencies, the measure of all things. When Paul tells Christian people to think on things grand and pure, which attract love and produce a solemn hush in the soul, no doubt he meant them to take into their field of vision the best samples of humanity in their fellow-men; but the scepticism of the day refuses to recognise anything higher than man. It will not do, my friends. It will not be enough to keep man even at his present level. He is sure to sink if no higher type is set before him than himself.

There are theories floating abroad about mankind having been developed from the lowest form of savagery; and there are speculators who would persuade us that human nature, having reached its present stage of perfection, can never retrograde. I do not feel so sure of this impossibility. To me the most frightful symptom of the times is the savagery that can be seen existing in the midst of our boasted civilisation. I do not know whether it be so in Chester, but in most great towns and in many country villages, you will find savages as wild and brutal, and in their conduct to their wives and children as little under the discipline of self-control—and that without the same excuse—as those South Sea Islanders who martyred Bishop Patteson.

Another thing sometimes moves me with alarm. It is the dread of lapsing into a glittering, but yet pagan, barbaric imperialism like that of Rome when, as one satirist of manners tells us, the rich thought happiness consisted in keeping yachts and driving four-in-hand, and the poor, as another adds, cared only for their victuals and the theatres. There is some peril lest, with wealth increasing so rapidly in every class of society without the accompaniment of a capacity to spend it upon proper objects and in a right way, we should relapse into types of life like these. We want Christ in the influence of His high example—Christ in the lofty motives of His religion—Christ in the power of His Spirit—we want Christ "to deliver us from the bondage of corruption into the glorious liberty of the children of God." We want Christ to save us, not only from the devil, *but from ourselves.*

Preached—At re-opening of Chester Cathedral, January 30, 1872

VIII.

THINGS HARD TO BE UNDERSTOOD.

"In which are some things hard to be understood."—
2 PETER iii. 16.

IF it has pleased Almighty God to make a revelation, a partial unveiling or manifestation, of Himself to man; it is not an unreasonable nor an impossible hypothesis that the disclosure should still be incomplete; or if not incomplete, in many of its parts at least incomprehensible and mysterious. Even those whom we believe to have been the instruments and media of the revelation, felt that the God who was thus making Himself known was still a God who "hid Himself" from their yearning gaze; that His judgments were unsearchable, His ways past finding out; that they knew in part, and prophesied in part; and their spirits inquired and searched diligently into the time, and method, and scope of that divine plan of salvation which they were commissioned, and felt themselves inspired, to proclaim. "The mystery of godliness," the manifestation of God, whether in the flesh or otherwise, the justification of His ways, whether spiritually or in what is called the "light of nature," the visions of Him whether by angels or by men, the preaching of Him whether to Jews or Gentiles, to wise or unwise, the measure both of belief and unbelief with which He has been received in the world, the final issue of the mighty purpose in that great harvest of souls of which the reception of Jesus Christ into glory is (so to speak) the first fruits; all these features of the dispensation under which we live are, and must be (as Paul felt them to be) under our present conditions of intelligence, a mystery, great, profound, unfathomable. And the higher we rise in the scale of knowledge, the more strongly we feel the limitations which the very nature of the phenomena with which we are dealing, imposes upon our desire to pass from the field of doubt, or gloom, into the realms of light and certainty. The philosopher is more conscious of his ignorance than the peasant of his. The highest minds are also the lowliest. "I seem like a child," said Newton, "playing on the sea-shore, and picking up a fair pebble here and there, while the great ocean of truth lies all undiscovered before me." "Nature is only conquered," said Lord Bacon, "by obedience," (*Natura parendo vincitur*).

It would be unphilosophical to postulate, or suggest, a revelation in those departments of human knowledge in which man's natural faculties are adequate to the task of invention or discovery. And yet so little do we know of what the actual method or moment of revelation *has* been or *could* be, so imperfectly can we understand the state of that mind into which a flood of supernatural light has been suddenly poured,—Moses' on Sinai, Elijah's at Horeb, Isaiah's when he saw the Lord sitting upon the throne, Jeremiah's when he felt a word burning within him as a fire, Peter's on the tanner's house-top, Paul's when caught up into the third heaven,—so sudden, too, and unaccountable, so little the conscious and apparent result of previous processes, even in the field of philosophical or scientific inquiry, have sometimes been discoveries pregnant with mightiest consequences,—as, for instance, the seeming accident out of which the mind of Newton evolved the great law of gravitation,—that it would not be very easy, nor very safe, to limit the sphere within which God vouchsafes to aid and quicken the faculties of man, nor to determine with any positiveness or precision what are the fields of knowledge in which the unassisted reason—the "dry light" of the human intellect—is supreme.

Still, speaking generally and popularly, man has discovered, or thinks he has discovered, slowly, gradually, precariously, but in the strength of his own intellectual resources, his relation to the outer world, and his relations to his fellow-men; the great laws which govern the physical universe of which he forms a part, the laws also by which society is governed, and by which civil and moral life become possible. "Whatsoever ye would that men should do to you do ye even so to them," may be the summary of a revealed law and of inspired prophets, and certainly has the sanction of the Divine Teacher Whom, in fulness of times, the Father sent into the world—but it had already been delivered among the precepts of Confucius, and is to be found, almost in the same words, among the moral aphorisms collected by Isocrates. It would ordinarily, therefore, be called a principle which the human intellect could develop without supernatural aid, and the fact that it is to be found among the precepts of the Gospel vindicates for it a divine *sanction*, rather than a supernatural *origin*.

But the relations of man to God, the religious and theological ideas which have exercised so mighty an influence upon the moral and social development of the race,—in spite of M. Comte, who regards them as a necessary condition of a certain immature stage of the human intellect, and of M. Taine, who considers them to be the product of two forces, the spirit of poetry and the spirit of credulity, working together,—can hardly with propriety, or with truth, be classed among human discoveries or treated as the result of human reasoning. In common parlance, I am aware, we talk of "natural religion"; and great arguments have been constructed upon its asserted principles: as, *e.g.* the argument from general consent; the argument from design; and the *à priori* class of arguments which postulate the idea of God as the necessary basis of correlative ideas assumed to be necessary and innate in the human mind; but of these, the argument from the general consent of mankind points rather to one common original, and probably supernatural source, than to an aggregate result of many independent concurrent inquiries; while the argument from design, though in my judgment unfairly discredited by some who now are leaders in the field of philosophical inquiry, has been seriously impugned; and we must all, I should think, feel that the argument, as conducted by Samuel Clarke, from *à priori* or metaphysical considerations, is altogether wanting in the element of cogency, and indeed fails to be generally comprehensible. "Canst thou by searching,"—was Zophar the Naamathite's question of the patriarch Job,—" Canst thou by searching find out God? canst thou find out the Almighty unto perfection? It is as high as heaven; what canst thou do? deeper than Hades; what canst thou know?" (Job xi. 7, 8.)

It is true that the evidences of natural religion (so called) are appealed to by St. Paul in two famous arguments. In his address to the heathen Lycaonians, sunk in the degradation of an anthropomorphic polytheism, he appeals to the rain from heaven and the fruitful seasons, witnessing to the beneficence of the living God who had made the heaven, the earth, the sea, and all things that are therein (Acts xiv. 15—17). In the terrible picture that he paints in Romans i. of the gross vices and degrading Atheism of the heathen world, which the Gospel of God was about to make a final effort to purify, the inexcusableness of all this ungodliness and unrighteousness is traced back to the fact that the invisible things of the Creator could be clearly discerned by the eye of the mind from the things that are made— even His Eternal Power and Godhead. And yet, in both these instances, the evidences of religion from the phenomena of nature are alleged, not so much as original or independent sources of truth, as (rather) collateral and subsidiary supports to ideas or convictions already in the mind—dormant perhaps, in the case of the Lycaonians, but only needing the utterance of some living voice to quicken them into the energy of an operative faith. And indeed from the natural argument in Acts xiv. 17, if it stood alone, an erroneous and even mischievous inference might be drawn. For the goodness and benevolence of God might be supposed to be, not only as the Psalmist felt, "enduring yet daily" and spread "over all His works," but indiscriminating in the moral as well as in the material world; not only "making the sun to rise on the evil and on the good, and sending rain on the just and on the unjust," but rewarding with equal measure, and with equal indifference, obedience and disobedience, those who resist, and those who love to do, His will.

And there is one terrible burden which men have to bear in the world, to which the knowledge of God's Eternal Power and Deity would by no means be an adequate counterpoise. I refer to the burden of the consciousness of sin. No phantom of a distempered imagination, brooding unhealthily upon its own disease; no figment invented by priests to bring the human conscience into bondage to their spells and charms; but a real and terrible burden, so real that we most feel its crushing force just when we lie most helpless under it—so terrible, that in such awful moments, when the soul comprehends the reality of what it had so long tried to represent to itself as a dream, the thought of God's power only adds intensity to its dreadfulness—would only plunge the conscience-stricken wretch into deeper depths of uttermost despair. And it is this consciousness of the presence of sin, coupled with the apprehension of its consequences, that makes us feel the necessity—or at least the need—of some authoritative revelation of the character of God, which shall harmonise all His attributes in such a way that our conscience may be satisfied that "mercy and truth are met together; righteousness and peace have kissed each other." "O wretched man that I am," cries Paul, after that terrible process of self-introspection, in the course of which he had discovered "a law in his members warring against the law of his mind, and bringing him into captivity to the law of sin which was in his members:" a law so mighty in its force that the good he would he could not do, the evil which he would not, he seemed to be doing continually. "O wretched man that I am!" cries the helpless, the almost despairing one, "who shall deliver me from the body of this death?" "I thank God!" he adds, as a brighter, better light dawns upon his soul, "I thank God, through Jesus Christ our Lord." It was the revelation of " there being no condemnation to them which are in Christ, who walk not after the flesh, but after the spirit "—" the revelation of the law of the Spirit of Life in Christ Jesus" which freed him from this crushing burden of the law of sin and death. In the midst of the sorrows which he had in his heart, God's comforts refreshed his soul. When the conscience has woke up suddenly, like David's, from the delirious dream in which some Siren-hand has steeped it, to a sense of its guilt—to a sense, too, of how far that guilt of ours may have compromised others now beyond our reach or beyond our influence, possibly beyond the reach or influence of any one—and to the further consciousness that not one jot or tittle of all that has been done can be undone; when the bitter shameful confession has been wrung from the lips, " I have sinned against the Lord; against Him, Him only, have I done this evil, and that too in His sight," it needs the presence of a prophet, of some one commissioned to speak to us in the name of God, at least of some voice which seems to come down from heaven, to make us feel that yet it is possible for the Lord to put away our sin, by a plenary act of pardon; effectively, entirely, once for all.

The method of this reconciliation, the conditions of this forgiveness have been revealed; are recorded in a book which the whole Christian world, though with perceptible variations in the meaning which is attached to the phrase believes to be " inspired ";—the Word or Message of God; the account which He has been pleased to give of Himself, the Creator, in relation to us, the creatures of His hand. The Epistles to the Romans and to the Hebrews are full to the brim of the high argument. The mysteries which it contains are deep, unsearchable. The very terms in which the doctrine is theologically conveyed are terms, familiar to us all as phrases, familiar to us also, alas! as the battle-cries of parties; terms which have exercised the wit of man for centuries, but of which the precise meaning is unsettled still. Need I remind you of all the strife, and controversy, and word-war that have gathered round the doctrine of atonement, the theory of justification, the mystery of the new birth, the everlasting sentence of God's predestination, the possibility of falling from grace, the certainty of salvation, the full assurance of faith, the eternity of punishment. In all, are "many things hard to be understood." In all there are what St. Paul calls αἰνίγματα—puzzles, riddles, hard sayings, paradoxes. In this searching of the spirit into the deep things of God, as in all venturous voyages, no small peril has to be encountered. "So convinced am I," said a thoughtful and religious-minded woman, precluded by sickness from the activities of life, and much given in consequence to speculation in this field, "so convinced am I that it is impossible to be well with such things always in one's head, that I would abandon these studies if I could, and plunge into active life, satisfied to do my duty as well as I could, and leave the rest to God's mercy. But, in utter loneliness, the mind turns inwards to search into its own nature and prospects, and this research shakes the mortal case shrewdly. Few can comprehend this; and I, who feel it, can hardly describe; but I certainly feel that those who eat largely of the tree of knowledge will surely die, and that soon."— (*Letters of Miss Cornwallis.*)

Happily for mankind, God, when He manifested Himself to the world in the Person of His Son, hid these things from the wise and prudent, and revealed them unto babes. The doors of the kingdom of heaven were easiest found by those that felt most their need of entrance there; by publicans and harlots sooner than by learned scribes, or proud contemptuous Pharisees. "*Non in dialectica complacuit Deo,*" says old St.

Ambrose, "*salvum facere populum suum.*" "Not by dialectic—by logical processes—was it God's good pleasure to make his people whole." "They that would do the will should know the doctrine." The word was spoken as men were able to hear it. Sometimes in sweet, attractive illustration drawn from the homeliest concerns of life; sometimes in brief, pregnant dogmas; sometimes in simple, intelligible precepts; sometimes in eloquent action; sometimes in silent suffering. And the simpler the act or the words, the fuller they seem to be of strength, and comfort, and satisfaction. From the sight of Jesus going about doing good, "and healing every one that was oppressed of the devil"; from the first showing-forth of glory at the marriage feast at Cana; from the raising up to life of the widow's only son, and the restoring him to his mother; from the staunching of the issue of blood in her who came timidly behind Him in the crowd, and touched but the hem of His garment; from the hand held out to Peter as his heart failed him amid the waves; from the tears shed at the grave of Lazarus; from the ministrations of menial service in the upper chamber of Jerusalem; we learn something of the nature and the purpose of that great redemption, whose highest mystery was transacted, whose bitterest sufferings were borne, I know not whether in Gethsemane or on Calvary. From simple, emphatic utterances, "Behold the Lamb of God, that beareth the sin of the world"— "God so loved the world that he gave his only begotten Son, that whosoever believeth in Him shall not perish but have everlasting life"—"This is life eternal, to know Thee the only true God,—and Jesus Christ Whom Thou hast sent"—"The Son of Man is come to seek and save that which was lost"—"The blood of Jesus Christ cleanseth from all sin"—"The grace of God which bringeth salvation hath appeared to all men"— from these and a thousand like utterances, which as you all know are the very symbols of the Gospel, there beams forth a clearness and a force of truth for which you will search in vain in "Institutes," and "Canons," and "Confessions," and "Articles," and abstract treatises of theology. These have their use in teaching Christianity as a system; but not in applying it remedially to human needs, as a power. And "the kingdom of God," cries Paul, "is not in word"—in a logically developed system, "but in power."

I would exhort you, in this day of confessed peril not only to Christian faith; to belief in a revelation having come from God and in a kingdom of grace being set up upon this earth by God: but of peril also, flowing from this unbelief or misbelief, to those high social and moral interests which involve all that is most precious in the life both of the individual and of the community, I would exhort you to build your faith on these simple dogmas; to frame your lives according to these simple rules.

The very principle of faith—and with it, I venture to think, the only sure and permanent guarantee of holiness—is imperilled from two opposite sides: from the dogmatisers who call upon us to receive, as truths, propositions from which sometimes our conscience, sometimes our reason, revolts; and from the men of science who bid us, as a duty we owe to truth, give up everything that the reason cannot explain. Both parties make upon us what I cannot but consider unreasonable demands. There are mysteries in science, as well as mysteries in faith : and if philosophers are not disloyal to science by accepting a "working hypothesis," which they cannot fully prove, but which explains phenomena sufficiently well for practical purposes, neither are we disloyal to truth or false to our duty as reasonable beings, for accepting as our hypothesis the principle of faith—faith which can give a reason for itself in part, though not wholly, and on which we think we can dare "to work out our salvation, albeit in fear and trembling." We believe; we think we have some experience as a ground for our belief that God is working with us; and, to borrow the words of a great and profound thinker, "He who has willed that we should so act," upon principles not absolutely indisputable, "co-operates with us in our acting, and thereby bestows on us a certitude which rises higher than the logical force of our conclusions." (Newman's *Apologia*, 324.)

But the perils from the side of ultra-dogmatism are perhaps even greater than the perils from the "oppositions of science falsely so called." Indeed, I am misapplying the Apostle's phrase; and the ψευδώνυμος γνῶσις of which he bids Timothy beware is not honest, legitimate inquiry into the laws which govern the physical world, but the daring or inane speculations of a gnostic theology, puffed up by a temper carnal rather than spiritual, and intruding into things which it had not seen and could not pretend to see. Under the specious names of Catholic dogma or of infallible truth, weak minds are lured to accept propositions about divine things which, if not simply unmeaning, are utterly incredible, and which, when examined, are not found to rest on any authoritative or undoubted warrant of God's word, but upon the precarious or over-subtle inferences of fallible man. And when this is discovered, the inevitable law of reaction comes into operation; and those who have believed most get to believe least, and the credulity of the *youth* is replaced by the scepticism of the *man*. "The simplicity that is in Christ," or as it would be more correctly rendered, "the simplicity that is *towards Christ*"—εἰς τὸν Χριστὸν—was the mental quality that St. Paul feared might get corrupted in the Corinthian Christians. (2 Cor. xi. 3.) The eye singly fixed on Christ as the centre of all our hopes, the source of all our spiritual strength, is the condition of clearness of vision in spiritual things. If you are lifting anything else into the place which He alone should occupy, whether it be the Sacraments, or the Church, or the Priest, or even what you call "the faith," which means your particular conception or formulation of truth, you are in effect drawing a curtain more or less thick, of more or fewer folds, between your soul and Him: and even the thinnest, and most translucent veil will dim somewhat of the glory of that countenance which is as the sun shining in his strength. No doubt we need *some* veil. Our eyes are not yet trained to gaze upon the fulness of that glory. But take heed how you multiply veils. To take for an example the question that is so keenly agitated amongst us now, and which has recently been brought into such special prominence, and that is the only reason for my selecting it, there is ground for apprehension, lest amid these subtle controversies about the mode, and nature, and time, and conditions of the Divine Presence in the Holy Eucharist, the very object and purpose of that Presence should be overlooked or thrown into the background; lest while we are speculating about the virtue of the words and act of consecration; or are waiting for the elevation of the chalice or paten; or are preparing ourselves for some act of adoration of the Lord "present," as we phrase it, "objectively under the form of bread and wine," we so occupy ourselves with these uncertain and, at the best, secondary things, as to neglect to ascertain what tokens there are of the Presence *there*, where alone it can possibly be of any benefit to ourselves—I mean in our own souls. There is growing up amongst us, I fear, a materialised conception of the presence of Christ in His Sacrament which is as far below the spirituality of the doctrine of transubstantiation, as received by intelligent Romanists, as that is below the spirituality of St. Paul's teaching that "the cup of blessing which we bless is the communion of the blood of Christ; the bread which we break is the communion of the body of Christ." There is, I repeat, a danger of the thing signified being utterly obscured and lost behind the veil of the signifying form; of the outward and visible sign hindering instead of furthering the reception of the inward spiritual grace. And the danger is not only the danger that always springs from a superstition taking the place of a spiritual or reasonable service; but the yet greater danger of the "form of godliness" making men indifferent to, or careless of, "the power." A ceremonial service has always had the effect of deadening the conscience to the claims and obligations of the moral law. King Saul needed to be told that "to obey was better than sacrifice, and to hearken than the fat of rams." In Isaiah's days men were offering their vain oblations, filling the air with the fumes of their incense, which was an "abomination;" keeping their new moons and sabbaths, which in the eyes of God was as it were "iniquity," "while their hands were full of blood." And another prophet had to teach those who were offering "their firstborn for their transgression — the fruit of the body for the sin of their soul"—what were the first principles of commercial honesty, of considerateness, and of fair dealing, and to remind them that the primary duties which the Lord required of them were "to do justly, and to love mercy, and to walk humbly with their God." With all the outward show of religion which surrounds us, I should like to be assured that this interest in ceremonial is commensurate with, and expressive of, a vital sense of religion's sanctifying, purifying power. If any of you that hear me are merely, or mainly gratifying an æsthetic sentiment in these matters, I may venture to tell you that you are indulging in a very perilous amusement.

And with regard to points of faith or doctrine, it was a memorable saying of Channing's that "men are responsible for the *uprightness* of their opinions rather than for their *rightness*." The desire to be truthful at all hazards is a nobler temper than the mere desire to be what men call "sound." The spirit of truthfulness is what Christ tells us the Father seeks in those who worship Him. There may be things hard to understand in the Pauline Epistles, and in the other Scriptures; but no one shall miss their meaning utterly, still less wrest or twist them to his own destruction, who seeks simply to know God's will for the purpose of doing it. No doubt ignorance and instability of character are serious hindrances in the search after truth: but there can hardly be instability where there is earnestness; and the ignorance that hinders is the ignorance of prejudice and self-sufficiency and shallow knowledge, rather than the ignorance which springs from the lack of cultivation or of educational opportunities. St. Paul had a strong conviction that differences of opinion among earnest men would ultimately be harmonised by the teaching of the Spirit of God, and certainly ought not to break up Christian unity. "Let us, therefore," he writes to the Philippians, "as many as be perfect, be thus minded; and if in anything ye be otherwise minded, God shall reveal even this unto you" (Philip. iii. 15). He has more confidence in the power of truth to prevail by its own weight, than those who would needs protect it by damnatory clauses. He reserves weapons of this kind for one class, and one class only: for an unbelief that was moral rather than intellectual, and that believes not the truth because it has pleasure in unrighteousness. "If any one love not the Lord Jesus Christ let him be anathema" (1 Cor. xvi., 22). He foresees the prospects of heresies or sects springing up within the bosom of the Church, not perhaps with satisfaction, but at least with equanimity. "There must be also heresies among you—δεῖ γὰρ καὶ αἱρέσεις ἐν ὑμῖν εἶναι—that they which are approved may be made manifest among you." He would not say, as some say nowadays, that the existence of diversity in religious opinions was a necessary condition of healthy and energetic religious life in individuals and in churches; he did not deny that schisms, on the part of those who wantonly make or cause them (but I beg you to remember that he who *makes* the schism is not always he who *causes* it, and in the lamentable schism of the last century, it is very doubtful who should bear most of the blame, John Wesley or the priests and bishops of the Church of England)—I was saying, Paul did not deny that schisms on the part of those who wantonly make or cause them, were products of an un-Christian temper, tokens of a carnal mind; yet he admitted they might have a moral purpose—δεῖ γὰρ εἶναι—and might be worked into the foreordained issue of the Divine counsels, and even accomplish their own cure or their own antidote, by manifesting, and indeed helping to create, a higher form of spiritual life in those who passed through this trial of their faith not only unharmed, but purified. For it must be remembered that the presence of divergence in religious opinion—and even of unbelief—amongst us, justly as it may be deprecated on other grounds, does give opportunity for the culture and exhibition of certain graces or virtues—and those not of a secondary or trivial kind—in which Christians, with conspicuous gifts of another order, have not unfrequently been found wanting. Fairness towards an opponent—the charity that neither thinketh nor imputeth evil—a mind so evenly and so surely balanced on the pivot of its own faith, as to be able to allow for the effect of partial conceptions of truth in the minds of others—power to discriminate between what is essential and what is accidental, what is vital in a system and what does not touch its heart—abstinence from exasperating language—restraint of the *odium theologicum*—the wisdom that knows when to resist and when to concede—when to circumcise Timothy, when to refuse to circumcise Titus,—these, and many more than these, are graces which in minds fashioned in the likeness of Christ's mind, are, it may be said, actually generated in an atmosphere of controversy.

And, further, it must be admitted, that those who are bound to uphold a particular system—especially if it be a traditionary system, reverend with the hoar of antiquity—are, so far as the system cramps their freedom of inquiry, less qualified to judge of truth with that entire absence of bias or prepossession which the subject requires. "How legible the book of nature becomes to me," said Goethe, "I cannot express to thee. My long lessons in spelling have helped me, and now my quiet joy is inexpressible. Much as I find that is new, I find nothing unexpected: everything fits in, because I have no system, and desire nothing but the pure truth." "I had no right, I had no leave," says John Henry Newman, in his *Apologia*, "to act against my conscience. That was a higher rule than any argument about the *Notes of the Church*" (p. 26). And on this ground I think we must all feel, that while a certain amount of agreement upon points of faith considered fundamental—though even here a reasonable latitude of opinion must be allowed, and the mind of a modern interpreter must not dictate the sense in which the terms of an ancient contract are to be understood by the recipient,—while, then, a certain amount of agreement upon so-called "fundamentals" is indispensable to that unity which is the condition of organised life in a Church, yet nothing is really gained, while much is lost, by multiplying such points, and the creed or the confession which avoids "curiosities of explication" (as Jeremy Taylor calls them), is at once the surest safeguard of the cause of truth, and the truest friend to honest consciences. Every one who knows the history of Churches must be able to remember many points to which they have formally committed themselves in articles, or catechisms, or confessions, which have subsequently, in the progress of opinion, proved dangerous and well-nigh fatal, to that faith which they were meant to sustain. Fabrics are weakened, not strengthened, by accretions round the foundations.

And so, men and brethren, young and old, the things to struggle for are not speculative opinions, which a zeal not according to knowledge has unwisely tried to raise to the rank of Catholic dogmas, but those truths— few, simple, comprehensive,—which you feel lie at the root of your spiritual life. I think it was a remark of Arnold's that only those heresies are condemned in Scripture, which took their rise in a vicious conscience, and issued in profligacy of life; mere differences of opinion are treated in another temper.

I have already reminded you how calmly Paul contemplates the possibility of the Philippians being otherwise minded to himself. He does so because he had confidence in what Channing calls "the uprightness of their opinions"—the clearness of their moral perceptions—their love of goodness and of truth. "Finally, brethren," he writes, "whatsoever things are true, whatsoever things are venerable, whatsoever things are just, whatsoever things are pure, whatsoever things are lovely, whatsoever things are of good report—if there be any virtue, if there be any praise—think of these things . . . . and the God of Peace shall be with you" (Philippians iv. 8). And amid all the fluctuations of opinion the soul may surely rest, without disquietude, on the great central truth of the unchangeableness of God. He sitteth above these waterfloods, and He remaineth a King for ever. "The Kingdom of God," cries Paul, weary of disputes about ceremonial observances, "is not meat and drink; but righteousness, and peace, and joy in the Holy Ghost." There may be some things in those Scriptures, to which we all refer for the credentials and criteria of our faith, hard to understand; but these elementary ideas are not among those things. The conscience knows when it is pursuing righteousness; the heart feels when it is possessed by peace and joy. Where these are, there truth is most likely to be. It was said the other day that, "it was better that men should be free than that they should be sober." It may be said perhaps, with still more emphasis, it is better that men should be righteous—truthful, generous, pure,—than that they should be orthodox. The solid foundation of God standeth,—ὁ στερεὸς θεμέλιος τοῦ Θεοῦ ἕστηκεν—steady amid all the rockings of human systems; as sang Arthur Clough :—

> "It fortifies my soul to know,
> That, though I perish, Truth is so ;
> That, howsoe'er I stray and range,
> Whate'er I do, Thou dost not change :
> I steadier step, when I recall
> That, if *I* slip, *Thou* dost not fall."

Preached—Westminster Abbey, June 23, 1872. St. Mary's, Oxford, November 17, 1872. Cambridge University, February 9, 1878.

IX.

PAUL BEFORE FELIX;
OR,
THE MORAL BASIS OF CHRISTIANITY.

"And after certain days, when Felix came with his wife Drusilla, which was a Jewess, he sent for Paul, and heard him concerning the faith in Christ. And as he reasoned of righteousness, temperance, and judgment to come, Felix trembled, and answered: Go thy way for this time; when I have a convenient season I will call for thee."—Acts xxiv. 24, 25.

WE know, all of us, more or less of the character of St. Paul, but Holy Scripture tells us little of him—at that moment the master of Paul's destiny—with whom the Apostle discoursed on these high arguments; these, as they might easily have become to him, perilous themes. And yet, without this knowledge, the narrative of St. Luke loses half its force, and St. Paul's reasoning all its appropriateness.

Antonius Felix, the procurator of Judea, had risen to his present eminence from the rank of an emancipated slave, through the influence of his brother, the freedman Pallas, the favourite of the Roman Emperor, Claudius Cæsar. Two sentences of the historian Tacitus throw all the light we need, for our present purpose, upon his character as a man, and his conduct as a magistrate. "Relying upon his brother's influence, he thought there was no misdemeanour he might not commit with impunity." (*Cuncta malefacta sibi impune ratus tanta potentia subnixo.*—Tacit. *Ann.* xii. 54.) "In every form of cruelty and lust, he exercised the power of a king in the temper of a slave." (*Per omnem sævitiam et libidinem jus regium servili ingenio exercuit.*—*Hist.* v. 9.)

Before this Roman magistrate, insensible to the claims of justice and humanity, gratifying every wayward lust and passion remorselessly and to the full; the most terrible of compounds, a slavish, brutal nature, endowed with sovereign, absolute power; the fearless preacher of the new principles that were beginning to "turn the world upside down," had the hardihood to reason, and apparently not without some success—at any rate so as to command respectful attention—of "righteousness, temperance, and judgment to come."

And as he reasoned—not perhaps so much in the form of logical argument as of solemn, passionate appeal, such as we find him using subsequently as he pleads his cause before King Agrippa—the dead, or stupefied, conscience of a thoroughly vicious, hardened man was stirred with a momentary compunction. As the satirist of that bad age expresses it with such terrible emphasis, "The torment-scourge within smote his soul" (*Tortore animum quatiente flagello*), he trembled; and not till baser passions supervened, and the corrupt magistrate began to hope that the bribes, for which he had so often sold his judgments, might once more be offered him by his prisoner, did the opportunity of a moral recovery pass away which, if we may reverently say so, the Spirit of God, like the wind blowing where it listeth, was waiting to use.

Sermons vary almost infinitely in character, in method, and in aim. The tendency just now seems to be mainly in the direction of the emotional, or the dogmatic, or the speculative aspects of Christianity; which perhaps stir the sensibilities or exercise the intellectual faculties, and by some are supposed to furnish food for faith, but are with difficulty discerned —possibly are not expected—to have any direct bearing on the government of daily life. When the public appetite is greedy of such highly-seasoned dishes, plainer but more wholesome fare is sometimes rejected with disdain; and hearers, seeking after some attractive or philosophical system, like the Greeks of old, forget how simple, and yet how solemn, are those truths which, again and again, in the history of mankind, have hid themselves, as by a Divine law, from the wise and prudent, while they have been revealed to, and discovered by, babes.

Distracted by controversy, perplexed by speculation, growing dizzy in the wild war of words, beginning to doubt of all things—whether there is a God, whether we have souls, whether we are free agents, whether we are responsible—let us try if we cannot once more gain a steady footing upon some solid bits of rock, which rise above the surf of controversy, which arrest the daring inroads of speculation, and which, as yet at least, survive the wreck of faiths and creeds, by help of which men once thought they could ride safely through the storm.

Such considerations, indeed, are eminently in harmony with, what I will venture to call, the calm and thoughtful temperament of the Church of England. It has even been made a reproach to her—not justly, I think—that enthusiasm of every kind is an offence to her; that she has always, like the astute French diplomatist, repressed and discouraged zeal. It would be fairer to say that her spirit is one of tempered piety, of sober, reflective religion; that she almost sternly subordinates the passions to the judgment; and that the charge of St. Paul to the young Cretan bishop, that he should teach men and women, young and old, "to be sober-minded," as well as sound in the faith, is specially congenial to her mind. "Next to a sound rule of faith," says Mr. Keble, in the preface to the *Christian Year*— that admirable manual of religious meditation which, I fear, is becoming year by year less known to the rising generation of English Churchmen—"next to a sound rule of faith, there is nothing of so much consequence as a sober standard of feeling in matters of practical religion; and it is the peculiar happiness of the Church of England to possess, in her authorised formularies, an ample and secure provision for both. But in times of much leisure and unbounded curiosity, when excitement of every kind is sought after with a morbid eagerness, this part of the merit of our Liturgy is likely in some measure to be lost on many of its sincere admirers; the very tempers which most require such discipline setting themselves, in general, most decidedly against it."

In the midst of our present restlessness, our unreasonable dissatisfaction with our position as a branch of Christ's Holy Catholic Church, our passionate craving after any new religious sensation, our over-readiness to gird ourselves with armour by whomsoever offered, by whomsoever previously worn, which we have not proved, and which neither suits our stature nor our more free and natural way of using our limbs, this warning voice of one who in his day, and that not long past, was justly deemed a master in Israel, may well be sounded from time to time in our ears.

The Gospel of Christ is a *discovery* rather than an *invention*. "The Old Testament," says our Church in her seventh Article, "is not contrary to the New," nor, it may be added, the New to the Old. The ideas of life, and even of immortality—true ideas many of them, so far as they went—were in the world before, and were probably, in spite of modern theories of the progressive evolution of civilisation, coeval with the history of man. Christ accepted them, illuminated them, placed them on a more solid basis, illustrated them by a divine example, sustained them by a new motive power.

The Gospel, according to St. Paul's conception of it, was a *φανέρωσις* ; an *ἐπιφανεία*. Christ was ὁ φωτίσας ζωὴν καὶ ἀφθαρσίαν (2 Timothy i. 10). The ideas, the facts, call them what you please, were there; He shed on them a new light; made them stand out from surrounding phenomena in fuller relief; breathed into them, so to speak, out of His own perfect love, a new and an invigorating spirit. They were no longer ideas set in a philosophical or theological system. Something more was required than the mere γνῶσις or knowledge of them; they were placed as motive forces in the centre of human life and activity; they had not simply to be understood in their scientific relations, as Plato or Aristotle might have tried to make men understand them—to be methodised or formulated—but to be believed in, realised, apprehended, applied. "I am come," said the Great Teacher, "that they may have life, and that they may have it more abundantly." The source of the stream was the same, but certain lets and hindrances which had prevented its free and equable flow were cleared away. Men could now drink of "the water of life freely."

And so we read the teaching of the New Testament in the presence of old ideas, rather than of new ones. As St. John says, "Brethren, I write no new commandment unto you, but an old commandment which ye had from the beginning;" and yet, in another sense, "the old things," as St. Paul speaks, "have passed away, and all things have become new"—new in their adjustments, new in their deeper significance, new above all, in their constraining power; because the same God Who, at the first, "commanded the light to shine out of darkness," in this His new creation shone with a directer and less distorted ray into men's hearts, giving "the light of the knowledge of the glory of God in the face of Jesus Christ."

And so there is really nothing strange in the phenomenon, though it may have perplexed us before we thought about it, that the last page of the Bible reads but as a revision and republication of the first; and the ideas of life and light (only a higher life and a purer light) are still the pervading idea of that revelation of Himself which, "in manifold parts and ways"— πολυμερῶς καὶ πολυτρόπως—the Invisible Father has been pleased to bestow upon man.

The theocracy is set up again; the kingdom of God emerges into view. We come once more unto the Mount Sion and the city of the living God, "the heavenly Jerusalem," and to the King Himself sitting upon His holy hill. There is still a blood of sprinkling, though it speaketh better things; still a law, though one of liberty; still a worship, but in the spirit of truthfulness; still a covenant, but resting upon better, because clearer and farther-reaching, promises; still a mediator, but Jesus, not Moses; still, too —and this must not be forgotten—"a consuming fire," but through which, though it shall "try the work of every man," there is a secret power (the presence and companionship of one "like unto a Son of God") that can, if we will trust faithfully, carry us unharmed.

(1) *Paul reasoned of righteousness.* The system of invisible, divine power with which we are surrounded, from which we cannot really escape, and to which we are required to conform our lives, is called "a kingdom;" and the essential laws of this kingdom, the basis of its constitution, have been eternally, unchangeably, the same. Christ did but republish, with fuller authority, more distinct utterance, the two great principles on

which all the teaching of law and prophets had really hung. When God revealed himself to Moses, we know not how, it was with these characters: "The Lord, the Lord God, merciful and gracious, long-suffering and abundant in goodness and truth, keeping mercy for thousands, forgiving iniquity, transgression, and sin, and that will by no means clear the guilty." (Exodus xxxiv. 6.) When Micah—if indeed the words are not really those of an older seer—would help men "to know the righteousness of the Lord," it is thus that he declares it. Putting aside all ceremonial propitiations or sacrificial atonements, he proclaims aloud, "He hath showed thee, O man, what is good: and what doth the Lord require of thee, but to do justly, and to love mercy, and to walk humbly with thy God?" (Micah vi. 8.)

How does this differ from the teaching of St. Peter, that "God is no respecter of persons, but in every nation he that feareth Him and worketh righteousness is accepted of Him"; or from that of St. Paul, that "the kingdom of God is not meat and drink, but righteousness"; or from that of St. James, that "pure religion and undefiled before God, is to visit the fatherless and widows in their affliction, and to keep oneself unspotted from the world"; or from that of St. John, "whosoever doeth not righteousness is not of God, neither he that loveth not his brother"; or from that of a Greater Teacher than all, "Seek ye first the kingdom of God and His righteousness, and all these things shall be added unto you"?

It is from iniquity that Christ came to redeem us,

rather than from hell; from sin itself, its dominion, its power, rather than from its penalties and consequences. The righteousness which His Spirit works in us, and which makes us, almost consciously, "free from the law of sin and death," is not, as some theological schools have pictured it, fictitious, forensic, imputed merely, but real, inherent, our own.

I do not say it can plead for itself, or would even desire to do so. Nay, to the last it cries, "O sinful man that I am, who shall deliver me?" To the last it acknowledges, "By the grace of God I am what I am." It cannot "establish" itself, or think to be saved, by its own merits, before the heart-searching Judge; or to claim reward as a wage fully and fairly earned. But even in its feeblest efforts, its modest victories, it is real and true. It *is* righteousness, and not unrighteousness. It is a striving of the human soul to grow more and more perfectly, though at an immeasurable distance, "unto the measure of the stature of the fulness of Christ." There is a real desire not only to know, but to prove—and to prove by making an honest endeavour to do—the "good and acceptable and perfect will of God."

It is, indeed, only through such an effort, that any real, profitable knowledge of the Divine Will is possible. Christian *gnosis* is the result and reward of action; or at least of the attempt to live up to the standard of a high ideal. "If any man *wills* to do His will, he shall know of the doctrine." As St. Paul lays it down, God reveals Himself to those who are striving to be perfect. (Phil. iii. 13-16.)

If there be, as has been maintained, a tendency in things to fulfil the law of their being; if there be a law, a power, external to us, "which makes for righteousness," certainly that teaching must be in harmony with this law, does not contradict or contravene this tendency, which proclaims loudly and on the house-top, "Follow holiness, without which no man shall see the Lord."

(2) The second topic on which St. Paul reasoned with Felix was *temperance*—ἐγκράτεια—"*self-control.*" The apostle, who quotes the Greek poets, was no doubt more or less familiar with the systems of the more prominent Greek philosophers. Felix, we are told, traced his origin to the old kings of Arcadia, and perhaps had read, in a dilettante way, the writings of Aristotle. In the ethical system of that teacher, the temperate, or continent man, is he who, feeling in himself the strain of vicious desires, keeps them in check, and finally conquers them, by asserting the legitimate supremacy of reason. Spiritualise this moral conception, make the conquest possible and the triumph assured by the aid of that Spirit, "Who helpeth our infirmities," that grace which out of weakness makes men strong, and there would be no quarrel between the heathen teacher and the Christian.

In the struggle to win the incorruptible crown, the Christian athlete, says the apostle, "is self-controlled in all things"—ἐγκρατεύεται πάντα. Passions, appetites, desires, affections, even the purest, even those which move in the religious sphere, are, with him, all held as with a bridle; all are under the restraining check of an enlightened spiritual perception discerning between good and evil; all are brought firmly, even sternly, yet cheerfully, under the dominion of Christ's law.

Excitement, tumult, ecstasy, are not the normal, nor the health-giving constituents of that spiritual atmosphere in which the Christian lives, and moves and has his being. I do not know that St. Paul himself was much the wiser, or the better, for that rapture in the third heaven, of which he knew not the physical conditions, and where he heard what he found it impossible to utter when the vision, or the ecstasy, had passed away. We know how the Lord Jesus rebuked—or at least calmed—the wild excitement of the woman who cried, "Blessed is the womb that bare Thee, and the paps which Thou hast sucked." "Yea, rather," was the perhaps unexpected reply, "blessed are they that hear the word of God and keep it." (St. Luke xi. 27.)

The most perfect picture of one whom Christ's Spirit has really and effectively subdued is that of the man whose soul had once been the home of a legion of devils, calmly sitting at the feet of his Deliverer, "clothed and in his right mind." You will remember the magnanimity which refused to take advantage of the enthusiasm of gratitude, but bade the man bear his witness and show his devotion where it was likely to be most influential. "Go home to thy friends, and tell them how great things the Lord hath done for thee, and hath had compassion on thee." (St. Mark v. 19.)

In the excitement and restlessness of the age, so unfavourable to sustained action, so apt to dissipate the energies in search of visionary or sentimental ideals, instead of concentrating them upon one noble aim; so prone to mistake impulses and impressions for purposes of more pith and moment; it is well to notice that in St. Paul's reasoning with Felix, self-control occupied the second place among the notes of the Kingdom of God.

(3) And then before he concluded his high argument, the teacher sought to lift his listener's mind to the greatest of all thoughts—I mean "man's relation to God." St. Paul spoke of "the judgment to come"— the great external fact which is the correlative of the sense of responsibility in man. "Every one of us," says the apostle elsewhere, "shall give an account of himself to God."

We will not cumber or perplex this simple but all-momentous conviction with unsubstantial or materialistic fancies about heaven or hell; nor with speculations about the nature or duration of future rewards and punishments; nor with anything that might be thought to belong to the class of "doubtful disputations." The simplest expression of the great conviction is also the most helpful.

The sense of accountability is one of those ultimate facts of human nature, inconceivable to my mind upon the modern molecular hypothesis, which any teacher who professed to deal remedially, or even philosophically, with that nature—Socrates as well as Christ—could not but recognise. And so it is stamped deep and legible on every page of the Gospel. We shall be judged according as our works have been; and the conscience, whatever its testimony may be worth, echoes, "Ay, we shall be so judged." Our Master may seem to have gone for a while into a far country, but "He will return," He says, "and reckon with His servants."

Banish from your system—destroy in your soul—the sense of responsibility and its accompanying hope of immortality, and it would, I fear, be found impossible to maintain, not only the principle of religion, but also the principle of morality in the world. If I understand him aright, Professor Huxley abandons the principle of free will. I do not see how, without that, you can retain the idea of responsibility. Mr. Greg abandons as an unprovable illusion the hope of immortality. The weightiest consideration in favour of a future state he admits to be the conviction that God enters into relations with man; and such relations, such communion, he holds to be inconceivable between a God and an ephemeris—a creature of a day.

"This consideration," he adds, almost with pathetic sadness, "no doubt must be decisive to all to whose spirits communion with their Father is the most absolute of verities, but, alas! to them only." "Passing away," says this eloquent writer, "is the destiny written upon every other of the works of God or the results of evolution—on the tree, the insect, the megatherium; on the lark, the sun, the star, the galaxy. Alas! why is it that each fresh argument for immortality which the ingenuity of desire excogitates should prove, when closely grappled with, just as baseless as its predecessors? Why must those who long the most to live for ever, whose hopes are the most aspiring, and whose energies the least worn out; who examine with renewed eagerness each new speculation that promises to be a proof, be compelled to fall back upon the old conclusion—that Faith may be undying, but that Proof there can be none?"

And in lieu of this sustaining and invigorating hope which, evidently with a reluctant hand, he thus cuts from beneath our feet, this clear thinker would comfort us, as Professor Häckel bids us be satisfied, with optimistic dreams, far enough at present from realisation, of the progress and perfection of the race. Man, he says, even without the prospect of a life in the world to come, is not a failure. "Do we really mean to assert," he asks with a solemn earnestness in harmony with the grandeur of his theme, "that man, with his wonderful capacities as yet only in their infancy, his strange happiness, often already so intense; with potentialities of joy growing more vivid and more varied as the ages roll along; with his accumulated stores of knowledge and discovery passed on, whatever we may say, from generation to generation; ay, and still more, with elements of character growing richer and nobler century after century towards the completion of God's perfect work—that such a being is not a conception worthy of the Creator we imagine? Take the best specimen of the race we have yet known or read of; picture him with his intellect furnished to the full with the hoarded wisdom of the past, his faculties trained to their ultimate perfection, his instincts and emotions disciplined by the experience of a thousand centuries, and his life lengthened to its natural limit by all that science will have taught him, and then fancy this being, this man at his culminating zenith, to be, not as the good are now, a mere rare and exceptional instance of what man might be, but a faithful portrait of the average man as he will have become! Consider all this—which is nothing more than Positivists and poetic Pagans alike anticipate—and then tell us, if you dare, that the realisation of such a conception may not fitly occupy the Creative Spirit during that long fragment of eternity called Time; and that He may not, as He looks upon His finished work, justly pronounce it to be 'very good' —ay, even though each individual of the race be doomed, after a life of noble energy and stainless joy, to pass into a dreamless and unconscious rest!"

In reply to which great challenge I can but answer that this fair vision seems to me, as he who pictures it forth himself calls it, to be nothing more than "a fancy"—a conviction of which "faith may be undying, but proof there can be none."

I live among toiling thousands, working out the sad and dreary problem of their lives in a ceaseless round of daily labour, and often under conditions most unfavourable to the development of the "richer and nobler elements of character"; whom the complex thing we call "civilisation," instead of elevating, depresses more and more; where, instead of life being "lengthened to its natural limits by all that science teaches," nearly fifty per cent. of the whole mortality is of infants under five years old; where one cannot so much as conceive the possibility of this "average man," unless the present secular conditions are wholly changed, and life is lived in the "new heaven and the new earth, wherein dwelleth righteousness," even when the "thousand centuries" have rolled by, and the moment of the "culminating zenith" has arrived.

Mr. Greg speaks, I can hardly suppose with indifference, of the present "scheme of things"—as Bishop Butler might have called it—as "either a word of God *or* a result of evolution"! Perhaps to the evolutionist it may be a matter of theoretical unconcern that, till the "thousandth century" has come, man's life upon this hypothesis is doomed to be imperfect, maimed, and so far frustrate; but to any one who believes in the "works of God," it must be a difficulty quite as great as any that encompasses the faith in immortality, to suppose that the "Creative Spirit" would allow a thousand centuries to roll away before the average man attains that perfection which, *ex hypothesi*, from the first was intended for the race, and which is to redeem even this present life from the reproach of failure.

Mr. Greg says we cannot *prove* the doctrine of immortality. We cannot prove it as we can prove the conclusion of a geometrical theorem. But are all the hopes and yearnings and aspirations of the soul—that "longing" which Mr. Greg admits, "to live for ever"— to go for nothing in the argument? How came they there if they are never to be satisfied? There are proofs *and* proofs. As Sir William Hamilton, not a cloudy thinker on such a subject, has said, "The existence of God and the immortality of the soul are not given us as *phenomena*, as objects of immediate knowledge; yet if the phenomena actually given do necessarily require, for their rational explanation, the hypothesis of immortality and of God, we are assuredly entitled from the existence of the former to infer the reality of the latter."

"If God did not exist, it would be necessary to invent Him," said Voltaire. I ask you fearlessly, upon any sober review of the situation, what would life be—not when the myriad ages has run its course and the "average man" has reached his "culminating zenith," but now, and as far back as historical investigation can penetrate, as far forward as the most sanguine anticipation that is not a mere wild dream can foresee—what, I ask, would life be, "in all the nobler and higher elements of its character," if you withdraw at once from the moral supports—which are all too feeble ofttimes to bear it up against the pressure of adverse circumstances—the sense of responsibility, the hope of immortality?

"*Non complacuit Deo*," said St. Ambrose, "*in dialectica salvum facere populum suum*" (Not by any methods of mere argument is it God's will to make His people whole). But when men have found the revelation of Christ come true in other respects, they will not think it likely to disappoint them here. They feel that to know the Father and Jesus Christ whom He hath sent *is* eternal life—inchoate and incomplete here, but the germ of what is to be developed and perfected hereafter. They cannot be wholly frustrate, these hopes the brightest, these thoughts the deepest that occupy the soul.

"But, *soul* say you," methinks I hear some sciolist from the school of modern physical philosophy exclaim; "how do you know we have a soul? With us, soul is regarded only as a function of matter, and passes, when the present molecular combinations are dissolved, 'into thin air,' as heathen poets used to say."

Well, if you really believe this, if you dare to act upon your belief, you may as well say, "Let us eat and drink, for to-morrow we die," as try to reach any higher standard, to live with any nobler aim. If men in general act upon this maxim, give a practical expression to this theory, *when* the "culminating zenith" will be reached, I would rather that you should venture to prophesy than I. But men are both better and worse than their principles. Though a degrading materialism seems to be infecting many types of religious thought, and some of our sacramental theories, which claim to be the highest, seem to me to drop into an almost unfathomable abyss of superstition and to lose the very character of an act of rational worship, yet I refuse to believe that there is any widespread determination to force theories to their terrible conclusions. Amid all the swayings of philosophical opinion and all the varieties of religious belief, you may yet, upon the solid basis on which St. Paul reasoned with Felix, build a life which, in its simplicity, in its high-reaching aspirations, in its calmness and peace and joy, shall realise the apostle's idea of a life, lived under the conditions of humanity, but, in its deepest springs, "hid with Christ in God." Amid the thousand false, low standards upon the commonest matters of morality accepted and acted upon by the young, the pleasure-seeking, the fashionable, the money-getting, the ambitious, it is well to try to accustom the mind to set before itself clearly and distinctly the principles that will govern—that we feel *must* govern—"the righteous judgment of God"; well to anticipate, to make ourselves seem to hear that terrible sentence which we know will pass against us if we are deliberately leading impure, selfish, false, dishonest lives—if we are resisting God's call to repentance and doing despite to the Spirit of Grace.

And as St. Paul reasoned, "Felix trembled." That craven fear never wrought true amendment. Repentance may begin in fear, but it is perfected by a nobler influence. It is the *love* of Christ which draws, which constrains to Him.

I would fain send you away hopeful, resolute. If what I have said has stirred thoughts in any of your hearts, I trust they are encouraging, not depressing thoughts. I trust you have faith enough to believe that a pure and noble life is possible even to the weakest, the most irresolute. "*All* things *are* possible to him that believeth." The Divine strength is perfected in human weakness. The old faith will still hold its ground in the hearts and consciences of men so long as it is seen to be not an organized hypocrisy, nor a lifeless system of formalism, but a power, bringing forth the fruits of righteousness.

Preached—Westminster Abbey, February 12, 1874; St. Mary's, Oxford, October 21, 1877; Westminster Abbey, June 20, 1880.

X.

DEBORAH.

"Awake, awake, Deborah: awake, awake, utter a song: arise, Barak, and lead thy captivity captive, thou son of Abinoam. Then he made him that remaineth have dominion over the nobles among the people: the Lord made me have dominion over the mighty. Out of Ephraim there was a root of them against Amalek; after thee, Benjamin, among thy people; out of Machir came down governors, and out of Zebulun they that handle the pen of the writer. And the princes of Issachar were with Deborah; even Issachar, and also Barak: he was sent on foot into the valley. For the divisions of Reuben there were great thoughts of heart. Why abodest thou among the sheepfolds, to hear the bleatings of the flocks? For the divisions of Reuben there were great searchings of heart. Gilead abode beyond Jordan: and why did Dan remain in ships? Asher continued on the sea shore, and abode in his creeks. Zebulun and Naphtali were a people that jeoparded their lives unto the death in the high places of the field."—JUDGES v. 12—18.

THIS magnificent lyric ode of the greatest of Israel's prophetesses labours, as is confessed by all, under manifold difficulties of interpretation. The language is full of figures and allusions; the transitions of thought and feeling are rapid and sudden; the spirit it breathes is fierce, and sometimes almost savage; the reconciliation of the poem with the history, or of the history with the poem, is a task by no means free from embarrassment.

Not a few difficulties, however, we have created for ourselves by that mischievous and often fatal habit of importing into the text of Scripture more than it actually and necessarily—or even by implication—contains. From the simple fact that Deborah is called a "prophetess" some tremendous but unwarrantable inferences have been drawn. It has been assumed that all her words were God's words, and that all her acts had a Divine sanction prompting and justifying them, and that even the fierce and ruthless spirit of her song was one that God inspired.

And so some have learnt to curse, and to curse bitterly, those who, like the inhabitants of Meroz, have stood coldly and timidly aloof when *they*, as they have thought, have been fighting the Lord's battles against the mighty; while others have taught the strange and revolting doctrine that a deed of cruel treachery like Jael's—for it was both cruel and treacherous—was yet defensible, and indeed righteous, because the Lord blessed, even if He did not command it.

So a paradoxical principle of interpretation has been adopted which has made it impossible, without violent and unnatural straining, to harmonise the ethics of the Old Testament with the ethics of the New; and a painful contradiction has been established, which has given triumph to the sceptic and perplexity to the believer. We have been scornfully asked to reconcile the deed of Jael with the ordinary maxims of morality accepted even by savage tribes; and the curse of Meroz with that Divine Voice, which proclaimed among the mountains of Galilee the New Law, "Love your enemies; bless them that curse you; do good to them that hate you; and pray for them which despitefully use you and persecute you."

I would only offer for your consideration two remarks in connection with these difficulties.

1. It is adopting a perilous principle to argue that an action must be right because, *as we suppose*, God commanded it. It is a safer rule of interpretation to infer that if an action, of which we know the details, or so far as we know them, is manifestly wrong—opposed to the instinctive sense of right, or goodness, or truth, or holiness, which, if the whole world were rocking beneath our feet, we still should feel to be immutable—it could not have been an act commanded by Him Whose essential characteristics are equity, goodness, holiness, truth. Indeed, it is nothing less than marvellous that men should accept without question the morality of a deed on the simple ground that God commanded it, when, without such presumed command, the conduct would excite feelings of abhorrence rather than of admiration, and be stigmatized as treacherous and bloody rather than be praised as an example of heroic courage and virtue.

Casuists, I am aware, have exercised their subtlety to define what deviations from the strict rule of truth and right war may excuse, if it cannot justify; but Jael's deed lacked even the pretext of a patriotic motive.

She had no personal nor national wrongs to avenge. Her wild clan, wandering Arabs of the desert, pitching their tents now here, now there, were aliens from the commonwealth of Israel, had no title to an inheritance in the "delightsome land." They did not belong to the oppressed race. There was peace between Jabin the King of Hazor and the house of Heber the Kenite. Sisera fled away to Jael's tent as to a place of sure refuge; she bade him welcome; he trusted her.

A Hebrew woman of undaunted courage but of fierce spirit, in the first flush of victory chanting her triumphant war-song, feeling that twenty years of cruel suffering and oppression had now been signally revenged, seeing the oppressor himself laid low and her nation once more free, may be forgiven if at the moment she thought less of the mode and instrument by which that freedom had been won than of the great result achieved,—may be *almost* forgiven, or at least understood, if, in the disturbed balance of her mind, the true measure of things failed to impress itself upon her conscience, and the end might seem to justify the means.

But this is a very different thing from saying that we, who have unlearnt, or ought to have unlearnt, somewhat of the fiery passions of a Jew, whose eyes have been enlightened by Christ to discern the more excellent way, are even, in an exceptional case, to invert our moral sense, and call a deed righteous from which we instinctively shrink as base and treacherous, because a Hebrew prophetess three thousand years ago, in an access of high-wrought poetic transport, breathing the fierce spirit of her race, rejoicing to see the enemies of the Lord perish by any hand, was moved to call her who wrought it "blessed above women in the tent."

2. Deborah's prophetic gift was, so far as we have materials for estimating it, rather an afflatus of poetic inspiration than anything deeper or more divine. She spake, as Miriam had spoken by the Red Sea shore, in older days than hers. The gift of poetry—certainly of poetry breathing a noble spirit, aiming at a noble end —must surely be reckoned among those beneficent endowments, those "perfect gifts" which, St. James tells us, come down from God. And even when the gift is desecrated by being released from the restraints of conscience and prostituted to ignoble purposes, yet the gift itself is part of God's dowry to the creature of His hand, whom, when He endowed him, He made free, and at the same time responsible for the use he should make of his freedom.

Nor, even if we were sure that Deborah was gifted with predictive powers, would that necessitate, or even justify, the conclusion that all her utterances, when not claiming to be spoken under special guidance of the Holy Spirit, were utterances of infallible truth or of immutable morality. "The spirits of the prophets are subject to the prophets," teaches St. Paul; and he guarded the Corinthians from confounding the words of one who had received grace to be faithful—of a man of ordinary or, if you please, extraordinary insight, but still a man—with the absolute and sovereign "commandments of the Lord."

Nor is there any proof that Deborah possessed, in the highest sense of the term, prophetic, that is, predictive power. In the opinion of the best modern commentators, and, indeed, according to Rosenmüller, of some of the most learned Jewish rabbis, the woman into whose hand she foretold Barak that the Lord would sell Sisera was not Jael, but herself. In the full confidence of a lofty and daring patriotism, she felt assurance of victory. She could not understand the hesitation of a *man* in such a cause; and *because* he hesitated, she felt that his name would not go down to after ages on the same level of honour as hers, who had never doubted, never paused, never quailed. In the words of her own hymn, the oppressions of her nation did not cease till "she, Deborah, arose; till she arose, a mother in Israel."

The gift of ratiocination, of high poetic song, we know she had; the gift of predictive foresight, the power of uttering infallible truth, we do not know that she enjoyed. And so her words have no claim to supersede that standard of right and wrong which we believe to be implanted in our consciences by God; and by which even words professing to be divine must, in the case of each individual responsible man, be ultimately tested and weighed. "Holding the mystery of the faith in a pure conscience," is, according to St. Paul, the attitude of mind and will in which a man may hope to escape the perplexities of unbelief, as well as to overcome the power of the more ordinary temptations.

I desire specially to dwell on the thoughts expressed in those verses of this noble song which I have selected for my text. The prophetess, even in her moment of highest exultation, cannot forget those who, in their country's critical hour, when freedom, honour, independence—everything that constitutes the real life and force of a nation, was in jeopardy, and one bold, united effort might achieve deliverance, stood apart in the isolation of rivalry, or selfishness, or in the inglorious love of ease, and "came not to the help of the Lord against the mighty."

From the fastnesses of Ephraim in the Mount of the Amalekites; from "little Benjamin"; from the cis-Jordanic portion of Manasseh; from Issachar; but above and before all, from Zebulun and Naphtali came forth princes and governors—pale, quiet students even—if we have caught in our version the true meaning of the words—more wont to handle the pen than the sword, but touched in their country's cause with the daring fervour of a sublime patriotism; from these half-dozen tribes there came a people ready to jeopardise their lives unto death in the high places of the field—for hearth and altar, such as Romans fought for—for their God and for their fatherland.

But the peril was common to all. For twenty years had this Canaanitish king mightily oppressed the children of Israel. The risk of encountering the peril was undertaken by few. Reuben, separated from his brethren by the dividing waters of Jordan, debated the question, thought about it much and often—"in the divisions of Reuben there were great searchings of heart"—but (a council of war, they say, never fights) finally preferred a safe and indolent repose, abiding among the shepherds, deaf to the war-trumpet, soothing his delicate ears with pastoral symphonies played on shepherd's reeds.

Gad dwelt in calm indifference among the highlands of Gilead, far from the scene of war. Dan and Asher, though near the peril, thought that their ships and proximity to the sea would enable them to effect a secure escape should the enemy's cause seem likely to prevail or the tide of war roll their way.

If help was looked for, none came from these. As so often in the history of great causes, the deliverance was wrought, not by the many, but by the few. An opportunity was lost, which peoples have no right to expect to be continually renewed, for knitting the nation together in those bonds of union created by a sense of common danger, by all shared and by all repelled, which seems to be, we may almost dare to say, God's appointed instrument for teaching a nation to realise its highest life—indeed, the very purpose for which it became a nation at all. "Blood," says the proverb, "is thicker than water"; but the greatest nations of the world have not always been, in the modern sense of the word, "of one blood"; the moral forces of humanity have always dominated the physical; and confederation in great causes has stirred even sluggish natures with a power, by the side of which the love of father and mother, brother and sister, ay, and of life itself, has seemed weak and cold.

May I venture to apply the lesson to our own circumstances?

There is a supine or a contemptuous indifference at the present day as to the result of great issues which are being tried at the bar of public opinion, and which profoundly affect the conditions of national life; which, so far as I may presume to form or express a judgment, is fraught with peril to the highest interests, both of Church and State—to all that we ought to hold most precious, both in the department of religious thought and practice, and in the department of social and political life.

Never, perhaps, was there more excitement about questions of the hour and questions of the surface—the trivialities that form the staple of the idle gossip of the club, the dilettante conversation of the dinner-party; never, perhaps, less serious thought about questions which go down into the depths, and which may affect the welfare of the Church, or of society, for centuries. In fact, a man who is in earnest is by common consent voted to be a bore, and I don't deny that sometimes he is a bore. Talleyrand's celebrated maxim about the danger, or the folly, of an excess of zeal, has passed far beyond those regions of diplomacy to which it was originally confined. An utter carelessness for the morrow so long as all is calm and undisturbed to-day is the supreme achievement of the philosophy—hardly a wisdom from above—which teaches men and women the conditions under which the duties of life are to be avoided rather than discharged. To escape a responsibility under cover of a happy phrase, or a skilful stratagem, is the kind of dexterity which the world seems most ready to admire.

It is not hard to trace this temper to its source. It is the product of the moral tissues, of a life—whether individual or national—tainted, enfeebled, degenerated by luxury, by affluence, by the love of ease, or pleasure, by adopting the principle of *laisser aller*. In some cases it may have been bred by disappointment; in others it is the not unnatural fruit of reaction, or of counter-action. The enthusiasm of ardent natures intensifies the cynicism of selfish natures. St. Paul and Festus represent the antagonisms of two mutually repellent moods of the human mind.

And so it comes to pass that, in great crises of truth or righteousness, or when some large problem involving conditions under which alone healthy national or social life is possible—such as are some of the great economical problems of the hour—requires the united thought and united effort of all for its adequate solution, men without high aspirations; men with much care for their party or their social status, but with little care for their kind; men who are reckoned wise in that wisdom of the world which neither sees, nor cares to see, much further than its hand, look coldly and sarcastically on, while a few are bearing the brunt of the fray; content to show the fruits of their victory, if victory is won; ready also, that they may not lose their credit for prescience, to raise the first cry of failure when failure is seen to be imminent, and the gallant band, for want of adequate support, is hurled back, shattered and discomfited, from the breach which, without duly measuring their strength, they had essayed to storm.

No one can blink, or be blind to, the fact that Christianity is confronted all over the civilised world by a gigantic foe. I know not by what better name to call it than "the spirit of unbelief:" a *moral* unbelief in the existence of truth, rather than an intellectual unbelief, staggered and perplexed by speculative difficulties. The latter spirit exists also, sometimes independently, sometimes in alliance with the former; and it is only when it is so allied that it becomes, in my judgment, truly formidable.

An honest mind, really loving truth, and goodness, and purity, will seldom go very far, or very long, astray. Practical doubts at least will clear, even if speculative doubts remain. If it be true, as old St. Ambrose has it (*non complacuit Deo in dialecticâ populum suum salvum facere*), "that it is not the divine will through logical processes to make His people whole," I cherish the conviction that imperfect knowledge, and even what may prove to have been speculative errors, where there has been a love and a yearning for truth and righteousness, will never shut a man out from the beatific vision, from the fruition of that fuller light in which we hope "to know even as we are known."

The real peril is from those who, in St. Paul's words, "believe a lie, because they have pleasure in unrighteousness." The heart that is loyal to virtue and truth is really loyal to God, Who is the essence of virtue and truth—as Plato used to phrase it?—"the Itself good, the Itself beautiful, the Itself true." And often found in company with the unbelief that has pleasure in unrighteousness—which is earthly, sensual, devilish—and working, though less directly and avowedly to the same end, is another type, which I observed called by a clever speaker "drawing-room unbelief"; hardly less mischievous and infinitely more contemptible, which springs up in a mind destitute of moral force—shallow, vacant, frivolous—repeating phrases at secondhand and supposing them to be true, if it really cares for truth at all, because they are new, or clever, or witty, or startling. The effects produced by this vicious levity are moral rather than intellectual, robbing life of its purpose and aim, disabling men for high and noble efforts, and making them no better than feathers tossed to and fro with every idle wind.

But pure and earnest minds, which perhaps have not been able to see their way to accept the Christian system as it has ordinarily been presented to them: who have been shocked either by the irrationality of doctrines or the inconsistencies of professors: or who, looking at the side of things which is most constantly present to them (in the intensity of their gaze seeming to forget that there is another side) cannot yet acquiesce either in the unbelief that springs from vice, or that springs from frivolousness. They still feel the need of a religion, of something spiritual that shall bind the soul to God; and of a Church, that is, some visible organisation that shall embody this idea, and express it, vividly to the world.

"I can conceive," said Professor Huxley, "the existence of an established Church which should be a blessing to the community, a Church in which, week by week, services would be devoted not to the iteration of abstract propositions in theology, but to the setting before men's minds an ideal of true, just and pure living; a place in which those who are weary of the burden of daily cares should find a moment's rest in the contemplation of the higher life, which is possible for all, though attained by so few: a place in which the man of strife and of business should have time to think how small after all are the rewards he covets, compared with peace and charity. Depend upon it, if such a Church existed, no one would seek to disestablish it."

And why should not such a Church exist? And further, why should not the Church of England, rising to the highest of her high functions—to express the highest, which is also the simplest, faith; to satisfy the deepest, which are also the calmest and most reverent emotions of the nation's heart—become such a Church? I feel sure that unless we have a national Church in the truest, broadest sense of the word, we shall never be able to offer a haven to restless, weary souls. Our innumerable sects and controversies do but multiply and intensify our perplexities. It is worth considering whether they who dwell in one house, and are most of them beset by common foes, could not make more successful efforts than they have hitherto made, to be of one mind; whether the variations of Protestant Churches are still to furnish the most effective weapon to infidel assailants on the one hand, and to Romanist assailants on the other.

I fear that national life without a national expressive expression of religion, that is, without a national Church, would be a feeble and maimed thing. "A national Church," says a recent writer, "is the only conceivable expedient under which there can exist at once very great varieties of spiritual conviction, and a perpetual circulation of thought upon those varieties. Surely men must see that a nation without any common meeting ground for the purposes of moral and spiritual life is a nation with one great organ of unity missing; a nation needlessly shorn and crippled of its highest opportunities of collective life and feeling."

Religion is not, as it has been called, the product of credulity and poetry. It is the product of the profoundest and truest instincts—at least if their universality is any test of their truth—of our nature. It is the product of the sense of a life higher than that which we actually live; of the sense, too, of a power *in* us but not *of* us, lifting us up to a desire for, an effort after, its attainment. All that constitutes the true nobility of human nature is proportionate to the influence of this sense in man. Without it you may have philanthropists, but you will not have martyrs: politicians, but not statesmen: good citizens, but not patriots: soldiers, but not heroes: respectable householders and fathers of families, but not saints.

Are we doomed never to realise the temper under which alone such higher results are possible? Shall we, broken up into miserable sects and parties, stand selfishly, or suspiciously, by, while Zebulun and Naphtali —the more generous spirits of the age—are jeoparding their lives unto the death in the high places of the field? Oh! how one longs to gather into one camp, or to mass together in supporting columns on the great battlefield, all those who, however differing on points of lesser detail, are yet united in this—the great uniting influence—that they love the Lord Jesus Christ in all sincerity! Oh, that some Barak would blow the trumpet in Kedesh, even if not more than ten thousand brave hearts should feel themselves stirred and go down to the battle after him!

Is no power, human or divine, no motive Catholic enough to dominate and subdue all sectarian rivalries, ever to bring about the reunion "for which all the best minds of all cultivated people are longing?" "He who believes in Christ," says the great leader of the Old Catholic party, "cannot shut himself out from the expectation that a not-all-too distant future will bring a Church which, in her purified form, as the true successor of the first uncorrupted centuries, shall have room and attractive power for those who are now sundered— a Church in which freedom with order, discipline and morality and purity of faith with intelligence and unfettered inquiry, may be able to exist together." When minds of such different temper, trained in such different schools, as Professor Huxley and Professor Döllinger are dreaming the same dream, must it be, need it be, *only a dream?*

I have no scheme of union to propound. Men's minds are hardly yet in the temper to entertain schemes. They are too captious, or too critical, or too prejudiced. A scheme of reunion which would furnish topics the next day for a leading article in every newspaper, and would be dismissed in that dainty, supercilious fashion with which we are all familiar, would not be started under the most favourable conditions of success.

And besides, God works out problems of this kind mostly at His own time, by His own instruments, in His own way. If St. Paul is to be trusted as able to estimate the forces that were operating round him, it was not by means of the wise, or the mighty, or the noble, that the Galilean conquered the world. When the same strong faith once more takes possession of the souls of men, the wave of conquest, which now seems ebbing back so far and on every shore, will again return with all the might of a resistless tide. When Christianity is again set up before men's eyes as the embodiment and expression, " of whatsoever things are true, whatsoever things are honest, just, pure, lovely, and of good report;" when science and religion shall meet no longer as foes, or even as nominal but mutually mistrustful friends, but as comrades in arms against common enemies—against ignorance, and superstition, and suffering and sin—then men's hearts will surely be drawn together to recognise the claims and the duties of a common brotherhood, and to maintain, as dearer than life itself, that liberty wherewith, as they will then feel, "Christ hath made them free."

Meanwhile, till the advent of that golden age, we may humbly and trustfully work with God in that direction to which all His purposes, all His providences, so far as we can read their lessons, seem to point. That His Church "should be one," was the Saviour's prayer. And so let us work, if not for that union which is external, at least for unity which may yet underlie manifold and obvious external differences. We may each, within the sphere of our respective influences, add something to the ground that is being won from suspicion, from uncharitableness, from prejudice, from jealousy, from rivalry. No doubt "there are many adversaries," but they that have a good cause, and engage in it with a loyal heart, may hope to "drive out the Canaanites, though they be strong and though they have chariots of iron." A poet's words may breathe new force into hands too inclined to droop, new hopes into hearts too ready to despond.

> "Say not the struggle nought availeth ;
> The labour and the wounds are vain ;
> The enemy faints not, nor faileth ;
> And as things have been, they remain.
>
> "If hopes were dupes, fears may be liars ;
> It may be, in yon smoke concealed,
> Your comrades chase ere now the fliers,
> And, but for you, possess the field.
>
> "For while the tired waves, vainly breaking,
> Seem here no painful inch to gain,
> Far back, through creeks and inlets making,
> Comes silent, flooding in, the main.
>
> "And not by eastern windows only
> When daylight comes, comes in the light ;
> In front the sun climbs slow, how slowly,
> But westward, look ! the land is bright."

And in this spirit, in this day, when as in that of the prophet, "the light is not clear nor dark"—not so clear as some of us may wish it were, yet not so dark but that we can discern some sure outlines of truth and rectitude—do not, I entreat you, do not yet despair of Christianity.

Preached—St. Mary's, Oxford, 1875 ; Westminster Abbey, June 6, 1875 ; Manchester Cathedral, June 6, 1880.

XI.

THE WORD OF LIFE.

"That which was from the beginning, which we have heard, which we have seen with our eyes, which we have looked upon, and our hands have handled, of the Word of life—for the life was manifested, and we have seen it, and bear witness, and show unto you that eternal life which was with the Father, and was manifested unto us—that which we have seen and heard declare we unto you, that ye also may have fellowship with us; and truly our fellowship is with the Father and with his Son Jesus Christ."—1 ST. JOHN i. 1—3.

ST. JOHN sets forth in his writings no theory of life. He cannot, or does not, formulate his conception of it into a system. Nothing is more alien from the spirit of a philosopher, whether physiologist or metaphysician, than the spirit of St. John the Divine. He simply feels a power, not of death but of life, working in his own soul. He is sure there is nothing in the world, or beyond the world, that can destroy it. Its evident tendency *to* God attested its origin *from* God. There might be other media to other men: to him it came through Christ.

Cicero tells us that Socrates was wont to say, that it

Virtue could only descend from heaven to earth in living form, all men perforce must love her. St. John had seen this incarnation of more than earthly loveliness. He had looked upon it with his eyes. He had handled it with his hands. It had stood before him in the person of the Master whom he had loved and served. It had penetrated his heart with a force that was not yet expended.

We are all in search of ideals. This was his. He had no need of a system or a theory. The life was manifested; and the impress it had left on his soul could be told in half a dozen words—which still sustain whatever can be called faith in the world—" We know that we are of God, and we know that the Son of God is come, and hath given us an understanding that we may know Him that is true, and we are in Him that is true, even in His Son Jesus Christ. This is the true God and the eternal life." It was, to use a well-known distinction of Aristotle, an energy rather than a mere state or condition. Beyond the reach of material, or even spiritual, analysis, it moved in a sphere, it put forth self-evidencing manifestations, which were exclusively its own. Its sphere is light : " the life is the light of men :" its characteristic tokens are the spirit of love, and the spirit of righteousness—" we know that we have passed from death unto life, when we love the brethren;" " If ye know that He is righteous, ye know that every one that doeth righteousness is born of Him." It culminates in that "enthusiasm of humanity," in which some have thought they discerned the central principle of the Gospel—" Hereby perceive we love," he goes back to his ideal, "because He laid down His life for us; and we ought to lay down our lives for the brethren."

These, and such as these, were the symptoms, the phenomena, of that life which God in Christ had given to the world; which, as it became known, was placed within the reach of all: and which, as it was embraced, became a light and a strength to all. It is the same great truth which is expressed with more passion and force, but hardly with more grandeur by St. Paul— "The law of the spirit of life in Christ Jesus hath made me free from the law of sin and death . . . for to be spiritually minded is life and peace;" "The Spirit itself beareth witness with our spirit, that we are the children of God; and if children, then heirs: heirs of God and joint heirs with Christ . . . that we may be glorified together."

The result was meant to be the same, though the processes were directly reversed in the philosophy of Plato and the theology of St. John. Each wished to help men to escape from a world of phenomena to a world of realities—from what *seemed* to what *was*, from the mists of error and falsehood and evil to the clear heavens of certainty, and truth, and goodness. By a dialectical process, by an intellectual effort to disengage itself from material surroundings, Plato thought that the soul of man might recover truths which it had lost when it submitted to gross corporeal conditions, and slowly and painfully attain the conceptions of the very truth, the very beautiful, the very good. Reversing the process, in the mystery of the

Incarnation, St. John thought that "the way, the truth, and the life," had been manifested to men. They are not his words, it is true, but the words of one who, in this matter, as we have seen, thought with him. "The God who commanded light to shine out of darkness, was He who shone in men's hearts to give the light of the knowledge of the glory of God in the face of Jesus Christ."

I cannot but think that St. John's method has, by its results, proved its title to be, I will not say the more philosophical, but the more effective for the moral guidance of the world. What is more, the method of Plato could never have been suited to any but the few: the "secret of Jesus"—as it has been called—is for all alike. The Greeks, as St. Paul tells us, in their conceit of wisdom, despised, what seemed to them, the folly of the message that there was One who had given Himself to be the life of men. But events have justified those who laid, in Christ, the foundations of the power that was first to revolutionise, and then to regenerate, the world. Even M. Renan, from his wholly unsatisfactory, and indeed incoherent, point of view, allows that the life of Jesus is the highest that has ever been presented to the eyes of men; and that, for all practical purposes, it may be regarded as unsurpassable.

There has been a certain type of life and character formed in the world, professedly on the model of the life, and character, and teaching of the Lord Jesus Christ. Making fair allowance for human imperfections and human aberrations, remembering that the treasure is in earthen vessels, can it fairly be said that the heights which have been attained by those who have truly lived the Christian life—heights attainable by all, and which have been as often attained by the lowly as by the high-born, by the illiterate as by the wise, and far oftener by the poor than by the rich—are heights which have been as often attained, and can be as easily attained, by disciples in the school of Plato and Seneca, Spinoza and Voltaire, as by disciples in the school of St. Paul and St. John.

Can we, without wishing to deny that the principle of life may have had other manifestations, and the truth (if you like to say so) other martyrs, deny that he who has fellowship with Christ, in St. John's sense, that is, who is baptized with God's Spirit and conformed to His example, becomes thereby transfigured into a higher type of moral excellence than any ethical system, appealing to ordinary motives and resting upon ordinary supports, has ever been able to achieve?

Righteousness, purity, love (St. John's three), are identical in fact, though not in phrase, with St. Paul's three—faith, hope, charity. For charity and love are the same, even in word; and purity is the fruit of hope —"he that hath this hope in Him purifieth himself even as He is pure;" and righteousness is the only proof of a really regenerating and saving faith—"if ye know that He is righteous, ye know that every one that doeth righteousness, is born of Him." This seems to me to be a Gospel for all ranks and conditions of men—as St. Paul puts it, "for Jew and Greek, Barbarian and Scythian, bond and free; for there is no difference."

I do not believe in the Gospel of Christ being a mere

system of magical arts—a mystery entrusted to a caste — such as was attempted to be practised at Ephesus by the sons of Sceva, the Jew. It may be expanded, as everything made up of a vast number of related truths may be expanded, into a philosophical system which you may call "the queen of the sciences"; as dealing with the highest subject on which the mind can occupy itself. But its power over the consciences and affections of men does not dwell there. It is in its simpler forms, as it can be taught to babes, that it is most effective.

As a rule of life, bidding us be pure and unselfish, and kindly affectioned; as a high ideal, stimulating us to forget the things that are behind, and to reach forward unto things that are yet before; enlightening us where we saw but dimly; enabling and capacitating us where we were feeble and incompetent; purifying us where appetite and passion were in danger of blunting the finer perceptions of the heart, the noble purposes of the soul; laying the foundations of an ampler and higher life, first for the individual, and then for society and the race—it was thus that the "Word of Life" presented itself to the mind of St. John.

If it had free course; if all who preached it practised it; if there were less cant and hypocrisy, and inconsistency in the world; if men with low, selfish motives were at once detected when they endeavour to conceal these motives from their fellow men under the mask of religion; if its opponents would condescend to debate the question with becoming seriousness, and its advocates would cease to advance arguments in its defence which cannot be sustained; if the failure of other systems to explain the phenomena of humanity, and still more to relieve its admitted ills and sorrows, were more fairly estimated and more fully known: perhaps it would be thought and seen that Christianity had not said its last word.

Christ's most common phrase for the system which He was setting up on earth was "the kingdom of heaven." If the two great curses of our modern civilisation —drunkenness and prostitution—were swept away, the streets in which you live would be more like heaven than they are. If men and women were true to one another, and to themselves; if they were honest —and when you speak of an honest man, still more of an honest woman—you mean something more than one who will not pick your pocket; there would be more types on earth than there are of what the Son of God was manifested to make us all.

We first frustrate the grace of God, do despite to it, trample it under our feet, and then call the Gospel a failure. We make Christian influence impossible, and then ask: Where is it to be found? We first grieve, and finally quench, the Spirit of God, and then say we can recognise no tokens of His presence, or His power. And yet, under all these circumstances of disadvantage, there are to be found in palaces and cottages, pure and brave and noble souls; and where one such soul lives and breathes, diffusing the fragrance of its beneficent influence, and the power of its saintly life, *there* is the proof of the truth of Christ's Gospel, *there* is the witness that God still leaves of Himself in the world.

I did not hesitate to speak, just now of "types of

moral excellence"; and to some pious minds that will seem a poor and feeble, even a disparaging phrase for the result of God's grace upon the soul. I desire to utter a word of not wholly unnecessary warning on this matter.

We have got into a way of talking which, I think, is strangely unreal and, in many cases, fatally misleading; a way which regards the supernatural, rather than the natural, as the proper sphere of the Divine energy; a way by which the *spiritual* appears to supersede and keep out of sight the *moral*. I am aware that the word "nature" is used in various senses more or less restricted; but the phrase "supernatural" leads people commonly to suppose that the ways of God's Spirit are fitful and capricious rather than stated and orderly; whereas there can be no reasonable doubt that the "reign of law," in the truest sense of the words, is as supreme in the spiritual as in the material world. Our Lord's comparison of the effect of spiritual action to the effect of the wind blowing where it listeth, pointed merely to the invisible character of that action, and was not meant to intimate or imply capriciousness. We know exactly what to do in order to receive a gift of the Spirit; and if the conditions are fulfilled, the gift is bestowed, and that quite as certainly as in a chemical experiment. What is this but saying that the effect is the result of a *natural* law, in Bishop Butler's large sense of the word "nature."

Oh! friends, beware lest you do an irreparable mischief to religion by separating it from morality, and that of the homeliest kind! Beware of dissociating religion from such moral qualities as chastity, honesty, truthfulness. When St. Peter has stirred our spiritual impulses by telling us, as St. John also tells us, of the exceeding great and precious promises by which we are, as it were, made partakers of the Divine nature, he at once brings us down from heaven to earth again by saying: "And beside all this, giving all diligence, add to your faith, virtue." When St. Paul would pray for the best gifts for his Thessalonian converts, he prays that God would sanctify them wholly, and that their "whole spirit, soul, and body might be preserved blameless unto the coming of our Lord Jesus Christ."

No man had a keener insight than St. Paul into the perils of that subtle form of self-deceit, which under the mask of religion, hides a foul and corrupt heart, and while claiming to possess a spiritual mind, leaves some of the basest and meanest passions all wild and unsubdued. "Shall we continue in sin," he asks, "that grace may abound? God forbid! How shall we that are dead to sin live any longer therein?" To put away a good conscience was the first step towards making shipwreck of the faith.

It is my firm conviction that it is not so much speculative difficulties which shake the faith of men in Christ's Gospel as the power of God unto salvation to the human soul as moral incongruities—as, for instance, when a man who has made a profession of godliness, who may have been even a leader of religious parties, is found out to be a swindler or a libertine, or is known by those who have any intimacy with him to be selfish, proud, covetous malevolent, revengeful. The natural judgment to pass upon religion, when we have seen it thus associated, is to pronounce the whole thing a sham. That such shams exist here, there, everywhere, and that they justly provoke such scoffs and sneers, is only too notorious. The marvel to me is that men think it worth while to wear such thin disguises, beneath which the true features are only too clearly seen. Can they possibly imagine that God will judge them on the principle of a set-off, as though two tradesmen were settling accounts together?

As I survey the phenomena of the age, the chief fear in my mind for the future of religion is lest it should get dissevered from morality; lest it should become a matter of dogma and ritual, that is, of opinion and sentiment rather than a principle of conduct. It has been truly said that "conduct is three-fourths of life." It is the main affair. Orthodoxy is good, but morality is better. Even truth, when of the purely speculative kind, in the sphere of theosophy or theology, is barren of results, unless it can be made to bear on the regulation of the life and the illumination of the conscience; and worship, unless it expresses and satisfies the yearnings of the soul, unless it is used and felt as a means of access to God, as a vehicle of that grace which we all so sorely need, is nothing better than an organised, though it may be a graceful and attractive, formalism.

It is from this point of view, and not because I have narrow Puritanical ideas upon the subject, that I dread the possible effects of the present extravagant attention to an æsthetic and even sensuous ritualism, which I trust has nearly had its day. It has gone to form a type of character which, I confess, is not much to my mind. There is a danger, of which St. Paul has warned us, of the forms of Godliness being scrupulously cultivated by those who are yet, in their hearts, strangers to its power. Men and women are making religion rather a matter of special observance than a principle of general self-control. The leaven, if it can be so called, affects a part of their nature only, not the whole. In their souls there are dark, foul chambers, into which the unclean spirit, once perhaps cast forth, has found his way back again: or they are haunted by the spectres of sins which they can hardly be said to have forsaken, although they are continually reiterating their confession of them; and instead of revolting the conscience, the memory of them, sometimes deliberately awakened, even gives a languid sense of pleasure to the imagination.

We build sanctuaries, in which we place, not God in any rational conception of His nature, but a fetish whom we worship and think to propitiate; not Christ, the Saviour of all men, specially of them that believe, but a Christ so localised and materialised that a stranger who passed by and beheld our devotion might think we believed in the power of charms and spells; and that His objective presence on an altar is deemed infinitely more precious than His subjective presence in the soul. We think in such sanctuaries, where the air is stifling with the vapid fumes of incense, we can offer to God a higher and more acceptable service than is possible in the outer world of activity and usefulness; where perhaps worship plays a less conspicuous part, but where there is no lack of calls to duty or of motives for disinterestedness and self-sacrifice. O that God would raise up for His Church Prophets, Evangelists, Pastors and Teachers who would inspire a passion for virtue! The Evangelists we have seen to me to stimulate the sensibilities, but hardly to quicken the conscience.

We have need to close our ranks in defence of virtue. Morals and religion have more to fear from those who attempt to discredit the Sermon on the Mount than from those who express (not always, it is true, in as measured language as one could desire) their dislike of the seeming hardness of some of the statements of the Athanasian Creed. It is time that we understood the meaning of that saying, "The Kingdom of God is not in word, but in power." It is time we appreciated the difference in value between the weightier and the less weighty matter of the law; to use our Lord's own comparison, "between mercy and sacrifice." And so strong is my own confidence in the essential harmony of things, that I feel sure that a clear and authoritative conscience will be found to be the surest safeguard and strongest support to a rational faith; and that he is not likely to wander far, or long, from the precincts of truth who keeps his feet firmly planted in the ways of rectitude.

I do not doubt "that the decomposition of belief which is going on so rapidly among us must—or at least may—involve the most profound, probably sincere, and yet alarming, recast of principles of honour and principles of self-restraint hitherto commonly accepted," and which constitute the substance of ordinary morality. But I believe that "the ethical basis of thought is deeper than the dogmatic; and to attempt to rehabilitate faith before you have restored the recognition of the supremacy of conscience, is to build a house upon the sand." "If the light that is in thee be darkness, how great is that darkness." So do not suppose that to preach morality is to empty the Gospel of the grace of God of its proper power, or to supplement the work of Christ by a righteousness of our own. The moral nature of man is the true subject of grace; and Christ is only truly *Lord* when He is thoroughly *obeyed*.

Preached—Westminster Abbey, June 25, 1876. Christ Church Cathedral, Oxford, December 7, 1881. Westminster Abbey, July 5, 1885.

XII.

IMMORTALITY.

"It doth not yet appear what we shall be."—1 St. John iii. 2.

This is Revelation's "last word" on a great subject, which theologians have too often forgotten in their positive statements and assumptions.

Our English version does not quite correctly represent the Greek original. It is not οὔπω φαίνεται, "it doth not yet *appear*," as a result of human inference or speculation; but οὔπω ἐφανερώθη, "it has not yet been manifested or revealed." God Himself still wraps our destiny among His "hidden things."

Even Paul, when wading in these perilous depths, and talking of the "change" that awaits all, and attempting to describe the properties of a "spiritual body," felt himself to be confronted with a "mystery;" and while satisfied that there would be a victory over the grave, and that mortality would be swallowed up in life, wisely brought back his readers' thoughts from dreamland to reality, by bidding them simply "be steadfast, unmoveable, always abounding in the work of the

Lord, forasmuch as they knew that their labour was not in vain in the Lord."

Nor can it be said that the Great Teacher Himself, when He most clearly proclaimed the doctrine of the Resurrection, drew aside for more than the briefest moment the curtain by which the mystery is veiled. "The children of this world," He said, "marry, and are given in marriage; but they which shall be accounted worthy to obtain that world, and the resurrection from the dead, neither marry nor are given in marriage; neither can they die any more: for they are equal unto the angels, and are the children of God and of the resurrection." One of those who heard Him tells us that the words conveyed no distinct idea to him as to what the after-resurrection state should be; and an equally reasonable faith, while clinging to the hope of immortality as the very anchor of the soul, which if let go life would drift helplessly amid the shoals and rocks that surround our course on every side, will still admit that coequality with the angels, and seeing God as He is, do not belong to the class of definite ideas, but to those vaguer shapes and imaginings which define little but suggest much, and of which, even when most consciously under their influence, we can hardly say whence they come or what they are.

To those who hold the merely physical theory of being—who see in matter the promise and potency of life in every form—who account for even the phenomena of what used to be called "volition" by the reflex action of a muscle or a nerve—the very existence of these imaginings, these hopes and fears, should be a problem of no slight difficulty. It is possible, as Professor Tyndall has said, that "Many who hold the hypothesis of natural evolution would probably assent to the position that at the present moment all our philosophy, all our poetry, all our science, all our art— Plato, Shakespeare, Newton, Da Vinci—are potential in the fires of the sun;" but it would seem to require a further reach of imagination in the province of science to conceive that the fires of the sun, itself one day to perish, could have implanted, even potentially, in the human soul the hope of immortality; still more so, if, as some loudly proclaim to-day, it is a hope destined never to be realised; not even one of those visions, in the language of the old Greek poet,

$$\text{ἐξ ὀνειράτων ἃ χρὴ}$$
$$\text{ὕπαρ γενέσθαι.}[1]$$

For there it is—a hope deep-seated in the heart of man; and, like every other phenomenon, it has to be accounted for. And as it is not pretended by any one to be within the range of mathematical demonstration or physical experiment, the most reasonable hypothesis must be accepted. As Sir William Hamilton has said, " The existence of God and the immortality of the soul are not given us as *phenomena*, as objects of *immediate* knowledge; yet if the phenomena actually given do necessarily require, for their rational explanation, the hypothesis of immortality and of God, we are assuredly entitled, from the existence of the former, to infer the reality of the latter."

[1] Æschyl. *Prom. Vinct.*, 485, 486.

Nor do intermediate hypotheses and secondary explanations *exclude*—rather they necessitate, or at least demand—a higher and primary account of things. If it be true that "between the microscope limit and the true molecular limit"—though I know not what mortal eye has penetrated to that unknown land—still, granting it to be true, as Professor Tyndall assumes it to be true, that in

> "The undiscovered country from whose bourn
> No traveller returns."

to tell us what he has actually seen, " the poles of the atoms are arranged, that tendency is given to their powers, so that when the poles and powers have free action, and proper stimulus in a suitable environment, they determine first the germ, and afterwards the complete organism," still there is room, and almost a necessity, for God ; and we know as a fact, under " the stimulus of a suitable environment," there has been either developed or implanted in the mind of man the hope of immortality.

And here the mere physicist is brought to a pause. He cannot explain the phenomenon consistently with his purely physical principles ; indeed, if these cover all the problems of life, it seems to me that he ought to try to *explain it away:* it is, to say the least, an awkward and unexpected result of a concourse of material atoms, whatever the arrangement of their poles, or the tendency given to their powers: and if he can neither explain it, nor explain it away, he is bound, upon his own principles, at least to listen to the hypothesis of one who has been studying in another, but not an antagonistic, school. If there is arrangement, is it not possible that there may have been an arranger? if a tendency was given, some one to give it? if an environment, an environer? if a stimulus, a stimulator? If this hope of an indestructible life is there, may it not have come from God? and is not the mystery of our being best solved, though not with the precision of scientific language, by the Old Book which tells us that "the Lord God formed man, and breathed into his nostrils the breath of life, and man became a living soul?"

For, admitting the fact of a Living Personal God, there needs be no insuperable or even serious difficulty in admitting the *fact* of a revelation, whether in the narrow sense in which the idea is sometimes confined to the inspired records of the Bible, or in that broader and more Pauline sense in which, even to the heathen, God is said to have shown His own attributes and their destiny (Romans i. 19, 20).

Not that revelation supersedes reason, or removes the things revealed from the field of legitimate, and even exact, inquiry. Rather it offers the noblest scope to a chastened and truly philosophic mind. As the great author of the *Analogy* has so truly said: "Not that reason is no judge of what is offered to us as being of divine revelation. For this would be to infer that we are unable to judge of anything, because we are unable to judge of all things. Reason can, and it ought to, judge, not only of the meaning, but also of the morality and the evidence of revelation." And we who call ourselves theologians have quite as much need to remember, and restrain ourselves in our speculations by remembering, these prerogatives of reason, as any other class of philosophical inquirers.

Nor, again, upon the same assumption of a Personal Author of the Universe, can there be fairly said to be any *à priori* objection to the *theory* of revelation. It is not a thing to be called impossible, or even improbable. As Mr. Davison in his introductory lecture on Prophecy has admirably said, "Antecedently to a consideration of the proper evidences of revealed religion, it cannot be said with any show of reason that it is a thing improbable in itself that a divine revelation should be made. Nothing that we know of the attributes of God or of His moral government, nothing that we know of the nature and condition of man, would make it appear unfit for God to bestow upon man an immediate communication of His will. On the contrary, the most just and rational notions we can frame of the providential care of the Deity would lead us to consider it as entirely suitable to His attributes and designs, that he should at times impart to His reasonable creatures whose whole existence and destiny are dependent upon Him, supplies of knowledge and direction. And on the side of man it is too clear, on a sober review of his condition, that he is not so complete in his own natural resources as to be placed above the benefit, or even the need, of such supervening assistance."

We have only each to keep within our proper precinct, and not to advance hypotheses and conjectures as though these were ascertained and irreversible laws, and there need be no quarrel, no antagonism even, between the physical investigator and the believer in revelation. Each is bound to give a reason for what he asserts and what he believes; and it is to my mind impossible to conceive that truth in one sphere of thought will ever be found to contradict or clash with truth in another sphere. That, according to the author of the Epistle to the Hebrews, God has spoken His last revealed word to man by His Son, while Science, undaunted and untired, is adding year by year to its wondrous conquests, proves to my mind nothing more than that God saw fit to satisfy man's *spiritual* yearnings before his *natural*—presumably, because they were the more important of the two.

I am astonished, indeed, at the dogmatic hardihood—sometimes supposed to be confined to theologians—with which it is asserted that "the whole world, living and non-living," has resulted from "the mutual interaction of the forces possessed by the molecules of which the primitive nebulosity of the universe was composed;" and that "a sufficient intelligence could, from a knowledge of those molecules, have predicted, say the state of the fauna in Britain in 1869"—the year, I suppose, in which these words were written—"with as much certainty as one can say what will happen to the vapour of the breath on a cold winter's day." But I do not go so far as Dr. Beale, from whom I borrow this quotation, and say that such a theory or doctrine "strikes at the root of the idea of a living God, and in such a scheme neither a superintending Providence, nor a personal God, nor Christianity could have place." I suppose a *sufficient* intelligence *could* have foretold all that has been evolved out of the nebulous condition of the Kosmos, if this is the true account of existing things; but till you have proved to me that spirit is merely a mode of matter, or that my conscience and will—all that I feel constitutes the *Ego*—will pass away when the breath leaves my body into other beings, whether living or non-living, so that the doctrine of personal identity becomes an idle dream, there is room, abundant room, for all I care to believe about God and my soul.

There appears to be a sort of necessity laid upon thinking minds to explain this strange and inexpressible yearning for a life after death, which all recognise as among the strongest and most ineffaceable instincts of the human soul. It may be worth while to notice two of the most recent attempts which have come under my own observation. The one is Mr. Frederic Harrison's theory, in the July number of "*The Nineteenth Century*," of a posthumous life of influence, reputation and renown—the influence exerted upon posterity by a Shakespeare or a Cromwell or a Savonarola—as an equivalent for immortality; the other, a view put forward with much ability—and as ably answered—by a writer in last week's issue of the *Spectator* newspaper, who holds, "as a hypothesis, that some men, possibly very many men, a large proportion, live again, but that all men do not; that the potentiality of continued existence, which we call soul, is not an inherent quality or attribute of the human race, but an acquired or given quality of some portion of it only." Both these views, though departing from such different points, seem to me to be modifications of that theory of a *corps d'élite* of the human race, which, under the name of Calvinism, has wrought such havoc in theology, and, in spite of its cruel hardness, by its inexorable logic, has exercised so remarkable a fascination, not merely on the fanatical and unlearned, but even on high and gifted minds. Both are struggles— I cannot but think ineffective struggles—against the dark and dreary creed of annihilation, which, whatever comfort it might bring to some powerful but strangely-tempered minds like that of Harriet Martineau, would to most men mean an end, certainly of all their fears, but, as certainly, of their brightest hopes and noblest motives. "We too," says Mr. Harrison, speaking in the name of the School to which he belongs, "turn our thoughts to that which is behind the veil. We strive to pierce its secret with eyes as eager and as fearless, and even, it may be, more patient, in searching for the realities beyond the gloom. That which shall come after is not of less interest to us than to you. We ask you, therefore, what do you know of it? Tell us, and we will tell you what we hope. Let us reason together in sober and precise prose. Why should this great end, staring at all of us along the vista of each human life, be for ever a matter of dithyrambic hypotheses and evasive tropes?"

In spite of this eloquent and impassioned appeal, we must be content to answer, with the Apostle, οὔπω ἐφανερώθη τί ἐσόμεθα. We cannot tell *what* will "come after;" but, to us, the Scripture's promise of conscious continued individual life, under conditions of indefinitely higher possible development than any we have known here, in a world to come, seems a truer and more verifiable account of that "great end which stares at all of us along the vista of each human life," than theories which, if they admit a posthumous existence at all, evaporate it into a metaphor, and regard even that as the privilege of a selected few.

But I must ask you to observe another utterance— another (so to speak) "view of life"—of the Apostle who has so far led on our thoughts, and who more fully than any other witness has treasured up his Master's deepest words for the Church and for the world. He who tells us so plainly that he did not know, because it had not been revealed, what we *shall be*, tells us with the most unfaltering conviction what we *are*. "Beloved, now are we the sons of God." Paul's great assurance, too, you will remember: "The Spirit itself"—what Plato might have called the $αὐτὸ πνεῦμα$—"beareth witness with our spirit that we are the children of God." And to know this, to be sure of this, was enough. The future was hidden, but the present was clear. "For the life was manifested, and we have seen it, and bear witness, and show unto you that eternal life, which was with the Father, and was manifested unto us: that which we have seen and heard declare we unto you, that ye also may have fellowship with us: and truly our fellowship is with the Father, and with his Son Jesus Christ." It was, perhaps, remembering the Master's own words, that the disciple wrote in this strain. "This is life eternal," said the Christ in His last great intercession, "that men may know Thee, the only true God, and Jesus Christ, whom Thou hast sent." It did not seem strange or vainglorious to those who had followed Him in His great career, as He "went about doing good," and opening their eyes to understand many things that were dark before, to hear such words spoken from time to time as these, "I am the way, the truth, and the life"—"I am the resurrection and the life"—"I am the light of the world"—"I am the bread of life; he that eateth Me, even he shall live by Me." His miracles authenticated His words; and His words explained His miracles. They were not mere signs or wonders, but, as He so often calls them Himself, *works*, wrought visibly on men's bodies to show what He was capable of operating invisibly on their souls. And we cannot deny, unless we are prepared to deny all evidence of testimony, nay the evidence, I should suppose, of our own frequent observation, that that faculty of the soul which we call "faith"—which, adopting Mr. Harrison's definition of the soul, means "the consensus of all the human faculties" throwing themselves and fastening with intense energy on a particular object—it cannot, I think, be denied that faith, possessing itself (so to speak) of Christ, living, as Paul lived, in Him, and by Him, and to Him, has had the power of elevating humanity to heights, not perhaps unattempted, but unattained before. Unless it be seriously maintained that the heathen philosopher was as perfect a specimen of the race in its moral aspects as the Christian saint—that there were as many elements of goodness as well as of greatness in a Socrates or Seneca as in a Paul—it

N

can hardly be gainsaid that in Christianity there has been a perceptible accession to the forces or powers that govern the moral development of mankind. If in the region "beyond the microscope limit," according to Professor Tyndall, a tendency is given to the physical powers, so that, "when they have free action and proper stimulus in a suitable environment, they determine first the germ and afterwards the complete organism;" so, in the region beyond the limit of physiological or biological inquiry, there seems evidence of a tendency given to the spiritual powers, so that, under the like favourable conditions, they develop, in our Lord's figurative language, "first the blade, then the ear, after that the full corn in the ear." And of this tendency and this development you, gentlemen, while observing primarily the phenomena of natural life, must have been as frequently conscious as we who, by our profession, are more concerned with watching the manifestations of life in the soul. In the dark and sorrowful hours of many a sick chamber—by the side of many a bed occupied, now by one struck down by some deathly disease in the full flush of youth and strength, now by some hoary head going down to its grave "as a shock of corn cometh in in its season," you cannot, unless your eyes have been strangely holden from seeing such things, have failed to notice with what tenacity the human spirit clings to that eternal life which it believes itself to have in Christ Jesus our Lord: as one testifies, "the outward man perishing, but the inward man renewed day by day—the eye the while looking not at things which are seen, but at things which are not seen; for the things which are seen are temporal, but the things which are not seen are eternal."

It is indeed surprising how little modern criticism or modern scientific inquiry has done to undermine those old foundations upon which all religion in its very idea, and Christianity as religion in its highest form, must ultimately repose. It is only one here and there who tells us that the idea of a personal God is an unverifiable hypothesis; and even such recognise in the circumstances around them a manifest stream or tendency that "makes for righteousness." It is only one here and there who defrauds humanity of its brightest hopes and most sustaining motives by denying to it immortality; and even such, as though conscious of their wrong, endeavour to provide a substitute for the idea which they have destroyed, which indeed proves illusory, but which they seem to feel to be indispensable.[1]

No doubt, there are some sad souls

> "Mad from life's history,
> Glad to death's mystery
> Swift to be hurled,
> Anywhere, anywhere,
> Out of the world;"

but, however much we may sympathise with them or try to rescue them from their blank despair, we cannot sacrifice the hopes of the human race to these. In the dim gloom that shrouds the land beyond the grave there

[1] Mr. John Stuart Mill, in his *Posthumous Essays*, admits that, though the doctrine of the immortality of the soul is probably an illusion, it is morally so valuable that it had better be retained.

is yet a streak of light, like some sudden lightning-flash, illuminating the darkness with hopes full of immortality; in the still silence of the chamber of death, there is yet a voice heard, sustaining the soul in its passage through the shadowed valley, "He that believeth in Me shall never die." Grant me a right to believe in a personal God—in a living Christ—in an indwelling Spirit—in a life of the world to come; and, like that ship driven up and down in Adria, upon which " no small tempest lay," I shall have, as it were, my "four anchors cast out of the stern," while I "wait for the day" (Acts xxvii. 20, 27, 29). Speaking for myself alone, this thought is my comfort in a day when so many old creeds are ruthlessly assailed, and even we who think that the attack has failed against the key of our position must, if we are honest, confess that many outposts, which we once thought of more importance than they have proved to be, have had to be evacuated; that we have had to part with some once cherished beliefs, or, if we hold them still, hold them with less tenacity and less confidence than before. If the four great ultimate truths that I have mentioned are wrested from us, then, I admit, we must surrender Christianity. But as yet, at least, we claim still to be in possession of so much Christian ground. And on this ground, as " in a suitable environment," the human soul can live, and thrive, and grow. It will find for itself, by a sort of instinct, the food that nourishes it best. One is, as it were, a babe, to be fed with milk; another can digest and assimilate strong meat. One draws most nourishment from prayer; another from sacraments. So long as each grows, it matters not much why or how. And the fact of growth is the best proof that the food was wholesome, and suited to the system which received it. The cases are numberless in which physicians, whether of the body or soul, must stand aside, and discontinue their nostrums, and see, in one case what *nature*, in the other case what *grace*, can do. As long as such " miracles of healing " are witnessed, men will not seriously doubt the truth of Christianity. As M. Alexandre Dumas said the other day in Paris at the distribution of some prizes in reward of virtue—a somewhat curious merit first to discriminate, and then to reward—" the study of these lives has done me more good than the finest treatise in philosophy or wisdom ; for genius does not explain God, but goodness proves Him."

Yes, I feel it : we shall have to come back more and more to the simplest proofs of the " things which are most surely believed among us." Christianity has been too much elaborated into a system or a philosophy. Erudite treatises, forcible arguments may have done much in support of faith ; but a holy life does more. It was the Bishop of Peterborough's great argument in Norwich Cathedral before the British Association for the Advancement of Science, and, I have heard, fully appreciated there. Portraying to their imaginations the character of a Christian man—self-sacrificing, brave, humble, patient, pure—he said, " Account for that man." If you cannot explain him by any known law of physical development, listen to his own account of himself. He will tell you, as one told questioners of old, " By the grace of God, I am what I am." Beyond that, no need, no place, for further questioning. He cannot explain the relation of cause and effect any more than you can in your physical researches. But he is aware of a chain of sequences which lead up his soul to God. And the invariableness of the sequences, and the spiritual growth of which he is conscious, have made him, in a very real, though perhaps not in a scientific sense, "*know* Him in whom he has believed," and he is content to trust the future to Him as well as the present, persuaded, with a persuasion that you will not easily wrest from him, that "He is able to keep that which he has committed to Him against that day." "Lord," he says, with the simple-hearted disciple of old, "to whom shall I go? Thou hast the words of eternal life."

I trust, gentlemen, representatives of a noble profession, that His Spirit, who, in the strong but not strained language of Paul, "illuminated life and immortality," may guide you, in your discussions, to the furtherance, within your own legitimate and important sphere, of those high human interests for which He lived and died.

Preached—Before the British Medical Association, in Manchester Cathedral, August 7, 1877.

XIII.

RIGHTEOUSNESS.

" For the kingdom of God is not meat and drink ; but righteousness, and peace, and joy in the Holy Ghost."—ROM. xiv. 17.

A MAN need not be a pessimist or a cynic who says that he is not cheered by the present aspects, and that he feels a kind of uncomfortable shudder at the dark and threatening future, of modern society.

I admit that it is easy, perhaps natural, to some minds to exaggerate this. Our impression and our generalisation are so much modified by temperament, by association, by limitation of view, by accidental grouping or contrast of the objects which present themselves to the eye at the same moment ; by defect, sometimes of imagination and sometimes of reasoning ; by inability to "look before and after," to discern causes and trace consequences ; and not seldom by a loss of stability in the moral centre, and an enfeebled, if not a shaken, faith in God, that our inferences are apt to go further than we are justified, upon the evidence, in carrying them ; and a more sanguine, as well as a more philosophic and religious, mind would bid us see elements of hope and light in what had filled our hearts with gloom and despondency.

I remember well on my last visit to Oxford, walking with a thoughtful friend, and his remarking, in a tone that struck and surprised me, that he had given up all hope of the birth or revival of great ideas in England for this generation. What the twentieth century might have in store he could not tell; but the nineteenth had "left off bearing." Something like this, you will remember, was the fancy of Aristotle in regard to races. "There is a cropping-time," he says, "in the races of men, as in the fruits of the field; and sometimes, if the stock be good, there springs up for a time a succession of splendid men ($ἄνδρες\ περιττοί$); and then comes a period of barrenness." I am not saying whether such views are true or false, nor denying that there may not be a dangerous trace of fatalism in them which would paralyse effort, and help the prophecy to fulfil itself; but they are natural; and at crises like the present, when there are very few objects, either in the political, or the social, or the religious field of view, on which a reflecting mind can rest with satisfaction, they are apt perhaps unduly to depress the spirit, and almost make us lose our heads in the appalling thought that the deluge is upon us, and that we are too weak, too disorganised, and, above all, too late, to do anything to arrest its devastating and fatal career.

I was strengthened myself recently by a passage which fell under my eye in the preface of Mr. Thomas Hughes's touching *Memoir of a Brother*, a brother whom I remember when I first became a fellow of

Oriel, thirty-nine years ago, as an undergraduate of the highest type there; a memoir, which you, young men, who would fight the good fight, and pass safely through the world's trials and temptations, and win its highest and purest rewards, would do well to read.

Deprecating dark and gloomy forebodings of the future of England, as though we were unable to do what our fathers had done, Mr. Hughes bids his reader look round upon and number up the various groups of families scattered up and down the land, in which we know that homely, simple, modest, pure lives are yet being led, and which vice and luxury and selfishness have not yet contrived to spoil, and he says we shall be surprised at the number of such homes within the circle of our own acquaintance; and there, he adds, lie the hopes and the future of England. And I acquiesced in the truth of the statement, and thanked God and took courage.

Of course, there is always a ground of hope in what I may call the inherent moral resources of human nature. Even the darkest and most hideous pictures of the condition of man—"far enough gone," indeed, as every one's conscience must witness, " from original righteousness," yet not so far gone as some theological systems, which exercised perhaps too great a spell over the imagination of our reformers, have loved to paint him—have happily never been able to suppress the faith of the human heart in its capacities—in what Bishop Butler would probably call its "natural tendencies." Sane men—of course one does not notice the wailings of morbid minds like poor Cowper's—

who, when under the necessity of acting, have broken through the conventional phraseology of their schools, have felt that they had, and that they could exert, a moral power; and that even when, through the failing resistance of the will, they allowed themselves "to be brought into captivity to the law of sin that was in their members," there was yet within them that consent of the conscience unto the law that it is good, and those visitings of compunction for the evil that has been done or the good that has been left undone, which are at least evidence of a nature not wholly corrupt, and guarantees that the divine image in which we were made, however much disfigured, is not absolutely marred.

Indeed, when our Divine Lord bids His disciples have faith in God, it almost follows as a necessary implicit inference that they should have faith in man, who, as St. James reminds us, "is made after the similitude of God." To despair of humanity—to bemoan its sad estate—to picture it as, since the great mystery of the Incarnation, still lying "fast bound in misery and iron" —to so misread the lesson of the prophet's vision as to say or think that nothing can be done in the way of preparation, and of necessary preparation, which may be the very condition of full success, till the breath of God comes forth and shakes the bones and breathes upon and quickens those slain—this supine and enervating "waiting upon Providence" or upon grace—by whichever name it may be excused or disguised—is as irrational as it is unscriptural; as false in theory as it is fatal in practice.

Of course, results are not ours; and we often form mistaken and too eager estimates of them; and like the half-hearted King of Israel, we smite but thrice upon the ground with our arrows, and stay; or ask in a murmur, which savours of mistrust, "Lord, wilt not Thou stretch forth Thy hand and destroy the enemy that hath done such dishonour in Thy sanctuary?" and forget the need and the discipline of that "long patience" (as the Apostle calls it) with which the husbandman waiteth for the precious fruit of the earth, until it receives the early and the latter rain, he having done, and doing still, his own part the while; but still there is evidence, and evidence enough, of a general law, and the blessing for the most part comes quick and ample and rewarding, where there has been effort, and the effort has been wisely calculated and adequately sustained.

Quite wonderful at times has been the vivifying power of great principles and noble ideas, even upon masses of men who before seemed steeped in inertness and lethargy. It needs but that he whom Carlyle calls the hero should give utterance to the voice; and if it is a true and inspiring one, every tongue catches it up as it were instinctively, and repeats it to its fellows.

There is a harmony between the inner sensibilities of the soul and the moral order and beauty of the universe, if we only have the skill to touch the note which wakens it. It was this harmony to which Paul so unhesitatingly appealed, in spite of all the subtleties of a sophistical philosophy, which so often made evil seem good, and wrong right, when he trusted that the Philippians could still discern for themselves, and love and honour whatever was true, and honest, and just, and pure, and lovely, which men would not have stamped with the name of virtue, or consented as with one mouth to praise, if they had not felt its intrinsic excellence, and recognised its genuine attractiveness.

Let no man speak lightly of, or lose confidence in, human nature. It was of himself, in what some people would call his unregenerate condition, that Paul said, "I delight in the law of God after the inward man." To forget, in any battle we attempt to fight against sin, whether in ourselves or in others, that truth is more natural to us than falsehood, and right than wrong— more natural, I mean, in Bishop Butler's sense of the word, more agreeable with the constitution of our nature, and more in harmony with its actual facts—is to go into the fray almost with our hands tied; is certainly to neglect to avail ourselves of a position from which we could operate with the greatest advantage. The facts of human nature are not against us, but for us; we may appeal to them, and trust to the effects of the appeal. And this surely is a great ἀφορμή: a coign of vantage of a practical kind, not, for the sake of any theoretical consistency or theological prejudice, to be lightly thrown away.

Society, doubtless, is not in a healthy state; it is easy to mark the symptoms of many a form of dangerous disease; but one would not say that gangrene has set in. Things have been in as desperate a plight before. They were far worse in the days of Juvenal and Tacitus; far worse when Paul drew with his scathing pen that fearful picture of the general foulness of the heathen world; of which one historian (Tacitus) himself could say that it was an age hostile to virtue —"*virtutibus infesta sæcula*"—and another, "We have come to this pass: we can neither suffer our vices nor their remedies." And yet this almost *insanabile vulnus* —this corrupted body, with no soundness in it from the sole of the foot even to the head, full of wounds, and bruises, and putrefying sores—the wholesome medicine of Christ's Gospel, applied by the hands of wise physicians, in a measure, healed.

Let any one who cares to do so compare the ἦθος of St. Paul with that of Seneca, or even that of Marcus Aurelius, and, if he has any feeling for such differences, he will recognise how it was that evangelists succeeded when philosophers had failed; how it was that the firm grasp of a few great spiritual truths (for it was so unsystematic that it could hardly be called a method at all)—how, I say, it was that the firm grasp of a few great spiritual truths, the exhaustless love of God to man being at the base of them all, and every true response from the human heart gathering itself round that, sufficed to convert and purify the world.

Since then we have theologised and theosophised, and developed and formulated doctrines, and framed our faith into creeds and articles, and defended it with anathemas, and made it systematic, and think we are now more fully armed than ever to encounter the armies of heathendom abroad and the armies of ungodliness and unbelief at home. "The Catholic Faith is this," we say: and we seem to expect as a matter of course that all opposition will disperse before it, as mists before the morning sun. It has hardly been so, as a matter of fact, of history. The great ages of formulating doctrines and of anathematising heretics were not the great ages of winning souls. The spirit of Paul was more truly missionary than the spirit of Cyril of Alexandria, or even, grand figure as his was, of Athanasius. The Council of Jerusalem, if we read its effects in their spirit, did infinitely more for the relief and help of the souls of men than the Council of Ephesus. When men testified everywhere the simple doctrines of "repentance towards God and faith towards our Lord Jesus Christ," I can understand what I am told about "pricked hearts," and "common people hearing gladly," and souls that had long seemed to be lying dead, or at least torpid, in trespasses and sins, made conscious (so to speak) of new powers, recognising responsibilities never felt, making efforts never attempted before, becoming, in the highest, truest sense, "new creatures" old things passing away, and all things seeming new.

When I spoke of a medicine just now, I used an image which may mislead. Our popular notion of a medicine is of something made up according to the prescription of a doctor, or the directions of a pharmacopœia, of divers drugs in due proportions, neatly labelled and put up in a graduated bottle, to be taken punctually so many times a day. Nothing could be less like than this to the freedom, the almost infinite adaptiveness and versatility of the first preachers of the Gospel. "To the Jews I became as a Jew; to them that are without law as without law: to the weak became I as weak, that I might gain the weak; I am made all things unto all men that I might by all means save some."

He is careful indeed to tell us that he recognised a law: he speaks of the duty of conforming to the customs of the Churches; he preaches distinctly that God is not the author of confusion; he would have everything done decently and in order; but the law was a law of liberty, not of bondage; the customs were few and simple, and their aim does not seem to have been a mystic symbolism, but practical edification; peace was secured and confusion avoided by the spirits of the prophets being subject to the prophets, and every one submitting himself to the higher powers; and an elaborate ceremonial, each part in which has to be rehearsed by its actors that the tableau may be complete with a kind of mechanical completeness, would have been perhaps as far removed from Paul's ideal of "decency and order" as anything conceivably could be. You may as well try to persuade me, as some silly people, I am told, have persuaded themselves, that the cloak which the apostle left at Troas with Carpus was a sacrificial vestment—a chasuble.

I was much struck the other day with a passage which I met in one of the late lamented Professor Mozley's reviews. He notices the "melancholy fact that persons have often been driven by the near presence of the Church's teaching into a worse infidelity than they would have had without it;" and while he admits that "the Church is not responsible for such an effect," he asserts that she is "responsible for any tendencies in this direction arising from unnecessary and narrow-minded intolerance," or "from obstinate continuances" in courses which have grown out of date "amid a wholly different state of things." (Essays, ii. pp. 88-9.) At the same time, with that balanced and impartial mind which was so characteristic of him, he recognises " the great practical difficulties which always lie on the side of change." " It does not appear," he says, " to be the habit of institutions to dissolve on the principle of accommodation, and yield a voluntary and rational assent to the proofs of uncongeniality which present themselves to their eyes. They expect their dissolution under another form of approach, and they generally wait for that final evidence, good or bad, of incompatibility, which forcible overthrow supplies." And, then applying his principles to the case he had before him, he adds, " The Inquisition did what all other institutions do: it went on till it was stopped."

I may utterly misread the signs of the times and the drift of events. What seems to me mainly a superficial, irrational, and wayward excitement — largely materialistic, largely sensuous, and almost entirely æsthetic and emotional—may be, though I don't think it is, a great awakening of the conscience, the beginning of a revived religious life of the nation in higher, nobler, more solid, and permanent forms. In the heat of the fray, it is not easy to withdraw to a post of philosophical observation: but certainly, while I see no evidence to support this view, that the present methods which many of us are so largely using are producing over any great and discernible breadths of society a moralising influence upon life—are making people better, purer, stronger—all the *à priori* conclusions that I should draw would go directly the other way. For all philosophy requires that causes should be adequate and proportionate to their effects; and though, of course, the grace of God—the Spirit of Christ operating as Himself pleases—is and must be adequate to any moral or spiritual effect, yet even here we expect the grace to operate after a moral and spiritual, and not after a magical, manner.

I do not believe that the doctrines of sacerdotalism and of sacramentalism which are so much in vogue, and in which some people would seem to wish to make the very essence of Christianity, as a power of sanctifying the human soul, to reside, are doctrines of a true priesthood, or of a true sacramentalism. They have been brought out of the ages that were plunged in the grossest darkness, not out of the ages that, both in time and in spirit, were nearest to the light. If they can rightly be called Catholic at all—and perhaps at one time—say from the 10th to the 15th century—they did largely pervade the Christian world, they are Catholic only in the sense of being mediæval, not in the sense of being primitive.

Hooker's definitions, whether of sacraments or of priesthood, will not satisfy our new school. He will have no "supernatural quality in the sacraments, because they contain in themselves no vital force or efficacy—are not physical, but moral instruments of salvation." The ministry of the Gospel he will allow to be called a priesthood—" although," with his wise caution he adds, "in truth the word presbyter doth seem more fit and, in propriety of speech, more agreeable than priest, with the drift of the whole Gospel of Jesus Christ"—but only upon the distinct understanding that "now properly it hath no sacrifice." To so-called "Catholic" minds, Hooker's theory would appear to rob the sacraments of all their grace, and the priesthood of all its power; and I am afraid they would be as much repelled by the larger, but, as they would probably call them, latitudinarian views of Robertson, who saw ten thousand avenues by which grace might reach the soul, and even recognised in Rome's extension of the word a wholesome protest against the limitations of the opposite school. "All the universe," he says in one of his letters, "is God's blessed sacrament, the channel of His spirit to your soul, whereof He has selected two things as types of all the rest; the commonest of all elements, water; and the commonest of all meals, a supper; and you cannot find Him except in seven! Too many, or else too few; but even in that protest against the Protestant limitation of grace to two channels, I recognise a truth; only distorted and petrified as usual."

There is hardly a more beautiful or touching passage in the whole of Christian antiquity than that description, in the eighth book of the Apostolical Constitutions (ch. xii., xiii., xiv., xv.), of the great primitive act of eucharistic worship, which in that particular form of it —and Bingham in his great and learned work regards this as the most perfect type or pattern of all primitive forms—tradition, whether rightly or wrongly, ascribed to the institution of the Apostle James, the brother of John. It is worth reading for its exquisite pathos and simplicity, and the strain of simple faith and piety that runs through the whole. It might almost become the liturgy of any modern Christian Church which would retain the old spirit and yet meet new needs, without the alteration of a usage or a phrase.

Some needlessly sensitive minds might be startled to find the bishop bid to put on a splendid robe (λαμπρὰν ἐσθῆτα); and that before he commences his noble prayer he makes the sign of the cross upon his brow; and that, including under the idea of the Church all those who in every age and clime had been redeemed by the precious blood of Christ, he is not afraid to offer and to pray for all the saints who from the beginning of the world, patriarchs, prophets, just men, apostles, martyrs, "have been well pleasing in Thy sight and whose names Thou knowest;" but there is nothing here that breathes an unscriptural or superstitious tone in my ear. The prayer is nobly, grandly, sublimely Catholic. It is emphatically the act of the bishop and the people. The word priest is not so much as once used from the beginning to the end. The simple offerings of bread and wine are called θυσία, but antecedently to the invocation of the Holy Ghost, which is the only consecration, and never afterwards. There is no invocation of saints, or of angels, or of a Queen of Heaven; no incense, no lights, no mixed chalice—at least, no chalice symbolically mixed—no elevation, or adoration, but simply a reverent and orderly distribution and reception—κατὰ τάξιν μετ' αἰδοῦς καὶ εὐλαβείας ἄνευ θορύβου—no non-communicating attendants, but all, men and women, partaking of the sacred meal—and then (let no zealous Protestant be alarmed at a custom which was harmless enough till it got abused), the deacons gathering up the fragments that remained, and, not reserving them in a tabernacle for exposition or for worship, but carrying them into the παστοφορία—chambers adjoining the church, and used for various purposes—where they were ready to be distributed to such as from sickness or other valid cause were hindered from attending the public ministry of the Church.

The point I wish to signalise is that there is nothing sacerdotal—nothing implying that the virtue of the offering depended upon anything that was done or said by a man, standing betwixt God and the people and mediating for them—in the whole rite. It is too simple, too primitive, too fresh as with the air of the Galilean mountains, or with thoughts drawn straight from the solemn converse in the upper chamber at Jerusalem, for that. You must wait for this till you come to liturgies of uncertain date, which, though bearing great and significant names—a Basil's or a Chrysostom's—were no doubt revised and interpolated again and again to make them favour the growing claims of priestly prerogative and the growing darkness of popular superstition, of a later, but not a better, age.

Here, whatever change, whether relative merely or supernatural, passes upon the elements, is ascribed solely and absolutely to the operation of the Holy Ghost. This part of the eucharistic prayer is so beautiful in itself, and ought to be so reassuring to English Churchmen, as showing us how exactly their own glorious liturgy is framed upon primitive lines, that I cannot refrain from offering you a somewhat uncouth translation of it. "Mindful therefore of those things which for our sakes He bore, we render thanks to Thee, O God Almighty, not such as we owe, but such as are all we can; and we thus fulfil His command. For in the same night in which He was betrayed, when He had taken a loaf in His pure and stainless hands, and looking up to God and His Father had broken it, He gave it to His disciples, saying, 'This is the mystery of the New Testament: take of it and eat: for this is My body which is broken for many for the remission of sins.' And likewise having poured into the cup a mixture of wine and water and blessed it, He gave it to them, saying, 'Drink of this all: for this is My blood which is shed for many for the remission of sins: do this for a memorial of Me. For as oft as ye eat this bread and drink this cup, ye do show My death till I shall come.'

"Wherefore remembering His death and passion, and His resurrection from the dead, and His ascension into heaven, and His second coming, when He will come again with glory and power to judge the quick and the dead, and to recompense to every man according to His works, we offer to Thee, our King and God, according to His institution, this bread and this cup, giving thanks to Thee through Him, that Thou hast deemed us worthy to stand before and offer this sacrifice to Thee (ἱερατεύειν σοι). And we beseech Thee graciously to look upon these gifts laid out before Thee, Who needest nothing, and that Thou wilt be pleased in them to the honour of Thy Christ; and that Thou wilt send Thy Holy Spirit upon this sacrifice, the witness of the sufferings of the Lord Jesus, that He may make (ἀποφήνῃ) this bread the body of Thy Christ, and this cup the blood of Thy Christ; that they who partake of it may be strengthened unto holiness, may obtain remission of sins, may be delivered from the devil and his wiles, may be filled with a holy spirit, may become worthy of Thy Christ, and may attain eternal life, Thou being reconciled to them, O Lord God Almighty."

Well, if there is sacerdotalism here—and there is sacerdotalism in so far as this, that we see a man appointed to a sacred office discharging the highest function of that office in a solemn and godly manner—it is a sacerdotalism which no pious or intelligent mind would wish to expunge from any liturgy or any ritual. Well had it been for Christendom and the world if the Church in all ages had been content with such a reverent and edifying form. I rejoice to think that no Church in Christendom has retained probably so much of its spirit and tone as the Church of England in that almost inspired Communion office, which, when reverently rendered and devoutly used, seems to leave nothing for the pious soul, seeking to realise its union with Christ, to desire. As Keble so beautifully and truly said (I cannot for myself accept the posthumous alteration)—

> "If with thy heart the strains accord,
>   That on His altar-throne
> Highest exalt thy glorious Lord,
>   Yet leave Him most thine own,
> O come to our Communion Feast:
>   There present in the heart,
> Not in the hands, th' eternal Priest
>   Will His true Self impart.
> Thus, should thy soul misgiving turn
>   Back to th' enchanted air,
> Solace and warning thou may'st learn
>   From all that tempts thee there."

But I must hasten on; and I have left myself but little space or time to emphasise the great lesson which I desire you, my hearers, and especially you, my younger hearers, to draw from the text, and from the lines of thought along which I would fain have led you. "Beneath, far beneath, all forms of sight and feeling," said F. W. Robertson, "I joyfully recognise the unity of that spirit which forms the basis of all true lives. At bottom, all good minds mean substantially the same thing." I thoroughly believe it also; and this is why all through my life I have never found any difficulty in working with any thoroughly earnest-minded man. The weighty matters on which we were agreed would have made us seem fools one to another if we had stayed to quarrel, or even to argue, on matters of less moment on which haply we might have disagreed. But there is a sad fact which we can neither hide from others nor ignore ourselves, which destroys all the comforts that would naturally flow from this conviction that all good men are really labouring for what they believe to be the extension of Christ's kingdom, the cause of righteousness, and the good of the souls of men—viz., the fact that excessive ceremonialism is often attended by moral torpor and religious decay.

Even the man who spends, as it may seem to me, most of his time, and strength, and care upon what I cannot but call the extravagances of superstition, which I cannot conceive as exercising any beneficial influence upon the human soul, based as they are upon pure irrationality, I can yet suppose, and, if he is a good man, I must suppose, from his own point of view, however inconceivable to me, intends this aim. But, by his methods, is he likely to realise it? To such a one I could only say, Friend, will you not be taught by experience? Can history point to a single age, from the womb of time, in which an excessive addiction to ceremonialism and the externals of religion was not accompanied by a corresponding and proportionate dulness of the conscience and deadness to the higher forms of duty? It was so emphatically in Isaiah's day. It was so again, though with a perceptible and instructive difference in outward manifestation—the hypocrisy was more highly organised, the mask more skilfully painted—in the days of Jesus of Nazareth.

How often, I wonder, as we have been reading those solemn chapters of the old Hebrew prophet which he spake to Judah and Jerusalem in the days of Uzziah, Jotham, Ahaz, and Hezekiah its kings, from the beginning of Advent until now, have the holy angels been waiting with awe and wonder to see whether anything would open our eyes to discern how many lessons all these awful warnings have for ourselves. We go on our wilful and heedless way, and trust our false prophets and prophetesses who still see visions of peace for us, who foretell a morrow as abundant as to-day; who point with triumph to the conquests of human skill and knowledge and enterprise, and ask, "Can there be any limit to wealth such as this?" who blur the once clear outlines of right and wrong, truth and falsehood, and argue that all must be right which is profitable, and that anything may be true which a man wishes to believe; and who tell the world like the cynic of old, as though it were the last and best philosophic discovery, that all things being doubtful, and immortality nothing surer probably than a dream, "there is nothing better than that a man should eat and drink and enjoy the good of all his labour that he taketh under the sun all the days of his life which God giveth him. For that is his portion; and who shall bring him to see what shall be after him?"

F. W. Robertson once said "My misfortune or happiness is power of sympathy. I can feel with the Brahmin, with the Pantheist, the Stoic, the Platonist, the Transcendentalist—perhaps the Epicurean." Well, I hope I am not narrow in my sympathies, either. I can feel for and with much that I observe moves some hearts to anger, or bitterness, or scorn. But with this Epicurean cynicism, cruelly mocking at life, itself secure; abjuring every high aim in the lofty pursuit of personal comfort; checked by no moral considerations whatever in its froward path of pure selfishness; carelessly wrecking woman's honour, wickedly shattering simple faith; discussing the most solemn verities—at least the most solemn questions, toothpick in hand, over olives and wine—with this unhappy, but only too legitimate, offspring of an age that has resolved religion into phrases, and God's service into a gorgeous ceremonialism, I do not feel disposed to hold either truce or terms.

Christ can have no concord with Belial, nor he that believeth with this type of infidel. There are limits within which even Charity must intrench herself, and say to him that is of the contrary part, "I cannot welcome thee here." But I hope it is not the lot of many who are listening to me now to be thrown into companionship, or at any rate into intimacy, with such as I have described. If you are, and if you would still preserve the innocency and integrity of your souls, you have no choice left. You must come out from among them and be separate. It is not safe to tarry. It is not prudent to look back. Even now do not your ears catch the tramp as of a great army, the voice as of a captain bidding you "Go forward?" Are there none of you with the noble enthusiasm of Gideon's three hundred? Are there none who will strike a blow for truth and righteousness?

There are lives worth living to be lived in England, even in this unromantic age—in country villages, in manufacturing towns, in the metropolis; in trade, in commerce, in the clerisy, at the bar, in Parliament. England needs, as emphatically as ever, men who will do—will try to do—their duty. And perhaps the very discipline through which we are passing, severe though it be, is clearing some films from the eye away. Who will bind the red cross upon his arm, in a nobler cause than any old crusade, and follow Christ through all the perils and swayings of the fight, strong in the conviction that the cause of righteousness must prevail, and that there are yet powers in the living Word of God, which, far from being exhausted, have as yet hardly been tried?

Preached—St. Mary's, Oxford, February 9, 1879; Westminster Abbey, July 8, 1883.

XIV.

INFLUENCE OF CHARACTER ON INTELLECTUAL PROGRESS.

"Know ye not that they which run in a race run all, but one receiveth the prize? So run, that ye may obtain. And every man that striveth for the mastery is temperate in all things. Now they do it to obtain a corruptible crown; but we an incorruptible."—1 CORINTHIANS ix. 24, 25.

DISCIPLINE is an effort, as well as a result, of will. No one who watches the processes of his own inner life will accept the most recent philosophical and scientific theories, that he is a mere result of environment acting upon physical organisation—a mere piece of reflex-acting mechanism. Even the mappings out of a sounder psychology are apt to mislead; they make us forget, by their separations and discriminations, the unity of the character of each individual. It may be convenient to parcel out the faculties; but after all, they start from, or converge in, a certain point; and that is the centre of the man.

According to Bishop Butler's theory, human nature is only rightly organised when all its parts—if an indivisible spiritual being can be truly said to have parts—

are duly co-ordinated and set a-working in harmonious adjustment, by conscience sitting on her sovereign throne. It is this that gives character to a man. Without it, there can be none. According to the Epistle to the Hebrews it is the *formed habit*—ἕξις—that gives the perceiving faculties their discerning power (Heb. v. 14).

Aristotle, in a well-known passage in the *Rhetoric*, distinguishes between stable and highly-gifted natures. I am not sure that these differences are so much natural differences, as tendencies, whence derived I know not, which develop, under certain training and treatment, into what they ultimately become. Lord Bacon thought that one of the effects of his new method of philosophical generalisation would be to equalise intellects, and place the great scientific achievements of the future more plainly within the reach of all, or any, who would use the necessary industry, and observe the prescribed conditions of success.

Intellectual *progress* is a different thing from, and should not be confounded with, intellectual *success*. "Genius," said Buffon, "is patience"—and patience is a part of character. "Genius," said Carlyle, "is nothing but a transcendent faculty for taking pains"—and industry and perseverance are parts of character. "If we have done anything to advance knowledge," said Bacon, "it has only been by a true and legitimate humiliation of the intellect—crushing its pride, its precipitancy; teaching it to know and feel its limitations, where it is weak as well as where it is strong."

No one could have had a more instinctive sense of

the limitations imposed by the nature of the case, on even the most gigantic intellect, than Newton, when he said, " I seem to have been no better than a child on the sea shore picking up a few stones here and there, with the great ocean of Truth lying all undiscovered before me."

To philosophise in this spirit implies not only that the philosopher has a character, but that that character has determined, or at least modified and even regulated, the spirit and the very methods of his philosophy. His intellect, so to speak, has been moralised. The man's conscience goes with him into the field of speculation. Devotion to truth, as such and for itself, is a moral quality; a part of character; that which perhaps more than anything else stamps the truly great, as well as the only good man.

The more a man is possessed with this ardour for truth, the less will he be ready to project upon the world, and demand immediate acceptance of, his crude, unformed hypotheses — his quasi-scientific guesses, which, to minds of a certain temper, are all the more welcome if they come into startling collision with previously received beliefs.

Wise men recognise the responsibility of their utterances, and shrink, in spite of the supposed necessity for rounding off an hypothesis, from shocking beliefs which, with all their imperfections and inconsistencies, are still found to lend a support that cannot lightly be dispensed with, to the moral purpose of mankind.

I admit that if atheistic science, or scientific atheism, could be proved in the same way, or to the same extent, as Newton's theory of gravitation, it would go hard with theology; but, at the same time, it would go hard with everything besides. The social life of the world would have to be reconstructed upon a new basis. If the materialistic hypothesis becomes the order of the day, it will have to be shown how society, as the word has hitherto been understood—the union of men under a sense of individual responsibility and with distinct relative duties—could be compacted together, could exist at all.

Now this modesty, this hesitancy in the proclamation of opinions, this absence of presumption, vanity, self-seeking, are moral qualities; are a part of character, and certainly have a connection with intellectual progress. Let no one suppose that that Athenian temper, always in quest of the latest forms of truth, is necessarily indicative of a fair, impartial, advancing mind. It may be nothing more than the feverish restlessness of one who has become so volatile and inconstant that he cannot rest long upon any intellectual conviction— hardly, perhaps, on any moral certainty. "He woke in the morning prepared to find everything an open question," may be a description of the condition of mind which recognises, and truly recognises, that upon no truth, other than mathematical, as it presents itself to a finite mind, can the last word ever have been really spoken; but it may also characterise a weak, foolish, purposeless mind, incapable of progress, because incapable of sustained application; not recognising the moral obligation of truth, and forgetting that light may perplex and dazzle, as well as guide and illuminate.

"More light," is said to have been Goethe's dying cry. I wonder what light it was his soul really craved for: the phantom light of some little accession to so-called human science, or the "unapproachable light" of the presence of God, which alone could satisfy the yearnings of the heart, and the highest searchings of the soul.

The impatience of society to have its questionings answered, and its problems solved, with the least possible delay — an impatience which many of the conveniences of our modern life so powerfully tend to intensify—aggravates the evil which I have attempted to describe, till it becomes indeed a very serious danger. It is not an unnatural but an excusable, if not a praiseworthy, desire to be abreast of all the best knowledge of one's age. Active minds like to be in the forefront of the struggle against ignorance and irrationalism. It is an achievement to be the first, or among the first, to destroy the idols, as we call them, before which the human intellect, we think, has too long bowed down. Men who think they have qualities to become prophets in their generation are too ready to try the perilous vocation, even though the spirit of the Lord hath not spoken; too ready to run, like Ahimaaz, the son of Zadok, though they have no complete or accurate message to deliver (2 Sam. xviii. 26—30). Enough if they can achieve the not difficult reputation of being the first to gain the ear, whether of the king or of the crowd, with their babbling paradoxes.

And to resist this temptation, particularly if the speaker or writer has been enriched with the gift of "utterance," requires no small self-restraint and moral courage; and these are parts of character. Portions, at least, of Daniel's vision would seem to be in process of being realised. The age of men running to and fro, with their doctrines and interpretations, has come: whether the age of the increase of sound, tested, profitable knowledge has come also, is another matter. It is in the patience with which he pursued his inquiries, "the long patience," as St. James calls it, as of the husbandman waiting for his fruits, and in the modesty with which he advances his inferences from them, that Mr. Charles Darwin seems to me to be such a conspicuous example of the scientific temper needed in this age, whether for observing phenomena or of drawing conclusions.

If all men would philosophise in this spirit, and keep their hypotheses within the legitimate range of their phenomena, there would be little danger either to morals or to religion; there would be no intrusion of the one into the sphere of the other. The exercise of the scientific faculty in this temper is a part of character.

It was, perhaps, inevitable that man, with that large faculty of reason, reaching before and after, should stretch forth his hand to gather the fruits of knowledge. Were they not sweet to the taste, pleasant to the eye, "things to be desired to make him wise"? But he was warned beforehand at what peril he tasted them. He might be in danger (to make a slight change in a well-known line), "*propter scientiam, sciendi perdere causas.*" His knowledge might give him weakness, not strength; death, not life; darkness rather than light, because it had been unlawfully gained; because "the motives with which it had been sought were not noble, high, and pure."

"Intellect without God," has been some one's definition of the mysterious power of evil. More than once in the history of the race the depravation of the intellect brought about what St. Paul calls "the vain puffing up of the fleshly mind." The prostitution of genius, in such cases as Voltaire or Mirabeau or Jean Jacques, has been followed by a scathing moral pestilence such as the same Apostle describes with such terrific power in the first chapter of his Epistle to the Romans. Let us beware lest we purchase too dearly even the fair and precious fruits of knowledge.

This is an age when young men especially are apt to think they are scarcely responsible for their opinions. My own observation is, that while opinions tell largely upon character—levity in one direction producing levity in the other—so, too, character is a powerful factor in the formation of opinions. It is nothing to be ashamed of if we are slow to resign old and helpful principles which have never yet been found false or foolish, in favour of some quite new system which, however apparently philosophical, has not yet stood the brunt of life, and is able to give no satisfactory account of the causes of things. My will may be nothing more than the reflex action of some part of my physical organization; but I am hardly prepared to accept that hypothesis as dispensing me from the claims of duty. The theory does not equip me better, but worse, for the battles of life. By the help of my moral sense—the primary intuitions of my nature—I struggle out of this darkness into something that is at least more like light again.

I have said nothing about the connection between the moral character of a place or society in influencing its general intellectual progress. The character of Oxford, *e.g.*, and the intellectual progress of Oxford, have been different at different times; different forty years ago from what they are to-day. To-day, as I hear, they know more of τοὺς περὶ 'Αριστοτέλην than of Aristotle himself. And yet knowledge at first hand is to almost all men better than knowledge at second hand. There is no doubt that a society has a character which is something different from the aggregate of the characters of the individuals who compose it, and which acts powerfully in the formation of individual characters. I am quite certain that conscientiousness in reading is one of the first conditions of intellectual progress; but it is only conscientiousness that will send men for their knowledge to original sources rather than to the compendium or the system-monger.

The age seems to be growing indifferent to moral considerations; estimates men and their works by other standards; would persuade you that if you have genius you may almost consider yourselves exempted from moral obligations. St. Paul says the "law is not made for a righteous man." Modern society says the law is not made for clever, brilliant, men; "genius is entitled to claim its privileges." But I ask you, if you have any ambition to lead worthy, noble lives, to get rid of these false maxims. If you are to grow even in intellectual stature, your life must be dominated by a purpose—controlled by a fear. It was not merely a moral platitude, a text for a sermon; it was the word of a man who had philosophised, not in shallow fashion, on the laws of his being, which said, "The fear of the Lord, that is wisdom; and to depart from evil, that is understanding."

Preached—St. Mary's, Oxford, February 13, 1881.

XV.

RELIGION AND SCIENCE.

"There are diversities of operations, but it is the same God which worketh all in all."—1 CORINTHIANS xii. 6.

PROFESSOR HUXLEY has given the scientific inquirer a choice between three theories. "Either he must believe that the innumerable variety of creatures now existing, and all the forms of the long geological series, have been spontaneously generated without any particular reason, or that each has been produced by a special creative fiat, or we must accept the doctrine of Descent."

But as this accomplished professor tells us he has "all his life had a horror of limiting the possibilities of things," I submissively ask, "Is it the province of science to tell me what I ought to *believe* or what I ought to *know*?" Whichever of these alternative theories be adopted, if no other is possible, I still fall back on the higher truth, "There are diversities of workings, but the same God who worketh all things in all."

A conflict between the claims of religion and the claims of science upon the allegiance of the human mind, as though they were naturally exclusive and antagonistic, is a conflict that no wise man would desire to provoke. For it would be a conflict raised upon a false issue. Each can pursue its own way, if it will only bear in mind its own limitations, without violating the territory of the other. "If it is borne in mind," said Sir Joseph Hooker in his presidential address at Norwich, "that the laws of mind are not yet relegated to the domain of the teacher of physical science, and that the laws of matter are not within the religious teacher's province, these may then work together in harmony and with good will." And he quotes Mr. Herbert Spencer's dictum, "If religion and science are to be reconciled, the basis of the reconciliation must be this deepest, widest, and most certain of facts, that the power which the universe manifests to us is utterly inscrutable." I suppose he means that it has depths which science, with its instruments, cannot penetrate.

"There is in reality," said Sir James Paget in an admirable address on the relations of Theology and Science, delivered at the Clergy School in Leeds last December—"there is in reality no article of any of the Christian creeds which can be the subject of direct scientific inquiry. . . The disputes begin in questions in which knowledge is neither clearly revealed nor clearly within the present reach of science,—in such questions as the method of creation; the relation of man to the lower animals; the nature and relation of mind and matter, or free will and law; or the possible nature and conditions of states of conscious existence other than those in which we live. No one can justly maintain that either revelation or science can supply nearly exact knowledge on these matters, or can make us sure of what may be inferred from what we think of them."

And he adds, "In these discussions it is generally believed that one side must be in the wrong. Yet in many of them both may be right, and their opposition may be due to their both being ignorant of some intermediate truth which, when gained by increasing knowledge, will combine the truths they now hold apart. . . . Both sides *are* right in that which may be claimed as *well-ascertained knowledge;* and distant inferences on one side should not be allowed to weigh against knowledge or great probability on the other. If it be maintained, as an inference from facts in science, that miracles are impossible, or a resurrection, or that God became man, so let it be; from the purely scientific point of view such things seem impossible. But from the religious point of view we may hold them to be not only possible, but sure; and the religious conviction has a right to be no less strong than the scientific. . . . Science cannot infer or define all possibilities."

Surely the great statement of St. Paul which I have prefixed to this discourse, and which contains the idea that I meant to run through the whole of it, and to redeem it from the charge of irrelevancy, is not in conflict with any great principle of science. Man may not be able by scientific processes to find out God; his microscope and telescope and chemical experiments stop on the verge of the "inscrutable," and cannot penetrate its abysmal darkness; but if another faculty can discern through the darkness "the hands that reach through nature, moulding help," there is nothing that compels us to reject these inferences of faith, which are not irrational, which rest upon their proper evidences, which in one form or other may be found universal, and which have commended themselves to minds which found no natural repugnance between science and piety. "Did the Christian mysteries give him no trouble?" was a question asked of Sir D. Brewster upon his death-bed. "None. Why should they? We are surrounded by mysteries. His own being was a mystery; he could not explain the relation of his soul to his body. Everybody believed things they could not understand. The Trinity or the Atonement was a great deep; so was Eternity, so was Providence. It caused him no uneasiness that he could not account for them. These were secret things that belonged to God. He made no attempt to reconcile the sovereignty of Grace with the responsibility of man: they were both true. He could *wait* to see their harmony cleared; they were not contrary to reason, however incomprehensible. . . . He thanked God the way of salvation was so simple; no laboured argument, no hard attainment was required. To believe in the Lord Jesus Christ was to live."

For the idea of God is neither unphilosophical nor unscientific. In two essays, published some years ago in the *Fortnightly Review* on "the Nature of Atoms," and "the Origin of Force," the late Sir John Herschel —an illustrious and venerable name—distinctly arrives at the conclusion that, except upon the hypothesis of a presiding mind—a hypothesis based on the phenomena of our own consciousness and the ascertained powers of our own will—the organisation of atoms and the derivation of force are both inexplicable and inconceivable. Certainly this hypothesis does not seem to me less reasonable or even less scientific than the theory of Lucretius, who, in a famous presidential address, was matched against Bishop Butler, and meant, I think, to have the best of the argument, who held that the atoms—the "*primordia rerum*"—had their source of motion in themselves, and that, by virtue of a certain "*clinamen*" that is given to them, and with the help of certain little hooks which are attached to each, they form their affinities—the atoms with most hooks forming the matter of greatest density—and so constitute the actual elemental substances of the world!

"But miracles," some one may say, "both from the scientific and from the philosophical point of view, are impossible. You cannot expect me to believe *them*." I cannot, of course, force you to believe them; nor am I prepared to say that a Christian faith cannot exist without a belief in them *as miracles*. And I quite feel the *à priori* objection to them as violations of, or at least variations from, known law. But, as Sir James Paget says, "science cannot define or infer all possibilities." Paley's position is impregnable: "Only believe that there is a God, and miracles are not incredible." And as to the philosophical objection to them, the same strong reasoner says, "There is a want of logical justice in a statement which, while affirming the incredibility of miracles, suppresses all those circumstances of extenuation which result from our knowledge of the existence, power, and disposition of the Deity; His concern in the creation and the end answered by the miracle; the importance of that end and its subserviency to the plan pursued in the work of nature."

"Hume's celebrated principle," says Mr. J. S. Mill, "that nothing is credible which is contrary to experience or at variance with the laws of nature, is merely this very harmless proposition, that whatever is contradictory to a complete induction is incredible. . . . A miracle," he goes on to say, "(as was justly remarked by Brown), is no contradiction to the law of cause and effect; it is a new effect introduced by a new cause. Of the adequacy of that cause, if it exist, there can be do doubt; and the only antecedent improbability which can be ascribed to the miracle is the improbability that any such cause had existence in this case. All therefore which Hume has made out is that no evidence can be sufficient to prove a miracle to one who did not previously believe the existence of a being or beings with supernatural power; or who believed himself to have full proof that the character of the Being whom he recognises is inconsistent with his having seen fit to interfere on the occasion in question."

Nor can the human heart be content with that dark and dreary view of the future which is all that science can pretend to yield. We feel that there are invisible things beyond the visible; we have hopes that stretch beyond the grave. We are not content with the assumed immortality of the *race*, nor with the cold comfort of the posthumous immortality of the famous and renowned. It does not satisfy me, who am neither renowned nor famous, to say with the old heathen—"*Explebo numerum, reddarque tenebris* ("My life work done, let darkness once more come"). The hope of immortality cannot be extinguished in the human heart. Conscience and feeling alike require, demand it. And the revelation of Jesus Christ alone has satisfied conscience and feeling. Just as the Frenchman said, "*S'il n'y avait pas un Dieu, il faudrait l'inventer;*" just as Professor Huxley told you on Friday that "if the Darwinian theory of Descent had not been presented to the palæontologist, he would have had to invent it to account for the phenomena before him;" so John Stuart Mill held that even if the hope of immortality were an illusion, it were well maintained, so helpful was it and comforting. Science certainly has neither the right nor the power to rob us of it. Humanity—at least the mass of it—is not so rich that it can afford to part with what, to it, is no illusion, but a revealed truth, which has proved to it by actual experience, in hours of darkness, temptation, sorrow, trial, an unspeakable comfort and stay.

It was the hope of Sir Francis Bacon, expressed in the preface to his great philosophical work, the *Instauratio Magna*, that by his new method of scientific inquiry he had established a true and legitimate union between the two faculties, the empirical and the rational, whose morose and ill-omened divorces and repudiations had thrown everything into confusion in the human family.

It is on the same ground that I humbly but earnestly deprecate even the appearance of a conflict between science and Christian faith. We are each of us—our teachers of science and our teachers of religion—being wounded in the house of those who ought to be our friends. It is a conflict in which, if fought out to the bitter end, some of the highest interests of society would be imperilled. It is an unnecessary and therefore an unrighteous and unjustifiable war. It would seem that no single resource of the human mind is adequate to bear the pressure or satisfy the demands of man's nature, taken at its best or at its worst; and the knowledge which feeds the soul and supplies motives to moral conduct is at least as helpful and as necessary for the mass of mankind as that which teaches them their place in the universe of matter, or explains the framework and mechanism of that physical body so fearfully and wonderfully made.

There is another side to this subject which ought not to be passed over. There are services which the spirit of scientific inquiry has rendered to the cause of true religion which it would be uncandid and ungenerous not to recognise. And upon this point I prefer repeating what I said in a sermon preached in Salisbury Cathedral just thirteen years ago, on the Sunday after the meeting of the British Association in the city of Norwich. The repetition will at least show that on this subject I have not changed my mind. I had chosen for my text a passage containing an incident in the story of the shipwreck of St. Paul, which had been read in the lesson for the day; and I remarked—

1. It is the prevalence of the scientific temper more perhaps than anything else which has redeemed religion from superstitious corruptions, affecting both faith and practice. Observe the crude and utterly unwarranted hypotheses by which those "barbarous" Maltese who received St. Paul and his shipwrecked companions attempted to account for any extraordinary phenomenon. They had kindly instincts; they believed in God and in the accountability of man—the two foundations of the principle of religion; but, reasoning as they reasoned, this mere belief was insufficient to give either clearness or sobriety to their judgment. Impatient of delay unaccustomed to weigh evidence, with a theory cut-and-dried to account for each fact as it emerged, entirely independent of any examination of the fact itself, they passed, apparently without any conscious shock, from the undoubting conviction that the man before them was a murderer to the equally undoubting conviction that he was a god. No sane man, since the scientific temper has been formed, would venture, in a matter of religion, to draw such random conclusions as these.

2. Again: the philosophic has taught the religious inquirer the proper frame of mind in which every inquiry, if it is to have a good result, must be pursued. It must be undertaken, not to fortify a foregone conclusion, but with the simple desire to discover truth. "How legible," said Goethe, writing to a friend, "the Book of Nature becomes to me! Much as I find that is new, I find nothing that is unexpected, because I have no system, and desire nothing but the pure truth." (Lewes's *Life of Goethe*," p. 288.) And perhaps the Book

of Grace would become as intelligible to us as the Book of Nature became to him, if we sought to possess ourselves of its contents with the same simplicity of purpose, and made our love of theological system and our reverence for ecclesiastical authority bend to the higher allegiance that is due to truth.

3. And once more. The philosopher has often shown more faith than the theologian in the conviction embodied in the maxim, "*Magna est veritas et prævalebit.*" He believes in the power of truth to maintain itself by its own proper evidence, without forming unnatural alliances or calling in extrinsic aid. He has seldom been willing to *force* his conclusions on those whom he cannot *persuade*. He seeks to impose no creed by mere authority. He feels that dogmas must rest upon sure, or at least probable, warrants before they can be thoroughly received. He would have every man able to give a reason, satisfactory at least to himself, for what he professes to believe. And in the selfsame spirit, Paul, who, whether while sitting at the feet of Gamaliel or from the natural tendency of his own mind, had caught the true temper of modern philosophy, tells us that the one aim of his preaching was "by manifestation of the truth to commend himself to every man's conscience in the sight of God," and was never satisfied with the result which he had produced unless he left "every man fully persuaded in his own mind."

It derogates nothing from the claims or value of religion to acknowledge those obligations which she owes to science. She has been rendered more precious,

more attractive by becoming more reasonable. It is a
"reasonable service"—a true spiritual worship, we are
taught on high authority, that Almighty God demands
from His creatures. He would be no wise man who
would wish to return to the bondage of superstition for
the sake of escaping the possible perils of scepticism.
There is a safe escape from these perils—perils which
I admit to be real, not imaginary. The peril would be
past, if only the spirit of inquiry were penetrated by a
larger measure of "reverence and godly fear."

Indeed, how can we better express the feelings which
must more or less touch all hearts to-day than in that
exquisite "*Invocatio Christi*," in which the poet who
best interprets the spirit of this yearning age sums up
his hopes, and faith, and fears:—

> "Strong Son of God, immortal Love,
>   Whom we that have not seen Thy face,
>   By faith, and faith alone, embrace,
> Believing where we cannot prove;
>
> "Thine are these orbs of light and shade;
>   Thou madest life in man and brute;
>   Thou madest death; and lo! Thy foot
> Is on the skull which Thou hast made.
>
> "Thou wilt not leave us in the dust;
>   Thou madest man, he knows not why;
>   He thinks he was not made to die,
> And Thou hast made him: Thou art just.
>
> "Thou seemest human and divine,
>   The highest, holiest manhood, Thou;
>   Our wills are ours, we know not how,
> Our wills are ours, to make them Thine.

"Our little systems have their day,
    They have their day, and cease to be;
    They are but broken lights of Thee,
And Thou, O Lord, art more than they.

"We have but faith; we cannot know;
    For knowledge is of things we see;
    And yet we trust it comes from Thee,
A beam in darkness: let it grow.

"Let knowledge grow from more to more,
    But more of reverence in us dwell,
    That mind and soul, according well,
May make one music as before,

"But vaster. We are fools and slight,
    We mock Thee, when we do not fear;
    But help thy foolish ones to bear,
Help Thy vain world to bear Thy light.

"Forgive what seemed my sin in me,
    What seemed my worth, since I began;
    For merit lives from man to man,
And not from man, O Lord, to Thee.

"Forgive my grief for one removed,
    Thy creature, whom I found so fair;
    I trust he lives in Thee, and there
I find him worthier to be loved.

'Forgive these wild and wandering cries,
    Confusions of a wasted youth;
    Forgive them when they fail in truth,
And in Thy wisdom make me wise."

Sermon (abridged) preached in York Minster before the British Association, September 4, 1881.

XVI.

THE GIFT OF PROPHECY THE SUPREME NEED OF OUR AGE.

> "Behold, I will send you Elijah the prophet before the coming of the great and dreadful day of the Lord. And he shall turn the heart of the fathers to the children, and the heart of the children to their fathers, lest I come and smite the earth with a curse."—MALACHI iv. 5, 6.

A STRANGE, weird figure is that of Elijah the Tishbite, suddenly projected on the page of history, a unique personage with a unique mission!

There had been prophets before—Samuel, Nathan, Gad, Shemaiah, Ahijah, and others; but Elijah is as of a new order. He covers a larger space, speaks and acts with greater authority. He becomes a type of the man of God, speaking to men as the messenger of the Lord of Hosts. St. John the Baptist was one of his spiritual successors—his greatest; Athanasius another; Martin Luther another; John Wesley, perhaps, another; or at least these latter have been like Elishas, catching up his mantle, baptised with a portion of his spirit.

They have been the men who have accomplished

the great moral and spiritual revolutions of the world; each according to the needs of his age, and with weapons suited to the need: rough, earnest, strong-willed men, most of them, not given to mince their words or to stand upon courtesies; but they have been the men to keep alive the flame of religion, and to prevent its dying out.

Mark their ages: Elijah's an age of coarse, brutalising idolatry. That old worship of Baal and Molech and Ashtaroth was accompanied with the foulest sensuality and cruelty. It was not for a phrase or a dogma that Elijah contended: the contest between Baal and Jehovah reached deeper issues than that. It was whether the springs of the moral life of the nation should be tainted at the source or not. Idolatry of this coarse type disappeared after the return from Babylon.

The next Elijah was he who came in the wilderness of Jordan, by the preaching of repentance preparing the way of the Lord. It was an age of cold and deadly formalism; all the more perilous because men who were blind thought they saw, and attempted to guide others, hardly blinder; with what result our Lord has told us.

And when the simplicity of Christian doctrine in the person and nature of Christ was in danger of being clouded, and lost, in the mist of oriental subtlety, the great Alexandrian bishop set the faith of Christ, once more, firm on the doctrine of the Incarnation of the Son of God; and built up the creed of Christendom in the form which the great Council of Nicæa proclaimed to be the faith which had once for all been delivered to the saints.

And, once again, in the fifteenth century, when a darkness of superstition that could almost be felt was settling down on the nations of Europe, and the Church of Rome with her priestcraft, and traffic in indulgences, and claims to a universal supremacy—which one of her greater popes had said were the claims of an anti-Christ—was setting up an intolerable tyranny over the consciences of men; the great German reformer, with his iron hand, burst the bonds, and taught men that their souls were free, and that neither pope nor priest could shut them out from heaven by an arbitrary will, or bar the right of access that each might claim through Christ to God.

And, yet once again, in England, but little more than a century ago, another prophet rose in like power and spirit, and, when the Church seemed—like Sardis and Laodicea—to have merely "the name of life when it was dead," and a fatal lethargy kept down all high spiritual aspirations, touched the deepest founts of the religious life, and bade men arise from a sleep which was like the sleep of death, and Christ should give them life.

Whatever spiritual gifts may have been necessary or profitable to the Church in other times, I am sure that the gift of prophecy is the most necessary and profitable now. "Christ sent me not to baptise," says the Apostle—others with lower gifts could do that—"but to preach the Gospel" and he adds, "I preached it, not with the enticing words of man's wisdom, but in demonstration of the Spirit and of power." Men felt the power and acknowledged the teaching; their listening to him was the Apostle's highest credential. Just as, in the former generation, they had felt the difference between the teaching of the scribes and that of the Galilean peasant Who " taught them as one having authority," and of Whom some said, " Never man spake like this man," so they felt the difference between a Paul and a Philetus.

Man may well pray for a portion of this power, and for grace to use it in the noblest cause. It is not eloquence, it is not popularity, it is not the power of attracting the crowd. It is something impalpable, but most real, when men bend their wills and hearts and consciences before the uttered truth, and find that this is indeed "the engrafted word which is able to save their souls." It is a spiritual power which can bow the hearts of a multitude as of one man, swaying them with a charm of strange, mysterious potency; a power which we feel, though we cannot describe it.

Men who are such instruments of the Spirit must always be rare. We have them in England—for there is no limitation of the gift to the Apostolic age—but they could probably be counted on the fingers. It is not the mere eloquence of the pulpit, or the platform, of which I am thinking. This is common enough, and though often utterly wanting in depth and reality, yet, in the uneducated condition of public taste, is mischievously over-valued, and leads men to look for the secret of spiritual power where it will never be found; in declamation which is not eloquence;

in vapid sentiment which is not feeling. Of this we have more than enough in all the Churches, and men do not seem to discover that it lacks the ring of the true metal.

Of this I am not thinking; but I am thinking of utterances such as, in my old Oxford days, I heard at times from John Henry Newman, such as I conceive to have been those of F. W. Robertson; such as would probably have been—if his calling had been to speak to his fellow-men of spiritual things—the utterances of the great "tribune of the people," as he has been called, whose knowledge of the Bible, and of Milton, have given to him so deep an insight into the thoughts that sway the hearts of men—I mean Mr. John Bright.

Such men must be rare. There were schools of the prophets in Israel; but I do not know that the great prophets of that wonderful nation were products of the schools.

This age wants, and is prepared to receive, not the priest but the prophet, not the man who claims to stand between souls and God, but the man who can teach them the truth, and help them, in their blindness, and waywardness, and ignorance, to discover the way of peace and righteousness—for men *do* feel their ignorance, and are thankful for light, and are not indisposed to truth. It is astonishing how the true pastoral character seems to win the heart of the people of England. It is marvellous to me, and yet most encouraging, to see how few of what the world calls "gifts" are needed to fill a church and to work wonders in the lives and conduct of a people. A preacher acquires the truest eloquence by daily contact with his flock. I do not think a *real* pastor could preach an uninteresting sermon. The letter "h" may not have its fair treatment, there may be some provincialisms of utterance, now and then even the grammar may not be perfect; but you cannot leave that church and your mental contact with that man without feeling that he has penetrated the true secret of spiritual power, and without some new and higher aspect of life standing before your eyes. Like the Chief Shepherd Whom he is trying to follow, "he knows his sheep and is known of them." Not only do they know his *voice* but his *life* also; and THAT is the power I pray God to multiply a thousandfold.

Never was there a larger or more fruitful opportunity for the preacher who is in earnest, who believes what he preaches, and who will speak to men intelligently, reasonably, sympathetically. The people are, in fact, almost too ready to hear, and forget St. John's warning about "false prophets," and that there is a need of some tests to distinguish these from the true. They forget our Lord's own warning, "Take heed what, and how, ye hear." In an age such as ours has been said to be, "of much excitement and unbounded curiosity," the danger is a very real one; and the itching ear requires its proper correction, lest what "should have been for our health become to us an occasion of falling." I lament the tendency to supplant the parochial principle by the congregational, as one of the worst signs of an age which has "itching ears, and often loves fables rather than truth," and fashionableness better than either.

Yet heat is a sign of life: coldness and torpor are symptoms of death. The prophet must be in earnest, or men will not receive him as a prophet; must himself believe his message, or he will carry no conviction to his hearers. And, indeed, how can a man speak in the name, and in the behalf, of God, and proclaim the love of a Father to His children, and tell of the great redemption wrought by Christ, and of the mighty powers of the Spirit of God, unmoved? How can he vamp up the same old sermon a dozen times, if fountains of fresh spiritual experience are ever welling within his own soul? Is it not because *we* are so cold and rigid that *your* hearts are so seldom reached; that *we* preach, and *you* are not edified; that great opportunities are given and missed; that, even in the best cases, ears often are tickled rather than lives improved?

And yet we have a message able to stir the most phlegmatic feelings, and to arouse the dullest conscience, if only we know how to deliver it. Of course there are the "terrors of the Lord," of which St. Paul speaks; but we do not so often, nor so gladly, employ them. We would rather use the arguments of love than of fear: rather appeal to the generous emotions than to the slavish ones. There are the hopes of heaven and the rewards of the Great Day, but these are more or less vague and distant; and it has not yet been revealed "what we shall be."

But if our hearts have found out the secret, we can speak of present peace and joy in believing; of the kingdom of God standing in righteousness; of the nearness of a Father to us in our dangers, difficulties, and troubles; of the "no harm that shall happen to us if we are followers of that which is good"; of the love of Christ and the comfort of the Holy Ghost; of the sweetness that can be got from the life that now is, if only we go the right way to seek it; of the strength that comes of faith, and the satisfaction that rewards obedience. We can point to examples, full of hope and encouragement, of saints that have gone before; we can tell of the perfect work of patience which we may have witnessed, and so bid others persevere.

There are those who can speak of these things with a strange and moving power, and their arguments will rise high above the clouds of doubt and speculation, till they seem to bring us almost face to face with God. Such men are in very truth the Lord's prophets. Such teachers build on immovable grounds the fabric of faith. They are sure and trustworthy guides, for they are leading men to God, through Christ, by the ways of holiness. They have themselves travelled the road. They are testifying to us out of their own experience. "They speak that which they know."

It is a faith thus quickened—"faith cometh by hearing"—that vitalises sacraments, prayers, worship. Without such faith all these things are dead. With it, they become living, quickening powers. It is the spirit of the prophet before all other gifts that the Churches need to enable them to evangelise the world. May God of His goodness soon pour it abundantly upon them!

It is the prophet with his large, true heart that is

needed—a heart as large as that of Moses when he rebuked Joshua's ill-timed zeal for his honour with the memorable words, " Would God that all the Lord's people were prophets, and that the Lord would put His Spirit upon them!" Men, living agents, are at this moment the Church's greatest need: not merely men cognisant of ecclesiastical proprieties, whether of costume or ritual; but men with living, loving voices—voices not merely repeating formulas, however reverend or ancient, as though there were a spell in the very words; (formulas not intelligible to the mind awaken no echo in the heart of this nineteenth century;) but voices quick to respond to the great throbs of the heart of the age, and to interpret their deep significance; their strange, unsatisfied, and often lofty yearning: voices resonant with that undefinable sympathy which is the one bond between soul and soul; the sweet music of Christian love being discernible in their every accent. These voices need to be heard and felt, and to work their charm not only in dark, unhealthy courts and alleys, but in the resorts of wealth and fortune and social influence, if England is to retain her Christianity.

Have any of you seriously considered how little of Christianity remains — I am not speaking of it as fashioning individual lives, in which there is still much that is noble, unselfish, Christ-like—but as a pervading, governing social power, characterising and shaping the life of the age? Read what comes forth daily from a teeming press; read the contemporary literature that you find on every drawing-room table. Does this proclaim the supremacy of Christian motive and Christian principle, or does it indicate that both are merely respectable, ancient traditions, which it is not convenient, or perhaps not decent, as yet, openly to ridicule or put aside, but which no one dreams of regarding either as incentives or restraints?

"I am no prophet, nor the son of a prophet"; but I see plainly enough the perils that threaten society—not the fashionable portion of it only, but the whole social structure in which we live and move—from the dissolution of religion in England. We do not put these things down by law, as they foolishly try to do in France; but there is a force operating among us which is at once stronger and subtler than any statutory enactment—that tendency of public opinion which is gradually ignoring the sanctions, and before long may even dare to repudiate the name of Christianity.

At such a time, even if we like not their methods, one dare not rebuke nor try to hinder any who are working miracles or casting out devils in Christ's name. Surely they are for Christ, not against Him. Instead, then, of finding fault with others, let us bestir ourselves. Too long the Church seems as though she had been sleeping—sleeping by the crater of a volcano. If we would not have the Lord "come and smite the earth with a curse," let us see whether by Christian hands, and Christian hearts, something cannot yet be done to arrest the moral devastation of society. If the battle goes against us, at least let us fall with our faces towards the foe, and with the spiritual weapons of our warfare in our hands. It is something even to have *fought* in Christ's name and for Christ's cause. Even in this nineteenth century, in the noble army of martyrs "yet there is room."

Preached—Westminster Abbey, June 25, 1882; Manchester Cathedral, August 21, 1884; St. Margaret's, Westminster, June 28, 1885.

XVII.

THE GOSPEL AND THE MASSES.

"The people pressed upon Him to hear the Word of God."—
ST. LUKE v. 1.

WHAT could have been this wonderful secret power by which the great Prophet of Galilee drew all men after Him? We know, because the people confessed it with their own lips, that He spoke to them as one that had authority; and all people are not very ready to welcome authoritative and somewhat dogmatic speakers. We know that He rebuked sin at times most sternly, and yet many of those whom He rebuked most sternly, somehow, could not resist the attraction to be among His hearers. He certainly was not one of those demagogues who pandered to what people call the proletariat by denouncing the upper classes. A great French revolutionist of the last century (Camille Desmoulins, I believe) said that Christ was *le bon sans-culotte*. An accomplished peer in the House of Lords the other evening spoke of Christianity as the most perfect system of democracy; but if so it is a democracy with all its virtues developed and all its vices eradicated, such as this world, at least, has never yet seen realised. The Sermon on the Mount, which, I am sorry to say, I find is not so familiar to all people as it ought to be, tells us that the Christ did not pare down His doctrine to suit the passions of the mob. It was a Gospel for humanity that He preached, and not a theory of republicanism.

We can, I think—imperfectly, of course, but with some measure of accuracy—trace some of the elements of this power. One simple and very intelligible element of it was the way in which He recognised the wholeness of human nature, that, at bottom, the peer did not differ from the peasant, nor the monarch on the throne from the villager in his cottage. He recognised the wholeness of human nature, that great truth of which St. Paul afterwards spoke, when he said that the Father of mankind had made of one blood all people that dwell upon the face of the whole earth. And not only did Christ recognise the wholeness of human nature but He recognised its many diversified needs. There are two kinds of physicians to-day—the specialist and the more generally trained physician. The one knows all the characteristics of one special disease. He has made it his special study. The other looks at men with a larger, more penetrating eye. Christ, the good physician, was not a specialist. He not only formed a true diagnosis of each disease, but He knew the remedy for the whole system.

Further, He was sinless—the spotless Lamb of God. " In Him," says St. John, " was no sin " ; and He came to redeem the world from sin, which was its one great primal curse—that which still presses upon it most heavily, and seems to make one almost despair of finding an effective remedy. He hated sin, and yet—and that is a strange thing—He never had a harsh word for the sinners, provided only that those sinners were not hypocrites. If they were, then He had no measure in His rebukes.

Once more. He had the tenderest feelings for those who had enjoyed the fewest opportunities. It is true that He recognised that great social law which sometimes seems to work so harshly—that to him that hath much more is given. Still, you will remember that other saying of His, "To whom little has been committed, of him little shall be required." That is a comfort, I think, when we look abroad upon these great cities, and see the depths of degradation in which, by the very necessity of their circumstances, so many thousands of our brethren are almost compelled to live by what we call, with a gentle euphemism, "our social arrangements," which should be rather called "our social disarrangements." Christ had, I say, the tenderest feelings for those who had enjoyed the fewest opportunities. As to the people, whom He taught and whom He described as sheep scattered upon the mountains without a shepherd, if they were ignorant, as many of them were, and if they were wayward, or hard to teach, as no doubt many of them were also, whose fault was it, but that of the persons who had so long neglected them, or had only taught them what had given them no real strength to resist temptation, and no guidance to walk in better ways?

And, once more, He recognised what I may call the natural or social wants which are common to all men.

He would feed those five thousand men, and their wives and children, who had followed Him out into the far wilderness; He would feed them before He sent them away to their homes. He would provide more wine for the innocent festivities of Cana. And, remember, that was not an orgy, but a simple friendly gathering of friends and neighbours, met together on an occasion interesting to all. He would provide more wine at that festivity when the bridegroom's own scanty store was exhausted.

And yet, again, He disdained no man. Nothing could be observed in Him like the habitual conduct and deportment of Scribes and Pharisees. The most needy had always His first care; and even women that had been sinners, the most outcast and debased ones of all, were not forbidden to approach Him and to express their penitence in their own simple, natural way. These seem to me to be the really civilising powers of the Gospel. It is thus, and no otherwise, that its teaching has the power of welding society together. I only ask you to think what society in England, in spite of its so-called civilisation, would become if, I will not say the restraints, but the motives of the Gospel were withdrawn—if Christ's teachings were as utterly obliterated as if the waters of Lethe had washed them entirely out of men's hearts and memories.

And the power of the Gospel has been none the less because it has worked like the great forces of nature— not by catastrophes and cataclysms, but, so to speak, almost insensibly. You and I go about our daily work, whatever it may be, one after this manner and another after that; but if we had the Spirit of Christ within us, we should do that daily work in a different spirit from that in which we should do it if we had it not. And it is this little leaven working here and there which, I will not say leavens the whole lump, but which does exercise a restraining influence upon those who have it not, and sets up a higher ideal before the imagination of us all. It is thus that the Gospel of Christ has worked in many directions—for instance, in the direction of the elevation of woman. Some people think that, even yet, woman has not received all her full rights; but, at any rate, her position in society is recognised as being something very different from what it was in the days of Socrates or in the days of imperial Rome; and yet no one could put his finger upon the precise year or the precise century when this great change began to come about. It has come about insensibly, each century, perhaps, contributing something to the result as it has learnt more of the mind of Christ.

So, again, it has been in the destruction of slavery, not fully wrought even yet, but accomplishing itself gradually in the ages according as men's hearts have opened themselves to receive what I have called the insensible teaching of the Gospel of Christ; and though some may be slow to believe it, the power of Christ's Gospel is working still towards the great aim of making war morally impossible—that terrible scourge which we talk of lightly when it is at a distance, though, when we are in the midst of it, we go about in sackcloth and ashes, weeping and gnashing our teeth.

Now, none of these things are done or have been

done perfectly, but the lines are laid down. Every one who has an eye for such things can see them. The ideal is lifted up, and the human race, impelled by what I may call an irresistible moral force, is advancing —I will not say steadily or without many retardations, but on the whole is manifestly advancing—in its higher and more enlightened conscience towards these goals. The world may never become perfect, probably it never will, but these are the aims of all its noblest hearts, and these are the objects which they are proposing to themselves.

A panic seems to have beset some sections of society, as though the people who pressed round Christ to hear Him were pressing upon the hitherto privileged classes, and as though the old institutions of the country were going down before the rush. I thought it was a wise and well-spoken word that the Archbishop of Canterbury used in the House of Lords the other night, when he said, "Trust the people; give them their proper rights as citizens, and have confidence that they will not abuse them."

It was a great and wise saying, also, of the late lamented Duke of Albany, in one of his last spoken utterances, delivered last winter at Liverpool — it showed an admirable "touch" with all the best aspirations of the age—when he said that society would move on both faster and safer if all moved on together. They were the last words of his speech, and they are worthy of being remembered by all. The privileged classes are afraid of the people. No doubt there are forces full of mischief at work amongst us, and at times some sudden development of these forces frightens us even amid these many hopeful signs; but I confess for myself that I echo with all my heart the Archbishop's generous words, " Let us trust the people."

And we who stand up in pulpits, and call ourselves ministers or prophets of God, and presume to speak to you in God's name, cannot we do something more successfully than we have hitherto done to move and win these people? I hear of the wonderful crowds who throng our fashionable churches, where there is either a gorgeous service or an eloquent preacher; but though I recognise the good that is being done and may be done among these, I confess that I feel more concerned for churches at the East End than at the West End of this vast city. There, and not in your great squares and magnificent roads, there are the " much people," whom, as at Corinth, in the days of Paul, the Lord has in this city waiting for the Word of God. Somehow or other, and in spite of many discouraging phenomena, nothing has shaken my faith in the power of the words of Christ to reach the hearts of men when they are truly, simply, consistently, and lovingly presented. These desperate theories of human depravity, which are so popular in some schools of theology, if I believed them, which I do not, would, indeed, cast my heart down; but I thank old Tertullian, little as I like his hot African temper at times, for that grand phrase of his, "*Anima naturaliter Christiana.*"—"the soul is naturally Christian."

If I had before me a congregation of ministers of God's Word, I would say to them, " Oh! fellow-ministers, there is something in all those hearts which can be reached—some chord that will give forth sweet music if only you have the skill to touch it." In our Church reforms as well as in our State reforms—and the Church, I think, needs reforms as urgently as the State—we must think more of the people. It was a suicidal folly of that old Sanhedrin that despised alike the popular ignorance which they had caused, and the popular aspirations with which they had no sympathy. They sent out some of their officers to apprehend Jesus, and when the men came back without Him the magistrates said, "Why have ye not brought Him?" The officers answered, "Never man spake like this man." Then answered the Pharisees, "Are ye also deceived? Have any of the rulers of the Pharisees believed on Him? But this people who know not the law are cursed."

There is no special gift in rearing prophets. If we, with our academic training and culture, cannot or will not speak to the people in a tongue that they can understand, we must not be surprised, and still less must we be angry, if they choose teachers for themselves. Mr. Spurgeon's views on many points of technical theology are not mine. We have been brought up in different schools, and trained to look at things, perhaps, under different circumstances; but who cannot recognise the great gift bestowed on that man to reach, not the ear only, but the heart of the people? In a parish at the East End of London it was announced that the Bishop of Bedford was going to preach. A tradesman in the parish, who had been a sort of apostle of the propaganda of atheism, thought that he would go and hear him. People in the church who knew the man were surprised to see him among the congregation, but he was there, and he listened; and when he went away he made this remark, "Now, if that Bishop had argued I would have fought him; but there was no arguing with him. He preached to us simply about the love of God, and that touched me."

I have no fear for our Church, if we could only reach the hearts of those that are sometimes called, without our fully realising what weight there is in the words, "the masses." It is not the parade of a gorgeous ceremonial, which, however it may please the taste, I believe has very little converting power in it. It is, I repeat, the simple power of God's Word. "The people pressed upon Him to hear;" what they felt was "the Word of God." Paul felt it. He says, "Christ sent me not to baptize, but to preach the Gospel." He did not mean to disparage sacraments, but he did mean to exalt preaching—not the gifts of the preacher, of which he himself, in the judgment of the Corinthians, did not possess many, for they said of him, "His bodily presence is weak, and his speech contemptible." It was not the gifts of the preacher, but the power of his message. Writing again to those Corinthians, he says that it was God's good pleasure, "through the foolishness of preaching, to save them that believe." That is our modern version, but the Greek is "through the foolishness of the thing preached."

Oh! that God would give to all them that essay to preach, and are called to preach, the grace to preach this foolish thing—foolish as men estimate the forces that shake the world; but, nevertheless, the wisdom of God and the strength of God, the little stone cut out without hands which has smitten and destroyed so many of those colossal images which the kings of the earth have set up in their dreams of pride. I say, Oh! that God would give us grace to preach fully, faithfully, wisely, lovingly, this foolish thing, this Gospel of our Lord Jesus Christ, more in that spirit and with that simplicity and that abounding sympathy with which it was first preached in the cities and on the mountain slopes and by the lake shores of Galilee; and then I believe that the people would be found pressing to hear it as they pressed then. Of course, where the population has been swept away, as in some parts of the city of London, perhaps it may be impossible to fill our churches with people; but I will undertake to say that every church in London round which there are people living may be filled if we only go the right way to work to try to do it. There must be this first, the preaching of the Gospel in its simplicity, lovingly, sympathetically, and then, the great law of proportion being duly observed, all other needful, proper, expedient, desirable things will fall naturally into their places.

Experiments might be ventured among people vitally Christianised that would be perilous—aye, more than perilous, certain to work mischief—if this great purifying leaven were not first there. Artificial safeguards, we all know, are not worth much. It has been repeated till one has almost grown sick of the phrase, that you cannot make people virtuous by Acts of Parliament; and of course we know that Acts of Parliament operate in a very narrow sphere. The principle must be planted deeply within. The man must learn to be a law unto himself. The conscience must be the supreme governor of conduct, and the arbiter not only of right and wrong but even of expedient and inexpedient. And what is so much talked about now, though some of you, perhaps, may hardly know the meaning of the word—"altruism," or a paramount thought for others—is surely no discovery of the positivist philosophy. They vaunt it as one of their great discoveries—as their Gospel; but it had its prophet and its ideal eighteen hundred years before Auguste Comte lifted up his voice and preached it. It is part of our Gospel—not the whole of it, for man has his duties towards God as well as towards his fellow-men; but it is the second great word of Jesus, like unto the first, "Thou shalt love thy neighbour as thyself." To show the true bearing of this in relation to the complex phenomena of modern life is our duty as preachers of the Gospel. It was the "life" which the angel meant when he bade Peter and John "Go stand and speak in the temple to the people all the words of this life."

We have no need to be apprehensive of results, though these are not in our hands. Words spoken in love and tenderness and sympathy—words like Paul's, in which "we seek not yours but you"—words which will make better husbands and wives, better parents and children, better masters and servants, better politicians and citizens—surely, words such as these. He who is with the Church always, even unto the end of the world, will never let fall wholly idle and profitless to the ground.

Preached—St. Andrew's, Holborn, July 13, 1884.

XVIII.

THE MIGHTINESS OF REDEMPTION.

'Stir up Thy strength, and come, and help us.'—PSALM lxxx. 2.

WHETHER we regard the system of this visible universe either simply with the eye of a philosopher, as the multitudinous result of a few great laws, or with the devouter sentiments of piety, as the silent witness of an Eternal Power and Godhead, it alike impresses itself upon the musing mind as illimitable and incomprehensible. Go forth on some star-lit night, and gaze upward on the spangled canopy of heaven, and the thoughts of the eighth and nineteenth Psalms spontaneously fill the mind. Look round upon the varied landscape of nature, consider the evidence of power, contrivance, forethought, adaptation, goodness, that it displays, and if there is any warmth of piety in our heart, we find the language of the glorious 104th Psalm more in harmony with our deep emotions than the cold theories of the geologist, or even the accurate descriptions of the physical geographer.

Not that science—true, honest science, is not the handmaid of theology, and the telescope and microscope may not help the spiritual eye as truly as the natural; but the thoughts which a survey of the universe raises in a rightly-educated mind are religious, rather than philosophical. David's utterances, as he considered the heavens, the work of God's fingers, " the moon and the stars which He had ordained," sound more congenial to our ears, more accurately express our own best moods of mind, than the profound demonstrations or subtle analyses of Laplace or even of Newton. They are evidences of Divine *Power*, or rather of a Divine *Personality*, that we delight to find—not merely indications of a *system* or traces of a *law*.

Yet there is something in the Psalmist's heart that, as often as his mind was in danger of being lost in the immensities of space, or merely occupied with a barren admiration of the physical world, brings it back, by a strange and generally sudden revulsion of feeling, to dwell upon the mystery of its own being; to ponder the unfathomable marvels that encompass and penetrate the mechanism of man.

In each of the Psalms to which I have referred the transition is remarkable for its spontaneity and instinctiveness. It is so sudden as to make it hard to catch the train of thought, the association of ideas, with which the religious philosopher passes from the contemplation of the moon and stars which God has ordained, to the thought of the son of man whom He visits " and crowns with glory and worship." It is hard to trace the subtle thread of feeling by which the mind, one moment gazing upward on the sun "coming forth as a bridegroom out of his chamber, and rejoicing as a giant to renew his course;" the next returning to muse upon that law of God, not which prescribes the course of the planets, or governs the music of the spheres, but "which converts the soul" and gives light to the eyes—a strain of feeling and thought which breaks forth into an ecstatic adoration of the *strength* of the Lord, not as his *Creator*, but as his *Redeemer*, with power to cleanse him from his secret faults and to keep him from the dominion of "presumptuous sins."

If we can analyse the state of mind which found its relief in the utterances of the nineteenth Psalm, we shall have gained the key to much that is dark and difficult not only in revelation, but in nature; and perhaps be able to understand why it was *Redemption*, rather than *Creation*, that filled the poet's mind with a sense of Divine majesty, strength, and power.

Let me approach the subject through a familiar, but apt, illustration. Paley, in the opening of his well-known treatise on Natural Theology, adduces a watch as one of the most obvious instances of artistic contrivance and design. From the examination of its parts, and the observation of their mutual action and adjustment, we should at once, he says, infer power and skill in the maker. It were difficult to find a plainer proof of human ingenuity. Now dash that curious piece of mechanism to the ground; crush it under your foot into a hundred fragments. Where is the workman who can put together those broken springs and wheels? He could make it; but he cannot *restore*. He could adjust the parts into harmonious action when each was entire; but their reconstruction *now* is beyond his power.

And is not man a shattered mechanism? Do not body, soul, and spirit bear marks of some deep-seathing influence having passed over them? Is not disease unnatural, and death a sort of rival of the Lord of Life? Are not the appetites sensualized, and the affections degraded, and the understanding darkened, and the will impaired, and the reason enfeebled, and the conscience shaken on her throne? And will not man's lofty spirit, that should pierce the clouds, and gaze undaunted on the things that angels even have not seen, bow down to stocks and stones, and accept the most monstrous and revolting creeds, and worship fetishes, and prostrate itself before the wheels of Juggernaut, and, even in enlightened England and America, believe in Mormonism, and pretend, through the medium of table-rapping and the ridiculous rites of modern necromancy, to hold—what it feels it needs—an intercourse with the invisible world?

Now we have reached the problem. Can this wreck of what was once so fair and perfect be restored? Can the body triumph over sickness and over death? Can the soul recover its purity, the will its strength, the reason its clearness, the conscience its ascendency? Can the spirit break the bonds of superstition and fanaticism, and rise once more to heaven with a pure and holy worship, and assert its divine birth, and claim anew that privilege of approach to its Maker which it felt that it had forfeited when "Adam and Eve hid themselves from the presence of the Lord God among the trees of the garden"?

David felt that it could. His whole heart rested on the hope that restoration was possible, *but possible only to Omnipotence:* nay, in the words of the text, that Omnipotence Himself must "*stir up His strength*" if He would "come and help us." He cries, as out of the great deep, "O Lord, my *strength* and my Redeemer!" He who had not merely philosophised on the nature of man, who had not merely drawn cold, scientific conclusions from the pathology of disease, whether of the body or mind, but who had *felt* in the depths of his moral nature the dominion of sin—"the mystery of iniquity" —had found all past watchfulness, the self-formed habits of years, the discipline of a life of trial, utterly unable, alone and by themselves, to stand him in stead in the hour of overmastering temptation. He who has presented to scoffers of every age the sad and perplexing spectacle of a "man after God's own heart," given over, apparently without compunction, to a deadly sin; bound hand and foot by Satan; steeped in a lust which for a time dried the fount of feeling and drowned the reproaches of conscience; he, by an experimental sense, knew what a mighty *strength* that must be which should redeem one so loved, and yet so fallen!

The greatest of all helps to realise the magnitude of the work of Redemption is the experimental sense, the inwrought consciousness, of "the exceeding sinfulness of sin." It was when St. Paul had felt the powerlessness of his own unassisted moral nature, witnessing though it did to the authority of the Divine law, to resist the law of sin which wrought so mightily in his members, that he cried out with bitter agony, "O wretched man that I am, who shall deliver me from the body of this death?" It was when he felt his "freedom from the law of sin and death," when he realised the blessing of a "Spirit helping our infirmities," that he painted with all the force of an inspired imagination the picture of the 'whole creation," now "groaning and travailing in pain together," delivered by Christ's work from its bondage of corruption "into the glorious liberty of the children of God."

His words sound strange and visionary to us, unless we have something of the same kind of spiritual experience. With our loose, light notions of sin, the excuses we make for it, the soft names we call it by, never suffering it, even in some of its deadliest forms, to disturb our slumbers or lessen our appetite, no wonder that such language sounds unreal and extravagant.

Take this for an axiom. *He* thinks lightly of the greatness of Redemption who thinks lightly of the power of sin. *He* regards Jesus as a superfluous helper who regards Satan as a contemptible foe. The two spiritual conceptions are co equal and correlative. It is when, like David, we cry out, "Innumerable troubles are come about me; my sins have taken such hold upon me that I am not able to look up," that, like David also, we stretch out our hands to our mighty Succourer, and feel the force of the prayer which may often have passed our lips before, "O Lord, let it be Thy pleasure to deliver me; make haste, O Lord, to help me. Thou art my Helper and Redeemer; make no long tarrying, O my God."

I refuse to limit the great work of Redemption to what is called, in the language of popular theology, "the saving of the soul." I regard it as co-extensive with the work of ruin. Wherever sin, in its remotest consequences, has reached, there Christ's work reaches also. I remember St. Paul's assertion, that "the whole creation" is looking for, and has an interest in, "the manifestation of the sons of God." I call to mind that Jesus of Nazareth Himself was as sensibly touched by the sight of physical suffering as of spiritual corruption. Every act of mercy wrought upon the earth is but a shadow of the great act of Calvary: every true illumination of the Spirit is from Him whose mission in the world is to "guide us into *all* truth."

We do a fatal injury, as it seems to me, to the work of Redemption, as a practical human idea, when we disconnect it, as some are fond of doing, from the temporal and even the material interests of mankind. It is my full belief that the Cross of Christ has done, proportionately to the matter on which it works, as much for us in this world as it will do in the next. The "kingdom of heaven," in the idea of its great founder, began with St. John's baptism—runs its first course in this lower world—throws its light on "*life*" as well as on "immortality." There is a good time coming. Who doubts it? Have not prophets foretold, and poets sung, and saints dreamed of it? Is it not a religious thought, though it may not be expressed by one whom men would call a religious poet?—

"For I doubt not through the ages one increasing purpose runs,
And the thoughts of men are widened with the process of the suns."

It is a satisfaction, and enlarges our ideas of the height and depth of Redemption, to think of the Cross of Christ as stamped upon everything that contributes to the amelioration of humanity—on hospitals, reformatories, penitentiaries, aye, if you will allow me to say so, though less distinctly and with a fainter impression, even on such material things as museums, treasures of art, railroads. I know well enough that all these things may be savours of death; but, for that matter, so may the Gospel too. On the principle of not judging anything from its abuse; looking at the high aims by which even the meanest attempts at social improvement may be sanctified; viewing things in their natural tendencies, all as parts of one great, harmonious whole, I will not rob myself of the comfort, which I believe the Bible permits me to enjoy, of feeling that "*every good gift* cometh down from the Father of light;" and that I may lawfully connect every endeavour to improve the condition, and even to raise the tastes and multiply the conveniences of men, with that great act of love which brought the Son of God from His throne in heaven to redeem a groaning and travailing world.

For the law of the Kingdom of God is progress—development—of the species, speaking generally; and of the individual too, where it has free course and is not frustrated. It is indeed, as our great dramatist says of human mercy, "mightiest in the mightiest." It works more effectually in the nobler parts of our nature; in the spirit than in the soul; in the soul than in the body. But there is nothing in human nature that is too high to need it, too low to be susceptible of its influences. Even "our vile bodies" are to be changed into the "likeness of Christ's glorious body," according to the working whereby He "is able to subdue *all* things unto Himself." The ilness of spiritual discernment—the great gift of heaven—first; sanctification, that which now worketh in us mightily, next; but "the redemption of the body" also has its place in the scale of regeneration, though the quickening spirit of the last Adam has not yet swallowed up death in the completeness of His victory.

I know not, when the Son of Man cometh, whether He will find faith upon the earth, but I fully believe that He will find the earth itself fuller than now it is of the tokens of the goodness and loving-kindness of the Lord. I know not whether men will recognise the *Giver*, but I believe, as the ages roll onwards, they will be surrounded more abundantly and more freely by the *gift*. Surely we ourselves have a richer inheritance—have our lot fallen in pleasanter places—than our fathers had; and our children *may*, probably *will*, be "better off" in every sense than we. Surely year by year more ground is won, or at least attempted to be won, from the domains of ignorance, and superstition, and vice, and sickness, and death. Surely, as in David's day, so in our own, the Lord is "renewing the face of the earth:" making, literally as well as spiritually, "its deserts to rejoice, and its waste places to blossom like a rose."

No doubt it is so, says some wise man of the world. It is what we philosophers have always maintained; but why connect it with the Redemption, or the Gospel, or Christianity? We do not wish to entangle ourselves with supernatural accounts of things when ordinary influences, within the reach of our own experience, will do as well. It is civilisation, the march of mind, the schoolmaster, that has accomplished all this.

Right, O sir, if you regard these as divine instruments, the material organisms of God's providence and grace—the wheels, as it were, of Ezekiel's vision, in which was a "spirit of life," moving, guiding, governing them; but utterly, fatally wrong, if you sever them from God's Spirit—which, remember, is the effluence of Christ's work—and attempt to magnify them as manifestations of *man's* power.

Civilisation! the march of mind! the schoolmaster! Have you never heard or read of a civilisation rank and towering, like the gigantic vegetation of the tropics, which did but beget and conceal the deadlier poison? If not, read the histories of Athens, Corinth, Antioch, Alexandria, Rome. Try the civilisation of Rousseau or Voltaire, and see what it *will* beget and *has* begotten.

The march of mind, again! Why "intellect without God" is some one's definition of Satan. Does the world afford no instance of the most highly gifted of the sons of men helpless victims to the tyranny of some foul lust, or brutal passion, or sordid desire? Can there be a more striking type of the greatness and littleness of

s

man than he who is the founder of all modern science, the great, but as all must add, the mean Lord Bacon?

And as for the school, what is it but the wisdom of this world made foolishness? What is education but another weapon put into the hands of Satan—unless God's law is its atmosphere, God's Spirit its light, God's Son its corner-stone? Build schools on this foundation, and they stand upon a rock: on any other, they will fall before the first storm, and will add but another, and that the saddest, element to the scene of desolation.

"But is it not rather 'far-fetched' to attribute all these mighty developments of human progress to the great act of Redemption accomplished and manifested by the death of Christ?" "*Far*-fetched," it is true; but if the philosophic maxim is correct, that every cause exists in its effects, a most legitimate inference nevertheless. I will venture on an illustration. George Stephenson, the eminent engineer, the first successful applier of steam-power to locomotive purposes, was once on a visit to the late Sir Robert Peel, at Drayton Manor. "One Sunday, when the party—which included Dr. Buckland, the geologist—had just returned from church, they were standing together on the terrace near the hall, and observed in the distance a railway train flashing along, throwing behind it a long line of white steam. 'Now, Buckland,' said Mr. Stephenson, 'I have a poser for you. Can you tell me what is the power that is driving that train?' 'Well,' said the other, 'I suppose it is one of your big engines.' 'But what drives the engine?' 'Oh, very likely a canny

Newcastle driver.' 'What do you say to the light of the sun?' 'How can that be?' asked the doctor. 'It is nothing else,' said the engineer. 'It is the light bottled up in the earth for tens of thousands of years— light absorbed by plants and vegetables, being necessary for the condensation of carbon during the process of their growth, if it be not carbon in another form; and now, after being buried in the earth for long ages, that latent light is again brought forth and liberated, made to work, as in that locomotive, for great human purposes.'"

And so the great original motive power in the moral and spiritual world, ay, and even in the physical, so far as it is subordinated to the moral and spiritual, is the light that issues from the Sun of Righteousness. Philosophers tell us that the beam which reaches the optic nerve this moment from some distant star, left its source perhaps twenty years ago, and has been travelling onward all that time in the greatness of its strength, unquenched, unextinguishable. So the "Day-Star from on high," which visited the earth more than eighteen centuries ago, still illuminates the dark corners, and will illuminate them to the end of time. It was the great manifestation of Divine love and Divinest self-sacrifice. It contained in itself, so to speak, the introsusception of all other sacrifices. As the Apostle says, "They were all gathered into one, in Christ." Those of the Law were not merely its *types;* so far as they brought peace to any conscience, they shared its *power*. Even the bloody rites of heathen superstition, in their purest and original idea as offerings of that which was

best and dearest, bore witness to the deep instincts of
human nature, and were feeble foreshadowings of the
Cross on Calvary.

> "What seemed an idle hymn, now breathes of Thee,
> Tuned by faith's ear to a celestial melody."

And what if its mighty power has at times been lost
under the corruptions of false religions, or obscured by
the pretensions of false philosophy: what if luminaries
that shine but by reflected brightness have seemed to
claim its light as their own: what if clouds have come
across its path and hid for a while its glorious radiance?
What does all this come to but an admission of the
truth which no one denies, that the power of the Cross
is subject to the conditions of humanity and of the
atmosphere that surrounds humanity?

It is no reflection on the Divine Power that in this
or that instance it may seem to us to have failed in
its purpose, or to have wrought out its end by imperfect
or even evil agencies. For to us is committed the
scarcely less wonderful power of antagonism; we,
worms of the earth, can frustrate as regards ourselves
— ay, and as regards others! — the grace of God.
We can offend ourselves, and we can cause a weak
brother to offend. It is the inexplicable mystery of
human free-will, concurrent with Divine omnipotence.
And if the treachery of a Judas, or the malice of a
Caiaphas, or the moral weakness of a Pilate, or the
fickleness of an ignorant crowd, were really agencies in
the salvation of the world, what can we do but admire
the resources of that omnipotence which by a Divine

alchemy can transmute human evil into human good, and vindicate its sovereignty even by submitting to the use of base instrumentalities, and, like the light of the blessed sun, can pass through the foulest media, clouded perhaps, and robbed of some of its brightness, but yet uncontaminated and undefiled?

Some minds have delighted, fancifully enough, to trace the very form of the Cross in every true archetype—or idea, as the old Platonists called it—of nature's creative power, as the "exemplary draught or pattern," to use Hooker's words, "on which in working she fixeth her eye." But it is no fancy, but a most certain and demonstrable truth, that the spirit, or so to call it, *the law of the Cross*, is stamped upon everything noble, and brave, and true, and good, that Nature has ever borne. It is the spirit of self-sacrifice—the law of love.

Gaze not on the Cross as the manifestation of Divine wrath—look to Sinai for that if thou canst bear the sight—but as the token and pledge of love inexhaustible, unalterable. Gaze on it till thou hast thyself drawn from it into the pores of thy cold, selfish heart the virtue of its warmth, its holy, kindling, purifying fire. Let the electric spark of Divine love thrill through thy sluggish frame. Place thyself under it, and ask what lessons it has to teach thee. Shrink not, though thou feel in thy hands the prick of the nails, or in thy side the thrusting of the spear. "Be crucified with Christ": so shalt thou live the better, the braver, the truer, the happier life. Then shalt thou learn, with St. Paul, "how to spend and be spent for the brethren." Then thou shalt still love on, though thou be little loved in return. Then shalt thou "fill up that which is behindhand of the afflictions of Christ for His body's sake, which is the Church." Then shalt thou lend thy aid, feeble in thine own eyes, of no account in those of the world, but marked and registered and prized in the book of God, in accomplishing, perhaps in hastening, the great issue to which all things have been tending from the creation of the world; which sin has hindered but has not been able to turn aside, which God eternally predestined, and proclaimed anew, and stamped with the seal of His unchangeable counsel at the death of His Son—"the deliverance of the creature from the bondage of corruption into the glorious liberty of the children of God."

Preached—St. Thomas's Church, Salisbury, Lent, 1858.

XIX.

ST. ANDREW.

"One of the two which heard John speak, and followed him, was Andrew, Simon Peter's brother. He first findeth his own brother, Simon, and saith unto him: We have found the Messias (which is, being interpreted, the Christ). And he brought him to Jesus."—St. John i. 40—42.

ST. ANDREW was a native of Bethsaida, a town of Galilee, on the coast of the Lake of Genesareth, and by trade a fisherman. His father's name was Jona, and he was the brother, as most have thought, the younger brother of Simon Peter. That he was, in spite of the disadvantages of an imperfect education, and a worldly calling that must have occupied much of his thoughts and time, a man of inquiring mind and sincere concern for the highest interests of his soul, may I think be assumed from his being found among the followers of that stern preacher of righteousness, St. John the Baptist.

He was no man of a wavering faith or lukewarm devotion who would consent to be a disciple of a teacher who read men's hearts so truly, and reproved their sins so unsparingly. When we can still listen gladly to a preacher who is no prophesyer of smooth things, so long as we feel that he is preaching to us God's truth, we may accept it as a token that it is a real hungering after righteousness, and not merely an itching ear, or a restless curiosity, that has possession of our souls. People do not like to be spoken to as plainly as John the Baptist used to speak, unless their desire is not to be humoured, but to be saved.

It was at the feet of such a master that Andrew originally sat; and by him, he was, in a measure, prepared for the discipleship of Christ. He had no doubt often heard the Baptist speak of the still Mightier Teacher who was to come after him. He had listened to him as he unrolled the ancient prophecies, and foretold their speedy fulfilment. He knew that his present instructor's work was but preparatory to the richer and more gracious dispensation that was on the eve of being revealed.

And so, as he one day stood with his master by the river Jordan, and saw a Person coming towards them, upon Whom St. John looking said, "Behold the Lamb of God," he seems to have felt himself irresistibly drawn to the stranger. "He followed Him, and came and saw where He dwelt, and abode with Him that day": and left Him a worshipper and a believer.

Any system, any philosophy, any human wisdom, however profitable and instructive as far as it goes, if it stop short of Christ, if it do not lead us ultimately to Him "in Whom are hid all the treasures of true wisdom and knowledge," must be unsatisfying to a soul that has a painful consciousness of its own unworthiness and helplessness, and is casting about, as yet in vain, for some sure standing-ground on which to build its hopes. Human teachers are useful in proportion to their faithfulness, and the power they have received of God, to hold forth the Word of life. But they are not Christ; nor can they stand in the place of Christ. They can but point out the road: it is left for our own free choice to follow it. Our salvation does not depend upon the gifts of any mortal guide, but upon our finding out for ourselves where Jesus dwells, and abiding with Him.

St. Andrew, then, was the first known follower of our Blessed Lord. But he was more than this. He was, so to speak, the first missionary, the first who put in his sickle to the corn in the Church's harvest-field. He did not spend that night with his new Instructor, in His lowly dwelling, without learning that the spirit of the new religion which he had accepted was eminently not selfish and personal, but disseminative and corporate. He realised the fact that Christ was come upon the earth not so much to pick up outcast souls one by one, or to make the greatest saints out of the greatest sinners—which is some people's notion of the *ordinary* results of grace—as to knit together His elect into one communion and fellowship—to set up a kingdom—to build a Church, and in doing so, to make the welfare of each individual more or less dependent upon the growth and development of the whole.

If there is one corrupt element in our nature more than another that the Gospel is framed to eradicate, it is *selfishness*, even religious selfishness—for there is such a thing—the notion, that is, that Christ died for us alone: that we need only concern ourselves about our own souls: that, as wicked Cain said, "we are not our brother's keeper": that it matters not if the whole world perish, so long as we ourselves and a few others who think like us—whom we therefore take upon ourselves to call the elect, are saved. You will look in vain through the New Testament for countenance for such views. As the Church is a universal brotherhood, so is it with a spirit proper to a member of such a community that every individual Christian must be actuated.

St. Andrew felt this. He did not think that when he had found Christ he had found a treasure to be hidden and selfishly appropriated to his own comfort and profit alone. No sooner was he convinced of the reality of his discovery than he wished others to share it, and be the better for it too. He is the first Christian example of the grace of charity and the power of brotherly love.

Be assured that this is the only true evangelical temper. Whatever gift or privilege, whether temporal or spiritual, by God's providence we possess, we double the enjoyment of it by communicating it freely with our brethren. As in worldly matters, "there is that scattereth and yet increaseth; and there is that withholdeth more than is meet, but it tendeth to poverty"; so in spiritual things, so far as I have observed, the religion that is self-absorbed is universally cheerless and gloomy. He who would fully know what the love of

Christ is, must be content, as was St. Paul, "to spend and be spent for his brethren." Whatever he lays out in such a cause will be as much for his own soul's health as theirs.

St. Andrew was, moreover, the human instrument in bringing the first Gentiles to Christ—"the Greeks who desired to see Jesus." They had heard of Jesus, and wished to see Him, and they applied for the purpose to Philip, apparently because he was the first of our Lord's immediate followers who fell in their way. And what does Philip do? He comes to tell Andrew. But why? Why not, himself, introduce them to Christ? especially as he was a man of like disposition, and had himself before been instrumental in awakening the curiosity of Nathanael to come and see the despised Nazarene? My own opinion is that he told Andrew because he was sure he should find in him a kindred spirit: one who would sympathise with these poor inquirers: one who would know no distinction of race: one who would be puffed up with no vain conceit of Jewish privileges in dealing with the strangers: one who followed the promptings of his own heart, and not the selfish calculations of pride or prejudice: one who delighted in any enlargement of the borders of his Master's kingdom, and who, by the instinct of a loving heart more than by the grasp of a powerful understanding, already anticipated the time when there should be neither Jew nor Greek, bond nor free, male nor female, *but all one in Christ Jesus.* The great mystery of the Gospel, hidden before both from priests and prophets, this unlettered fisherman of Galilee, by the unerring discernment of an affectionate and unselfish soul, I will not say *com*prehended, but *ap*prehended, and acted on. As he was the first of the Apostles to make Christ known to the Jew—his own brother Simon—so may he, with equal truth, be said to have been foremost to "open the door of faith unto the Gentiles." He united the opposite missions of St. Peter and St. Paul. He preached the Gospel to the circumcision, and to the uncircumcision also.

The affectionate, brotherly temper which St. Andrew cultivated must have served as a valuable preparatory discipline for that act of sacrifice and self-renunciation which, in about a twelvemonth after his first interview with Jesus, he was called to perform. For some months after he and his brother Peter had been first brought to the knowledge of Christ, they pursued their ordinary occupation as fishermen on the Sea of Galilee.

I daresay often on those deep waters, as they sat in their boat, those two brothers had mused and talked together of the wondrous teacher of Capernaum, whose deeds and sayings were in all men's mouths, and of whom they themselves knew more than most who spake of Him. And doubtless also the all-seeing eye of Jesus often fell on them as they mended their nets upon the shore, or perhaps conversed about Him with their partners, James and John; and read their hearts, and saw that they were men fitted for His purpose, and watched His opportunity to make them indeed His own. We need not doubt that God does always choose His instruments; and those instruments, however unlikely they may seem to our eyes, are the fittest and most proper for the work He has for them to do.

And so when Jesus would gather round Him a small company of faithful followers for the attestation of His mission, and the future building of His Church, the first He summoned to Him were Simon Peter and his brother Andrew. He bade them leave their nets and follow Him—Him, a despised outcast who had not where to lay His head; "who had no form nor comeliness," nor any beauty that they should desire Him—Him they were to follow and He would make them fishers of men. It was free to them, of course, to have refused. They might have alleged the occupation of their trade, the age of their father, the necessities of their families, their unfitness for the work, the doubtfulness of success. They might have bargained, or asked for security, or taken exceptions, or sought to qualify the sacrifice in one or other of the thousand ways which worldly people always find to evade the simple acceptance of a call which they cannot help hearing but have no inclination to obey.

But these less clever fishermen did nothing of the kind. They heard Christ call them, and without stopping to consider what worldly ties they were breaking—whether it would be better for them in a temporal point of view or not—they followed Him without delay. What a noble faith! What a glorious venture! What a costly sacrifice! They gave up all things cheerfully *because Christ bade them.*

The sacrifice of self! How hard a thing it is, and yet the root of the whole matter, the necessary essential foundation of the Christian character in every age! It is not likely that any of us will be called to make sacrifices of the same kind, or to the same extent, as were St. Andrew and the first followers of our Lord. Their work was different from ours—different from the work which any set of men ever had to do, either before or since. They, for a specific purpose, were required to resign their homes, their families, their trades, their possessions, to follow One Who had higher aims, and wider spreading duties for them in view. *We* have to follow Christ *in* our homes, *among* our families, *on* our farms, *in* our daily labour and trade.

We should be mistaking our vocation if we thought Christ bade us, as he bade His Apostles, "go forth into all the world and preach the Gospel to every creature." We are only too ready to make a kind of vague, general interest in the success and enlargement of the Church serve as a substitute for the definite personal duties that meet us at our own door. But these homely duties cannot, any more than can missionary calls, be discharged without the spirit of self-sacrifice. Christ certainly calls us all to give up *something*, "and follow Him." Let it be our care to find out what that "something" is. It is what we shall find very near our hearts, intimately associated, as we think, with our daily happiness and comfort; very pleasant perhaps, and hard to part with; a different thing in different men, but in all *so far* the same that it is a something which is absorbing too much of our thoughts and care—which carnalises instead of spiritualising them; which makes them earthlier instead of heavenlier,

and which like the cherished right hand or eye, if it be
not cut off or plucked out, may *ultimately* be the cause
of their whole body being cast into hell.

But I must compress the remainder of this history
into a very few words. When the multitude who had
followed Jesus into the wilderness of Bethsaida were
fainting with hunger, and his brother-disciple Philip
was utterly at a loss to think how their necessities
could be supplied, it was St. Andrew who drew our
Blessed Lord's attention to "the lad there, who had
five barley loaves and two small fishes," which were so
strangely to be multiplied into a meal for five thousand
men. It is true that his faith in his Master's almighty
power as yet was scarcely strong enough to make him
hope that his suggestion would be of any avail: "What
are they," he asks, "among so many?" But we see
before us the same man whose portrait all along we
have been endeavouring to draw, ever alive to the
wants and exigences of others, and here as tenderly
solicitous for men's *temporal*, as at other times he was
for their spiritual, needs.

The only other special circumstance related of him
is, that he was one of the four disciples who asked our
Lord privately to explain to them more fully the mysterious words He had dropped about the throwing down
of the stones of Jerusalem, and with whom He sat down
on the Mount of Olives three days before His Passion,
and confided that awful picture of the latter days when
the stars of heaven shall fall, and the Son of Man shall
come, and the elect shall be gathered in, and the Divine
Purpose towards the lower world shall be fulfilled.

Here again we see the same inquiring, yet reverent and meditative, mind which first took the Galilean fisherman to John the Baptist, and then led his riper judgment to believe and to follow Jesus Christ.

We catch his name once more in the sacred pages of the Scriptures. He is one of the eleven who meet together in the upper chamber of Jerusalem to complete anew the apostolic number, and fill up the vacant bishopric from which Judas "by transgression fell." Ecclesiastical history tells us that he prosecuted his missionary labours with great success in the countries bordering on the Caspian Sea, and sealed a life of devotion to his Master's service by a blessed martyrdom, being crucified as his Lord had been; and, true to his character even in his death-agonies, still having strength and boldness enough to exhort the standers-by to "look unto Jesus," and, if need were, "to resist even unto blood, striving against sin."

In the same spirit he, though dead, this day still speaks to us. He makes us feel, with as constraining an influence as ever, the power and beauty of those twin sisters of grace—the love of the brotherhood, the sacrifice of self. We still have our sacrifices to make, though we do not look to them for expiation. We still have deeds of brotherly love to show, though we claim for them no recompense at God's hand on the score of merit. We know that we are saved by grace, and we should be slow to rest our title of acceptance on anything but the free and undeserved mercy of Almighty God. But still, Christ is our Example as well as our Atonement. He, too, has taught us that the love of others, and the sacrifice of self, are things which God delights in, and which He has promised to reward. If we cultivate these graces we shall not only be walking in the steps of St. Andrew, but of Jesus also.

Not unfitly therefore, as exhibiting in his life and character some of the fairest fruits of faith, no less than on historical grounds as the first-called of the Apostles of the Lord, does St. Andrew's name stand foremost in the catalogue of Christian saints. He is a representative man, a type of the power of grace, of the measure of possible, rational holiness. There is nothing *extraordinary* recorded of him—no ecstasies, or special illuminations, or catchings-up to the third heaven, or visions, or revelations of the Lord: no almost superhuman acts either of doing or suffering, of patience, or courage, or saintly heroism. His is simply the history of a calm, affectionate, teachable heart, ripening, educated, developed into features of singular loveliness under the discipline of the doctrine of Christ, by the secret, permeating influence of pure and guileless motives—the habitual, almost instinctive, discharge of homely, active duties.

Such a character pictures forth to us "the beauty of holiness" in colours that, to my eyes, are at once harmonious and lovely. It is so easy for each one of us to say and to feel, "I may go and do likewise." We are taught, by the example of a life that runs in lines parallel to our own experience, what is meant by "taking up our cross and following Christ." We find that it indicates a life, not of morbid asceticism, but of practical piety; a life, not of selfish spiritual isolation, but of social intercourse and an exercise of the affections; giving a free, though governed, scope to the best and purest instincts of the heart.

I cannot imagine where men get their narrow, gloomy views of the Gospel from. At least *I* have not so learnt Christ, nor dare I so preach Christ. The voice of my Master that I seem to hear most distinctly with my soul's ear is this—" Go cheerfully to thy work : do heartily whatsoever thy hand findeth to do: do it as unto Me, and not unto men : and thou shalt not have to go far to seek, or long to wait, for thy reward."

Preached—Newton Toney, St. Andrew's Day, 1853.

XX.

THE DIVINE CALL AND THE HUMAN CALLING.

As illustrated in the Call of St. Matthew.

"And as Jesus passed forth from thence, He saw a man, named Matthew, sitting at the receipt of custom: and He saith unto him, Follow me. And he arose, and followed Him."—St. Matthew ix. 9.

As Jesus passed from the house in which He had proved, by a mighty sign, that the Son of Man had power on earth to forgive sins, He called Matthew. A pretty picture for the imagination to attempt to realise, this call of the wealthy custom-house officer of Capernaum to follow the Teacher who had not where to lay His head! There, in his booth, with bills of lading and invoices all around him, sits Levi, Alphæus's son, taking toll and custom-dues from all that brought their wares into the busy harbour from lands across the sea.

A keen, quick-eyed, peering man, be sure, was this "Matthew the publican," as he calls himself. Not at all of the strict Pharisaic school, who would not have touched shekels thus earned with the tips of their fingers, but a money-making citizen of a laxer type; not troubled possibly with many scruples about the lawfulness of his trade, and, as it would seem from the company that seated themselves at his table, not over particular in his choice of friends.

St. Mark calls him Alphæus's son: and in default of any further mark of distinction it has been usual to identify this Alphæus with the father of James the Less; in which case St. Matthew will have been nearly related by birth to our Lord. If so, he must have been one of those "brethren" of whom St. John tells us that, as yet, their incredulous hearts refused to own the Messianic tokens of Jesus of Nazareth.

Whether this be so or not, it is most probable that Matthew—to call him by the name which he probably assumed to commemorate this crisis in his history, for it signifies, like the Greek name Theodore, "One given by God"—had many times, before this day, heard of, perhaps seen and listened to, the great Galilean Teacher, who, for more than a year past, had made Capernaum His home, and Whose fame was so widely spread in its neighbourhood.

These sudden conversions were not, perhaps, so sudden after all. Men's hearts, no doubt, as in the case of Cleopas and his companion at Emmaus, had ofttimes "burned within them"; deep questionings, and searchings of conscience had arisen, and perhaps again subsided; yearnings after higher truth than scribes and Pharisees could teach had been felt, and half purposes of confessing the despised Nazarene Prophet formed, before conviction became irresistible, and the promptings of the inner and nobler self could no longer be disobeyed.

This is most probable because it is most natural; most according to experience and the ordinary methods of God's grace; most like what we observe in others, or feel in ourselves. We cannot doubt that our blessed Lord, with that perfect propriety that marked His whole character and conduct as a man, in choosing His more immediate followers chose those whom, as God, He foreknew to be the fittest instruments of His purpose. Nor can we doubt either that His call was one that might not be heeded; and that men were free to accept, or refuse, the invitation offered to them. He would have fit servants, but not unwilling ones. They who, when called, began to make excuse, were not fit for the kingdom of God—at least not fit for its high and special places of trust, not worthy to have their names written on its foundation-stones.

When Christ bade a man follow Him, be sure He had marked, and waited for, His opportunity. He took him at the critical point of his spiritual history. It was the death-struggle between the generous, instinctive "first-thought" and the prudential, reflex "second-thought"; between conscience and interest; expediency and principle; the loss of comfort, and ease, and security, and the higher aspirations of which we have all, I suppose, been conscious at times. The doom of that man, perchance, as far as regards the growth and issues of the moral and spiritual life, was sealed by the choice he made. St. Matthew was called, and his heart leaped up at the Master's voice, and he obeyed the calling; and for his reward, "in the regeneration, when the Son of Man shall sit on the throne of His glory, he shall be one of those who shall sit on the twelve thrones, judging the twelve tribes of Israel."

This divine call reached St. Matthew in the very midst of circumstances that, of themselves, would be most likely to stifle and make it abortive. A man seems hardly in the fittest frame of mind to listen to, and obey, the summons of the Spirit, when he is under the excitement of a thriving business. Yet God has often chosen such times to utter His first— His last—call. He calls Matthew from the receipt of custom. He calls Simon and Andrew, James and John, from their father, their hired servants, their boats, their fishing-nets. He called Saul, even while he was persecuting Him. He called another, but whose ears were deaf and his heart cold, while the corpse of his father was lying unburied in his house. "Unlikely seasons," we may be ready to say. Yet God chose them; and, we may be sure, chose them, not without a purpose, wisely and well.

And in every case the call demanded, and was accompanied by, a sacrifice. It cost something then, as ever, to follow Christ. There was a "right hand to be cut off," or "a right eye plucked out," the stern excision of many a carnal appetite and many a pleasant dream, of many a fond anticipation, of not a few welcome, but perilous, memories. They that walk *with* Christ, and *after* Christ, must be new creatures. Matthew closed his booth, gathered up his books and money-bags, gave "a great feast in his own house," a sort of farewell entertainment to his old acquaintances and friends, and "then arose, left all, and followed Christ." It was a sacrifice surely—a sacrifice of which, no doubt, the cost was counted before it was made. It was not a mere impulse, which might be retracted, but a deliberate act, irrevocable.

Not that God calls all of us to such sacrifices. *Some* sacrifice, *something* laid on His altar, be sure He requires from every man; but not always, not even generally, a sacrifice so entire, so absolute, so unsparing as this. Every Christian may be, and if he has any adequate sense of the necessity that is laid upon him, is bound to be, "a fellow-labourer with God": and neither you nor I can labour with God without making sacrifices. I do not say that the sacrifice shall not be repaid you— repaid with good measure, pressed down, and shaken together, and running over—but at the moment you make it you shall *feel* it to be a sacrifice, it shall cost you a pang, a regret, perhaps a tear.

These touches of natural infirmity —of the power of which our blessed Lord Himself perhaps knew something in His agony in Gethsemane—shall not impair its integrity and preciousness, even in the sight of God. We may give up a thing which we have loved, heartily, absolutely, unreservedly, for ever; and yet at the moment of separation, and even afterwards, till the lesson of resignation is fully learnt, sorrow shall fill our soul. God's converting spirit does not *crush* our nature, though it changes it.

There was another publican, the object of our Lord's notice, a child of grace, an elect vessel, a true son of Abraham, whom yet Jesus did not bid forsake his trade and follow Him—I mean Zaccheus of Jericho. Matthew was taken, Zaccheus was left. The one became an Apostle, the other remained a publican.

The first and most natural inference I draw from this is that neither in the dispensations of God's Providence, nor in the leadings of His grace, are all persons called upon to renounce the same things. Indeed, knowing the wonderful delicacy and subtlety of the links that bind together the inner and the outer world, the subjective and the objective, the spiritual and the material, we should at once allow that the same thing is not the same to all persons, nor are all persons the same in their relations to the same things. A business, for instance, an occupation, a line of life, that either inherently in itself, or from its inevitable associations, would be fatal to the mind's peace or the spirit's prosperity in one man, may be, and often is, the lawful, God-appointed calling of another. There is no law in these things, or, if there be a law, it is assuredly in the region of spiritual matters, beyond the powers of our analysis, and each case must be judged and determined by its own circumstances.

As though to make man conscious of his freedom, and of the high despotic sovereignty of his will; as though to give the lie at once, and for ever, to that sordid philosophy which would represent humanity as but the complex result of the influence of multifarious external things—the creature of circumstances—we notice it, as one of the most indisputable facts of ethics, that people who move in precisely the same orbit in relation to externals—whom God's Providence has placed in exactly the same envelope of circumstances, are yet by the action of some deeper and unanalysed law working in their moral nature, nevertheless most diversely influenced by their surroundings. The things that, in the highest moral and spiritual sense, are one man's wealth, become to another " an occasion of falling."

The calling of a publican, for example, viewed in itself—if we are justified in viewing any calling in itself, and irrespective of the person by whom it is pursued—could not have been favourable to godliness: must have been a sore hindrance to the development of saintliness, and even to the maintenance of common honesty. St. John the Baptist, in his outspoken way, warned men of its dangers. Zaccheus, by his well-known offer of restitution to any whom he might have wronged, would appear to have experienced, or at least to have become awakened to, them. It surely was not without that admixture of truth and shrewd observation which generally characterises proverbs and common sayings that the whole class was thrown together in one comprehensive description; and to be a "publican," in most men's estimation, was much the same thing as being a "sinner."

Yet in this calling, which St. Matthew was bidden to renounce, Zaccheus was suffered, perhaps commanded, to remain. There lay his discipline. In it he was to be proved. By and with it he was to work out his salvation. There that conscience, which had become quickened by the gracious words of the great Teacher to the claims of poverty and the responsibilities of power, was to assert its inherent sovereignty, and exhibit the miraculous virtue of Divine grace, even under the most untoward circumstances, to purge and elevate and sanctify the human soul. It was otherwise with St. Matthew. For some secret end of Divine predestination, for some deep reason which we can but guess at, and cannot, need not penetrate; whether because the traffic was too absorbing, and its accompanying contaminations dangerous to the purity of his heart, or for his special fitness for a higher and nobler work, Matthew was bidden leave, then and for ever, the receipt of custom at which he sat, and follow Him that called him.

But I would quit the detail of particular cases, and enter upon broader ground. Just here, on the frontier of cases like the two quoted, lies the debateable land of morality and sociology. Just here is the region of what, in the history of human speculation, has sometimes been dignified with the title of a science, but what after all is a mere empiricism—the region of casuistry. Oh! what a blessed thing is this Gospel of the Lord Jesus Christ to extricate us from the tortuous perplexities of casuistical divines! Truly they have laden men with burdens grievous and heavy to be borne. The casuist decides cases, as they never can be decided, *in the abstract;* but the Lord's Gospel, with respect to persons. The one lays snares for our feet, yea, and sets traps in our way; the other gives, and helps us to realise, a liberty that makes us free indeed!

What grand principles are those so fearlessly thrown down as gauntlets of defiance before all hair-splitting dogmatists by St. Paul! What an area of different ground do they cover, where men may spin their cobwebs and pursue their abstract arguments for ever, without arriving at helpful, practical results! They were not learnt at the feet of Gamaliel, or in the schools of Tarsus, but at the feet and in the school of Christ. "Let every man," he says, "be fully persuaded in his own mind." "Happy is he that condemneth not himself in that thing which he alloweth." "All things are lawful for me, but all things are not expedient." "Why is my liberty judged of another man's conscience?" "Who art thou that judgest another man's servant? To his own master he standeth or falleth. Yea! and he shall be holden up; for God is able to make him stand."

I know, and St. Paul knew, that such liberty, which is the moral prerogative of the children of God, may be abused into an occasion of the flesh, or into a cloke of maliciousness. But that fact really enhances the preciousness of the gift. Our Heavenly Father deals with us not as with babes who need to be fed with milk, but as men capable of digesting and being nourished by strong meat; and with our senses exercised, "by reason of use," to discern between good and evil. He thinks we ought to be able, without danger, to use edged tools. He bids us be free and make proof of our freedom. He raises us thereby in the scale of being; and He quickens our consciences at the same time with the keener sense of our responsibilities. It is terrible when we mark the evil that has sprung from the gift to realise the idea of human freedom; but God, foreknowing the evil, has nevertheless seen fit to make and leave us free.

And so we do not venture to dictate to others the

callings in life that they shall pursue. We dare but pray God to tell ourselves what He would have us to do, and to give us hearts prepared to follow, when He has opened our eyes to discern the, *to us*, more excellent way. We delight to believe that God's Providence governs, and His grace sanctifies, every honest, lawful human calling.

No one line of life, regarded simply in itself, has a right perhaps to call itself better, or higher, than another. Each is evoked by the exigencies of human nature. Each in its place and time is carrying forward the eternal purposes of God. For this or that man or woman, one calling may be more suitable than another, but they have to determine that for themselves. "Let every man," says the Apostle, with that far-reaching insight into the laws of human nature which is of the essence of true wisdom, "let every man, wherein he is called, therein abide with God."

The philanthropy and benevolence, and even the Christian feeling of the day, lack this mark of earnestness, and want this condition of success—that they are not *abiding*. The evidences of *faith* are more frequent than the evidences of *patience*. The general restlessness and excitement of the age infect even its religious enterprises. Our desire to work for God is intermittent, capricious, fitful. We grow weary of monotony, and crave for change. We forget that

> "The trivial round, the common task,
> Can furnish all we ought to ask—
> Room to deny ourselves—a road
> That brings us daily nearer God."

And this restlessness of mind vitiates our work and makes it unfruitful: it impairs the faith which should be the parent of our labours. The faith needs the occasional sustenance of sight. If the vision is ever tarrying, ever hidden, the heart sinks, the spirits droop, the energies are paralysed. God, in condescension to human infirmity, permits the faithful workman to see from time to time, even "while he lives in the flesh," the fruit of his labour: but it is only when he has the temper of the husbandman who "waiteth for the precious fruit of the earth, and hath long patience for it, until he receive the early and the latter rain."

What we have each to look to seems, to me, to be this: What is the definite work to which God, by His providence or grace, is calling us? And when that is clear and distinct to our consciences, we must act it out in the spirit of the Divine maxim, "Whatsoever thy hand findeth to do: do, it heartily, as unto the Lord." Let us see, each one of us, that in our calling we there "*abide* with God." The more nearly our calling *professes* to abide with Him—the more nearly it approaches, and touches, and deals with Him—the more need to see that this abiding is *real*, and that *His* glory is indeed the constraining, animating motive of all we do.

Be sure that God's Blessed Spirit came down from heaven upon this earth to sanctify, not spiritual callings only, but *every* calling. "Every man," it is written, "has his proper gift of God; one after this manner and another after that." It is no affectation, or unreal figure of speech, to denominate our walk in life, whatever it may be, a "calling," a "vocation." If it is not consciously so to us, it ought to be. It is a Divine calling, God's very voice to us, His method in which He would have us work out our salvation—the process through and by which our regeneration in baptism is to issue in our regeneration in glory.

Every work that a man can undertake with a good conscience he shall find, if he seek it, God's blessing resting upon. We need not forsake or exchange our earthly calling because we desire to serve God. If we wish to be owned at the last Great Day as those who heard Christ's call and followed Him, we shall find a thousand opportunities rising up unexpectedly, but not casually, at our very doors; by the right use of which we may render unto Him as acceptable a service as if we ministered at His altars, or gave up ourselves, like Matthew, wholly to the ministry of the Word. Did not He "that loved us, and washed us from our sins in His own blood," make us, one and all, by the self-same act, "kings and priests unto God and His Father?"

We who are priests of the Lord, if we know ourselves, if we have really measured the true nature of the calling wherewith we are called, ought to be the last in the world who should dare to say to any fellow-man, "Stand by thyself: come not near to me, for I am holier than thou." We whom the Lord has called with a specially responsible—I will not venture to say a specially holy—calling, ought to be the last who should desire to magnify our office. Even St. Paul, when "compelled" to vindicate his Apostolic prerogatives against those who depreciated them at Corinth, does so with an almost painful sense of unseemliness. If there are men who should shrink from boasting of the power which the Lord hath given to them, save under the pressure of some overwhelming necessity, it is we.

Finally, let us all try to realise, more and more perfectly, the holiness of our several callings. What God requires of every man—what He enables every man to do—is to " live soberly, righteously, and godly in this present world"; doing his work "heartily, as unto the Lord, and not unto men." If he leaves some of us freer than others, in respect of restraints of a more conventional kind, be sure we are all equally under the obligation of an immutable morality. In this region of things, what is lawful and permissible in a layman is lawful and permissible in a clergyman—and neither less nor more. We are all under vows—or under obligations as binding as vows. Whether distinctly called to the work of the ministry, as Matthew, or suffered still to pursue a secular business, as Zaccheus, for both there is but one road to the same entrance into the city of God. Christ has but *one* answer for all who ask Him, " Lord, what must I do to be saved ?"—" If thou wilt enter into life, keep the commandments."

Preached—Salisbury Cathedral, St. Matthew's Day, 1859.

XXI.

THE REVELATION OF GOD'S LOVE THE DISTINCTIVE CHARACTERISTIC OF THE GOSPEL.

" God is love."—1 ST. JOHN iv. 8.

WHAT has Christianity done to make good its claim to the proud title of *the* Gospel—*the one* good message of glad tidings to mankind?

It were easy to enumerate many eminent *social* blessings, many conspicuous elements of *individual* happiness (which we appropriate and use without stopping to think whence we get, or to what we owe them) which can be distinctly traced to the Christian dispensation as their only authentic source; but if I were asked to name what has been its greatest gift of all, what has most contributed to human progress and human happiness, even as philosophers measure those terms; what it is, more than any other element of knowledge, that has set free the intellect; more than any other principle of conduct has instructed the conscience; more than any other object of desire has elevated the affections; I should say unhesitatingly that it is the unveiling of the face of our Father which is in heaven; the revelation, all the more pregnant and influencing from the way in which it was made, that "God is love."

We must remind ourselves of other forms of religious thought and belief before, perhaps, we shall be ready to admit this. According to Herodotus, the theory of the relation in which the Supreme Being stood to the world which prevailed in his time—*i.e.*, 450 years B.C.—in Greece, in Egypt, in Persia, not only among the illiterate, who might be supposed to be open to the influences of superstition, but among kings, philosophers, statesmen, was that the Deity was a malignant mischief-making Being who, in the possession of happiness Himself, grudged a share of it to His creatures, and even felt a malevolent joy in their sufferings.

The Scandinavian mythology—which was the religion of our forefathers, and which has still left historical trace of its existence in the names of the days of the week—as exhibited to us in the Eddas, prepares the mind of the worshipper from the very beginning for "one all-destroying catastrophe," points to "a creation doomed by necessity to a fatal and final destruction," in which life is nothing else but the alternate ascendency, under different symbols, of the principles of good and evil till the cyclus of the great tragedy is completed by the fiery snake consuming universal nature with all-destroying flames, from which the best and greatest of the sons of earth struggle to escape in vain.

In the far East, 500 millions of minds are crushed to the earth by two degrading superstitions; in one of which, Buddhism, the burden of independent personal existence is represented as intolerable, and the only rest for human nature is its re-absorption into the divine: in the other—Hinduism, the favourite Deity is not the beneficent Vishnu but the merciless Siva; and the horrible tortures inflicted on themselves by the worshippers attest their conceptions of the character of the God whom they serve.

Wherever, again, the faith of the Arabian prophet is professed, and the voice of the muezzin summons 250 million hearts to prayer, there, though the belief in the supreme sovereignty of God has kindled sufficient religious enthusiasm to propagate its creed by sword, yet the fact that the believer's mind dwells solely on the unbalanced idea of the Divine Omnipotence—the fact that the evening cry heard from every minaret of Islam is "God is great," not "God is love," has, perhaps, while stimulating the fanaticism, at the same time crushed the moral energies of the people by that natural product, fatalism—which, whether in a Christian or in a non-Christian, or merely philosophic form, always seems to generate "either desperation or a wretchlessness of most unclean living, no less perilous than desperation."

And if we turn for relief to the religious conception of the Jew, even in the purest age, it is evident that he regarded the God of Abraham, the God of Isaac, the God of Jacob, with much the same feeling of awe as a Greek might regard the terrible Eumenides. The patriarchal sentiment still lived in all its force—was as strong in Gideon and Manoah as it had been in Jacob—that to see God's face, to hear His voice, to speak with a messenger from the unseen world, was a death-summons to a sinful man. The dark side of the law—which St. Paul tells us in its essence was a ministration of death—under the influence of this sentiment was continually growing darker still.

The whole history of Judaism, as I read it, is a history of the religious deterioration of the people under the influence of a conception of the Divine nature—true and wholesome in itself and in its place, but false and mischievous as they distorted it—the conception of "God as a consuming fire." It is plain that the prophets and psalmists struggled against this downward current of public opinion, and national belief, in vain. In vain they preached the axioms of a higher morality. In vain (as Mr. Davison says) "they taught the doctrine of repentance with a clearness and certainty which were not admitted into the original law." In vain better and nobler spirits felt and testified that it was a vain oblation to give one's first-born for a transgression—the fruit of one's body for the sin of one's soul. In vain David wrote the fifty-first Psalm. In vain Elijah prayed to the Lord God that His people might know Him, and that He would turn their hearts back again. In vain the piety of Jehoshaphat, or Hezekiah, or Josiah, tried to revive the Mosaic worship in its ancient purity.

The gravitating tendency of human nature, under the pressure of the one paramount idea that the God whom it served is a God *to be feared*, was too mighty to be resisted, or even sensibly retarded. The administration of Manasseh followed in quick succession upon the reformation of Hezekiah: and even while there was a voice sounding in Jerusalem, "speaking comfortably to her, and crying that her warfare was accomplished and her iniquity pardoned," and promising abundant mercy to every wicked man that would forsake his way, "the heart of the people was fat, and their ears heavy, and their eyes closed." The charmer charmed, but the adder was deaf, and in the valley of the son of Hinnom, where the first high place to Moloch was set up by the very king who had built the splendid fabric of the Temple upon Mount Moriah, "Tophet was ordained of old," and parents ruthlessly immolated their offspring to the abomination of the children of Ammon; and if they could not silence the beatings of their own hearts, they could at least drown the screams of their murdered innocents in the roll of drums or the clang of sistra.

Under the discipline of that old divine law, human nature stood—should we not rather say, lay prostrate—before God, like David before Nathan, with the confession of his shame upon our lips—"I have sinned against the Lord "—and there was no prophet near who spoke loudly enough, or clearly enough, or authoritatively enough, to raise each penitent from the ground, and pour into his heart the reassuring word, "The Lord also hath put away thy sin: thou shalt not die."

This posture of the soul seems to be the natural, necessary consequence of the *consciousness of sin*. The law gave the knowledge of sin; and one who had been trained under its discipline, and had sought to fulfil its righteous will with all the force of his fiery, earnest soul, tells us how it fared with him: "The commandment came; and sin revived; and he *died.*" "And so the commandment, which was ordained unto life, he found to be unto death:" and though he "delighted in the law of God after the inward man," and felt and acknowledged that "the commandment was holy, and just, and good," yet upon his conscience it lay with such an intolerable burden, convincing of sin, but opening no door of escape to the sinner, that all he could do was to resign himself hopelessly to what seemed an inevitable destiny, crying out, but with little hope that he should be heard, "O wretched man that I am! who shall deliver me from the body of this death?"

Though, as Mr. Davison has admirably shown, the action of the combined influences of the moral and ceremonial laws *ought* to have produced in "serious and reasonable men a temper eminently Christian," and a disposition to accept, if it were offered them, a better atonement than could possibly be procured by the blood of bulls and goats, or the ashes of an heifer sprinkling the unclean, yet the mass of men, instead of being "serious and reasonable," were "carnal, sold under sin." The actual result of the "terror" which the law "created, but could not relieve," was to drive men, in their impatience or their fear, to worse atonements, instead of waiting to see whether God would provide a better. Under the influence of the conviction that it was impossible for the "blood of bulls and goats to take away sin," they sought for ease from troubling thoughts either in more fantastic and bloodier rituals, each man setting up his imagery after his own heart; or else they yielded to a blank and demoralising atheism, saying, "The Lord seeth us not: the Lord hath forsaken the earth."

This is only saying that the Law was not the Gospel. It was not a message of great joy. Though it was possible to *conceive* the beautifulness of his feet who should bring upon the mountains tidings of good, and publish peace to Sion, as yet the conception seemed but as a dream. Deep in the womb of time lay hid the mystery which one day should make all men know the "love of Christ, which passeth knowledge, and fill them with all the fulness of God."

The law, as such, was not the vehicle of grace, and therefore not the message of reconciliation. The sense of its types was latent. Its sacrifices, even the expiatory, were not atoning. They could but "cover" sin, not take it away. Though the prophets searched deep and long, and spake at times of what the "Spirit of Christ which was in them did signify," and almost had their hand upon the veil to draw it aside, yet St. Peter tells us that they ministered rather to *us* than to their contemporaries. Men "believed not their report," or did not understand it; and one of the goodly fellowship, whose lips had been touched with a live coal from off the altar, and who had seen the vision of the Lord sitting upon His throne, yet found that light, shining upon his unaccustomed eyes, as dazzling as the very darkness, and cried out as one giving up the search for truth from very hopelessness and perplexity, "Verily, Thou art a God that hidest Thyself, O God of Israel, the Saviour."

Had not the Lord said, "I will dwell in the thick darkness"? and though there was the sure word of promise that He would "destroy in His holy mountain the face of the covering cast upon all people and the veil that was spread over all nations," the time of unveiling was not yet come. "Men waited for the light, but walked in darkness."

And so God, having spoken in time past partially and variously by the prophets, in the last days, when the time was full, spoke unto the world by His Son. The darkness passed away, the true light shone. The day broke, and the shadows fled away. One who had lived under that darkness, and *felt* it, describes, in vivid and emphatic language, the change that came over the spirit of his mind when, as one of the Israel of God, he found himself blessed with light in his dwelling. "If any man be in Christ," he cries, "he is a new creature." "God was in Christ reconciling the world unto Himself, not imputing their trespasses unto them. . . . For He hath made Him to be sin for us, who knew no sin, that we might be made the righteousness of God in Him."

Christ, says Clement of Rome, was taught His message of glad tidings by the Father, and the Apostles were taught theirs by Christ. And what is St. Paul doing here but attesting afresh, and weaving into the tissue of his own kindled thoughts, the original words which proclaimed the love of God to man—"God so loved the world that He gave His only-begotten Son, that whosoever believeth on Him should not perish, but should have everlasting life. For God sent not His Son into the world to condemn the world, but that the world through Him might be saved?"

I do not know that we are much helped to understand these deeply instructive, deeply comforting, words by having put before us what are called "theories of the atonement." I never yet met any such theory that did not leave unanswered half the questions which it prompted me to ask. But, sitting down before these words of Jesus and of St. Paul, I am not disposed to be a questioner or a disputer at all. I *feel* their power: and it is vain to attempt to analyse a feeling. It is instructive, and moralists tell us that, its legitimate object being present, it must needs be excited. What I *feel* and *need* is a Mediator between my sinful soul and my most Just and Holy but most Merciful God.

The Gospel was not only an Atonement, it was a Revelation. Not only was God in Christ reconciling the world unto Himself, but God also was in Christ making Himself known unto the world. The Son by whom He spoke to men in the last days was the "brightness of His glory, and the express image of His Person." "He that saw Him saw the Father." Or, as St. Paul puts it, "He was the image of the invisible God."

As we gaze on Him going about with that calm, steadfast mien, doing good and healing every one that was oppressed with the devil, sitting among publicans and sinners and eating with them, preaching deliverance to the captives, recovering of sight to the blind, liberty to them that were bruised, a gospel to the poor —to all, the acceptable year of the Lord—we gaze, as it were, on the very face of God, and see it bent upon us with an ineffable expression of pity and tenderness and love. "He willeth not the death of a sinner;" that is His unchangeable purpose. "Ye will not come to Me that ye may have life," is His sharpest reproof, and *that* uttered in sadness rather than in anger, to all who are not *obstinately* hardening their hearts. "My Father Himself loveth you;" there is the balm to every doubting or wounded soul. By the discovery that "God loves me," many a soul has been "overwhelmed with pathetic joy." If the heart is open to religious convictions at all, it must be penetrated to the quick by such a conviction.

There seems to be only one perversion of which this doctrine of the love of God, manifested in Jesus Christ, is capable; and that is, if it should make us think that the High and Holy One, who inhabiteth eternity, is *indifferent to sin*. But against this possible misuse of its glad tidings the Gospel has guarded itself to the full, as effectually as did the law. "The wages of sin is death" still, as ever. In the Epistle to the Hebrews, as well as in the Book of Deuteronomy, "Our God is a consuming fire." "Vengeance is mine, I will repay, saith the Lord," is an eternal principle of justice demanded by the conscience, and which could never drop out of any Divine Law. "Knowing the terror of the Lord," as well as "constrained by the love of Christ," St. Paul "persuaded men."

The doctrine of the love of God, when imbibed not speculatively or conventionally, but really and practically, not as the badge of a party, but as a conviction of the soul, is little liable to perversion. Antinomianism in a religious mind seems to me to be an impossible moral phenomenon. For whom are we more likely to obey—one whom we love, and whom we know to love us, or one whom we simply *fear?* Who renders the more willing service, a son or a slave? Surely, under a "law of liberty," all obedience, freely paid, becomes by that very freedom more hearty, more trustworthy, more true.

The reformation of the ills of modern society must come from a higher conception of duty, animating the consciences and governing the lives of us all. The first reform we all need, I take it, is of ourselves. We cannot be made better or happier by Acts of Parliament. They may remove an unwise restriction there, or impose a wise restriction here; but after all, the real improvement must take its source within. Less selfishness, less impatience, less vindictiveness, less brutality, less lust. Do not you think, my friends, that you and I could make this world a little better than it is *if we tried?*

In itself it is a terrible thought that the past is irrevocable, but taken in connection with the assurance of the love of God, the thought of the immutability of the past almost ceases to be disturbing. At least there is no need, unless it be a case of very special deep-dyed guilt, for the memory or the conscience to dwell upon it with morbid, superstitious fear: no need to go in quest of strange atonements:

> "No need to bid, for cloistered cell,
> Our neighbour or our work farewell."

The surest remedy against bitter regret, the strongest proof of true repentance, is to throw ourselves on the future—or rather on *the present*, which alone is ours—strong in the confidence that the God who spares our lives has not cast away our souls, with a steadfast purpose to serve our Master more loyally for the time to come.

And though nothing shall derange that principle of the great assize which shall reward every man "according as his works have been," yet it has happened once, and may well happen again, that he who did not *begin* his work until the eleventh hour, but began it then heartily, without an excuse and without a murmur, when called in to take his wage, found to his surprise and joy that he received as much as those who had borne the burden and heat of the day.

Preached—St. Thomas's Salisbury, March 25, 1863. (Sermon preached at Oxford in previous February largely worked in.) Portions of Sermon also preached to Ashbury's men, Openshaw, April 24, 1871.

XXII.

CHRIST, THE HEALER.

"There went virtue out of Him, and healed them all."—ST. LUKE vi. 19.

A CONSIDERABLE, and to some minds a distressing, difficulty emerges, when a man, observing the phenomena of the world, endeavours to fit them into a preconceived theory, and to reconcile them with what he believes to be the attributes and revealed character of Almighty God. And this difficulty is quite as apt to disconcert reason as to startle faith. It is even a more formidable embarrassment to the mere Deist than it is to a believer in a revelation which *recognises* the fact of the difficulty, even if it does not *explain* it.

The difficulty to which I refer arises from the presence of evil—of sin, suffering, disease, death—in the world; and the apparent incompatibility of these evils with any conception that it is natural to form of a beneficent and benevolent God. If God be Benevolent, and if He be also Omnipotent, why, we are tempted to ask, does He not prevent misery, and sin, and all that, to our eyes, seems to mar the perfection of His Creation, and to rob the great redemptive act of its completeness and efficacy? Can it be true—as the fervid Oriental mind attempted to solve the problem—that there are two Gods: a principle of good and a principle of evil; an Ormuzd and an Ahriman; a Θεός and a δημιουργός, engaged in a perpetual conflict, of which this sublunary world is the scene, and poor humanity the victim? Is Manicheism the soundest philosophy, the truest religion, after all?

If such dreams and speculations ever chance to exercise an attractive influence upon our minds, there are two or three cautions that deserve to be remembered before entering upon them.

In the first place, that they are *mere speculations*, dim guesses or random gropings after truth; vain attempts of the human mind to construct, out of its own resources and by its own unaided powers, a satisfactory "philosophy of the Universe;" "systems" (as Mosheim calls the Gnostic speculations in the first age of Christianity, of which many of these modern theories are but the reproduction or modification)—"systems which have no solid foundation, and are indeed no more than airy phantoms blown up by the wanton fancies of self-sufficient men."

In the second place, we should recollect the limit put upon all such speculative enterprises by the very constitution of our own mind, and the utter inadequacy for such high flights of thought both of our faculties and of our language. We have no formula, nor even the capacity for framing one, to express, with any completeness, the full relation of Almighty God to His rational creatures, or to His material world. "All grand truth," said Frederick Robertson, "is the statement of two opposites; not a *via media* between them, nor either of them alone." God is good, yet evil exists: God exists, yet evil is permitted. These are truths which we must hold and act on separately, but which, till the dawning of that day which shall see us "equal to the angels," no breadth of intellectual grasp, no keenness of intellectual vision, will enable us to harmonise or comprehend.

Of course I am speaking of *theoretical* comprehension, of *logical* harmony. I am not aware that the *believer* ever found his steps practically hindered or embarrassed, even for a moment, by his faith in the goodness of God being suddenly confronted with the presence of evil—whether material or spiritual—in God's world. The phenomenon may sadden, but it does not perplex, him. He does not pretend to have a theory of the Universe, beyond the very simple one that all is in God's hands. The believer has a distinct vision of duty, and, for his comfort, he fancies he can see how the very existence of evil has a transmuting power, and gives to the moral and spiritual capacities of the soul a scope, an energy, a development which, without it, would be unknown. Even He who undertook to redeem a lost world was, in the mystery of His Temptation, brought into certain relations with the very essence of sin, in order to capacitate Himself for His high mission, and to endow Himself with that quick sympathy for the infirmities of others which *they* are ever first to feel who, though they have escaped the *taint* of evil, have known and been tried by its *power*.

Perhaps, as Bishop Butler has pointed out, our conception of Almighty God as of a Being of pure benevolence is an incomplete, and therefore an erroneous one. He who has made Himself known as a God of love has also revealed Himself, and on the page of the Gospel too, as "a consuming fire." It is an idle, and indeed not a very innocent employment, to ask why He who made all things good does not more visibly interfere to reconstruct His world after a pattern presumed to be more in accordance with the recognised features of His character. "Perhaps," says Bishop Butler, "there may be some impossibilities in the nature of things which we are unacquainted with. Or less happiness, it may be, would on the whole be produced by such a method of conduct than is by the present. Or perhaps the Divine goodness, with which, if I mistake not, we make very free in our speculations, may not be a bare, single disposition to make the good, the faithful, the honest man happy. Perhaps an infinitely perfect Mind may be pleased with seeing His creatures behave suitably to the nature which He has given them; to the relations which He has placed them in to each other, and to that in which they stand to Himself: that relation to Himself which, during their existence, is even necessary, and which is the most important of all: perhaps, I say, an infinitely perfect Mind may be pleased with this moral piety of moral agents in and for itself, as well upon account of its being essentially conducive to the happiness of His creation. Or, the whole end for which God made -and thus governs the world may be utterly beyond the reach of our faculties: there may be something in it as impossible for us to have any conception of as for a blind man to have a conception of colours."

Whatever be the *hypothesis*, the *fact* of the actual constitution of things remains : and what is more, it is the fact with which we, as moral agents, have to deal; and upon our mode of dealing with which the formation of our present character, as we find by actual experience, and the determination of our future destiny, as we are taught in the page of revelation, principally depend. In that magnificent vision which is unfolded of the King upon His throne, dispensing, in the presence of the innumerable angels, the award proportioned to the work of every man, of "what sort soever it has been," the ground of acceptance or rejection is *the character*, shown by the eye which men have cast upon the various forms of human suffering: whether they have sought out, or endeavoured to avoid, objects of sympathy: whether they have heard, or passed unheeding by, calls for aid: whether or not in the disguise of some poor, shivering, tattered, emaciated fellow-creature they have discovered their Master's form ; whether in the great parable of life they have played the part of the Priest and Levite, who passed by painful cases that they encountered, shrugging their shoulders, regretting them, able, possibly, to draw down tears of sympathy as they told the piteous tale, their own hearts all untouched the while ; or shared *his* nobler spirit who, finding a wounded, half-dead traveller on the road, "went to him, and bound up his wounds, pouring in oil and wine, and set him on his own beast, and brought him to an inn, and took care of him."

Surely, if Christ's words be true, *they* will be nearest to Him, when He sits upon His throne, who have been likest to Him; who have imitated His character and conduct in those points in which, to frail, sinful men, it was most imitable; who, as He, have "gone about doing good," and healing, as far as God had given them the gift, all or any of those who "were oppressed of the devil."

The heathen, who had nothing to console himself withal but the fragments of a shattered faith, which lived on its feeble life, apart from the illuminating influences of a divinely authenticated law, and anterior to the dawning of the Gospel day, looked out upon a world that seemed to him a chaos, with feelings little, if at all, higher than despair. The earth had lost its youth, its freshness, its beauty. The age of iron had come. Nor day nor night was rest from woe. The gods themselves grudged mortal men their brief, rare, intermittent happiness. Degeneracy was the law imposed by fate on all things. As one of their own prophets sang,

"Thus from bad to worse
All things are backward borne, by God's hand doomed."

It is easy to see how such a faith, or rather such a conviction—for there was nothing in it of the hopeful temperament of faith—must have prostrated all human energy; must have made men utterly self-seeking, and living for the hour; must have reduced the list of possible virtues; must have arrested the progress of all improvement by deadening the conscience, chilling the affections, blunting and enervating the sympathies of the soul.

Before the "enthusiasm of humanity," as it has been called, can be raised to any very high energy, you and I must get rid of the depressing influence of the heathen creed, that this earth is lying under God's curse—is unimproveable; and we must believe that the Father of lights, "with whom is no variableness nor even shadow of turning," is working out through us, in our place and degree as His instruments, even as in His place and degree He wrought out by the hands of His Consubstantial Co-eternal Son, "the regeneration of the world."

It is to spiritual, rather than to material, forces that the increase of human purposes and the enlargement of human thought are due. It is the Gospel, penetrating and fashioning what is called "the spirit of the age," that has elevated woman. It was the Gospel that struck the fetters from the slave. It is the Gospel that has mitigated, and is mitigating still, the horrors and barbarities of war—would to God it could make war impossible! It is the Gospel that has replaced the savage instinct of cruelty by the civilised instinct of tenderness. It is the Gospel that created the idea, in its highest sense, of a gentleman. It is the Gospel that proclaimed, without perverting to revolutionary or communistic ends—without even showing any preference of one form of government to another, but with that wonderful breadth of spirit which made it possible to become the religion of mankind—the great principles that should underlie *all* government. It is the Gospel that uttered the great *political* creed of the *equality* of men, and the great *social* creed of the *fraternity* of men. For those whom God hath made of one blood must necessarily be equal, those whom He hath adopted into one family must necessarily be brethren.

I used just now the phrase "the regeneration of the world." I used it advisedly, and in the sense, I believe, in which our Lord Jesus Christ used it, when He spoke to His Apostles of "the regeneration, when the Son of Man shall sit on the throne of His glory," and when they also should sit on thrones at His side. There is a first regeneration and a second, even as we are told there is a first and a second resurrection. Baptised with the spirit of the first, we must labour to realise, and even to hasten, the glories of the last. Every conquest over evil, whether material or spiritual, whether physical, moral, or social, is an advance towards the "day of the restitution of all things"; is what St. Peter calls "a hasting of the coming of the day of God," in which all the elements of evil which mar this present economy of things shall be burnt up by the "fervent heat" of the purifying fire, and a renewed heaven and a renewed earth shall be made, meet for the dwelling place of God when He shall "take up His abode" with men.

Every effort that you make for the alleviation of the

ills and sorrows that encompass humanity in this low state, if made in a Christian temper and with a Christian view—if an offspring of a sense of duty to God rather than of that vague and somewhat ostentatious thing called "philanthropy"—is what St. Paul would probably call a "fellow-working" with God in His grand, "increasing" purpose of saving the world. Christ cared for all the wants of that nature which He assumed into fellowship with His own—for men's bodies as well as for their souls; for those that hungered after perishing meats as for those whose hearts craved for the bread of life; for those who lacked health as for those who lacked instruction. His commission to the Twelve was almost equally emphatic in both directions: "Preach the Gospel; heal the sick. Freely ye have received, freely give."

Do not let us attempt to divide what God has joined together. The physician of the body is as truly, in his vocation, a minister of God, as the physician of the soul. The "gifts of healing" are as distinctly enumerated by St. Paul among the manifestations of the Spirit as the gift "of prophecy," or the "word of wisdom." To no man has God denied the privileges and the prerogative of being a worker together with Him in His Kingdom.

A hospital, in its place and for its purpose, is as truly a consecrated building as a church. It is consecrated, not by a ceremonial act, but by a spiritual—by the very presence of Christ within its walls in His sick, His maimed, His poor. The services rendered unto the least of His brethren He reckons rendered unto Himself. "I was sick, and ye visited me." A hospital is emphatically a Christian institution. It was a thing almost unknown in the old pagan world. The heathen had their temples where, in their ignorant way— though ofttimes doubtless with a devout purpose— they worshipped God; but to provide places where the aches and ailments of men might be cared for, and healed, never entered into their conception of philanthropy.

And, as a Christian institution, a hospital claims the support of Christians on the broadest terms. In these days of narrowness and isolation, it offers a platform on which all "who love the Lord Jesus Christ in sincerity" can meet and practise at least some of their Master's precepts, and copy a portion of His example.

I spoke just now of the physician as "a minister of God." Such a phrase is quite intelligible to any one who remembers the mode in which the dispensation of the Spirit was regarded by St. Peter and St. Paul —to any who recollects, for instance, St. Paul's account of the civil magistrate, "He is the minister of God to thee for good." Of course I am not thinking of the ministration of the Word or Sacraments; I am thinking of him as one on whom God, in the distribution of His gifts, has bestowed that beneficent faculty of healing which the Apostle Paul has placed so high in the list of endowments wherewith God has enriched and illuminated His Church. "God hath set some in the church, first Apostles, secondly prophets, thirdly teachers, after that miracles, *then gifts of healing*, helps, governments, diversities of tongues." " Honour a physician," says the wise author of Ecclesiasticus, "with the honour due to him for the uses which ye may have of him: for of the Most High cometh healing: and He hath created him."

Every one who has ascended a mountain-height knows the charm of what is called a panoramic view, which takes in nestling villages, and verdurous valleys, and silver streams, and sloping uplands, and snow-clad peaks crimsoned, it may be, by the slanting rays of a summer sun. So, too, I at least, am glad to mount the calm heights of religious contemplation, and extend the horizon of a view too often narrowed by the limitations of party, or obscured by the mists of prejudice, and survey, as from a vantage ground, untrammelled and unimpassioned, the grand all-embracing purpose of God in Christ to man. There, for a moment, we can discern the magnificent proportions of a Gospel meant to be commensurate with the uttermost—the lowest as well as the highest—needs of man; not dwarfed down to the puny stature of our imperfect conceptions, nor distorted in the glare of our miserable sectarian animosities.

And as we gaze, the form of Christ, transfigured as on the Mount, stands out clear and palpable as the Healer of the Nations. The work of the Spirit is seen manifesting itself in every high desire, in every noble effort, in every chivalrous deed, that ever kindled the heart or strung the energies, or rescued from baseness the character, of man. And before the glory of the vision fades, and the cloud of our sordid, every-day, trafficking life again overshadows us, a voice, which the quick instincts of our heart recognise as our Father's shall fall on our entranced ears, saying, "This is my beloved Son, and this is the truth to bear witness to which He was born and came into the world."

Preached—Salisbury Cathedral, September 24, 1868. St. Marylebone Church, July 10, 1870. Lincoln Cathedral, November 3, 1870. Manchester Cathedral, February 3, 1873. St. Martin's, Leicester, July 20, 1879. St. Peter's, Cranley Gardens, June 15, 1880.

THE END.

Messrs. MACMILLAN & CO.'S PUBLICATIONS.

UNIFORM WITH THIS VOLUME.
PAROCHIAL AND OTHER SERMONS.

By the Right Rev. JAMES FRASER, D.D., Second Bishop of Manchester. Edited by Rev. JOHN W. DIGGLE, M.A. Crown 8vo, 6s.

JAMES FRASER,
SECOND BISHOP OF MANCHESTER:
A Memoir (1818—1885).

By THOMAS HUGHES, Q.C. With a New Portrait. New and cheaper Edition Crown 8vo, 6s.

The *Athenæum* says:—"Whoever desires to study the character of a brave, earnest God-fearing man who was, in the highest sense of the word, useful in his generation, should read the life of James Fraser as it is told in Judge Hughes's admirable volume."

The *Record* says:—"It is impossible to read this succinct and interesting account of Bishop Fraser's life without rendering a warm tribute to a noble character."

The *Times* says:—"A book which will be widely read. . . . It is a book which reflects very well the admirable character of Bishop Fraser, his simplicity, his earnestness, his interest in all the great movements of contemporary life, his energy, and his sincerity."

The *Saturday Review* says:—"Mr. Thomas Hughes's 'Life of Bishop Fraser' is in some respects exactly what a biography ought to be. Written from abundant knowledge and with a full heart, it sets its subject before us with remarkable clearness and vigour. . . . For the most part however the Bishop tells the story of his own life; for the volume is largely made up of his letters and extracts from his speeches and sermons, selected generally with good judgment and arranged with skill. And Fraser's letters are characteristic of the writer; they are eager, honest, and warm-hearted."

GODLINESS AND MANLINESS.

A Miscellany of Brief Papers touching the Relation of Religion to Life.

By JOHN W. DIGGLE, M.A., Vicar of Mossley Hill, Liverpool; late Lecturer and Postmaster of Merton College, Oxford. Crown 8vo, 6s.

The *Scottish Leader* says:—"Readers . . . . may readily appreciate his reverence of spirit, his thoughtfulness, and the frequent beauty of his style."

The *Liverpool Mercury* says:—"The work is pervaded by a spirit of the broadest catholicity and the tenderest respect for the opinions of others. . . . In style Mr. Diggle's work is eminently distinguished for its perspicuousness and vigour. While entirely and peculiarly an individual style, with all the charm of individuality, it approaches perhaps most nearly to that of Emerson. It is always clear, often elegant. The diction is forceful and choice, and many of its phrases are epigrammatic. . . . From a literary point of view the author is to be congratulated on the excellence of his work. The book is one which will be read with pleasure and interest not only by those whose sympathies are in union with the topics treated of, but by all who have a nice appreciation of cultured, scholarly, and graceful effort."

The *Saturday Review* says:—"Mr. Diggle has struck out a new and really brilliant idea, one so infinitely welcome to readers of sermons, that we fear our cordial recommendation of these printed, practical, and thoughtful little essays will be accepted with some discount. Each is complete in itself, readable, reasonable, and conclusive, a sermonette as unlike as possible to the ghastly skeletons called sermon notes."

The *Guardian* says:—"He speaks obvious truths in excellent language."

The *Record* says:—"The title of Mr. Diggle's book is well chosen; the book answers to it. The papers are godly, they are miscellaneous, and they are brief. There are in the papers many striking observations of a kind to leave a mark upon the reader's mind, and to quicken and to strengthen faith."

The *Rock* says:—"This is a book full of beautiful thoughts, finely conceived, and expressed in a style truly charming."

MACMILLAN & CO., LONDON.

Messrs. MACMILLAN & CO.'S PUBLICATIONS.

By ROUNDELL, EARL OF SELBORNE.
A Defence of the Church of England against Disestablishment. With an Introductory Letter to The Right Hon. W. E. Gladstone, M.P. Third Edition. Crown 8vo, 7s. 6d.

Ancient Facts and Fictions concerning Churches and Tithes. Crown 8vo, 7s. 6d.

Thoughts on Revelation and Life. Being Selections from the Works of CANON WESTCOTT. Arranged and edited by Rev. STEPHEN PHILLIPS, M.A., Reader and Chaplain of Gray's Inn. Crown 8vo, 6s.

WORKS BY CHARLES KINGSLEY.

Village and Town and Country Sermons. Crown 8vo, 6s.
Sermons on National Subjects, and the King of the Earth. Crown 8vo, 6s.
Sermons for the Times. Crown 8vo, 6s.
Good News of God. Crown 8vo, 6s.
The Gospel of the Pentateuch, and David. Crown 8vo, 6s.
The Water of Life, and other Sermons. Crown 8vo, 6s.
Discipline and other Sermons. Crown 8vo, 6s.
Westminster Sermons. Crown 8vo, 6s.
Out of the Deep. Words for the Sorrowful. From the Writings of CHARLES KINGSLEY. Extra fcap. 8vo, 3s. 6d.
Daily Thoughts. Selected from the Writings of CHARLES KINGSLEY. By His Wife. Crown 8vo, 6s.
From Death to Life. Fragments of Teaching to a Village Congregation. With Letters on the "Life After Death." Edited by His Wife. Fcap. 8vo, 2s. 6d.

By GEORGE SALMON, D.D. Regius Professor of Divinity in the University of Dublin.
Non-Miraculous Christianity, and other Sermons. Preached in the Chapel of Trinity College, Dublin. Second Edition. Crown 8vo, 6s.
Gnosticism and Agnosticism, and other Sermons. Crown 8vo, 7s. 6d.

By J. M. WILSON, M.A., Late Fellow of St. John's College, Cambridge, and Head Master of Clifton College.
Sermons Preached in Clifton College Chapel, 1879-1883. Crown 8vo, 6s.
Essays and Addresses. An Attempt to treat some Religious Questions in a Scientific Spirit. Crown 8vo, 4s. 6d.

By the Rev. PHILLIPS BROOKS, Rector of Trinity Church, Boston, Massachusetts.
The Candle of the Lord, and other Sermons. Crown 8vo, 6s.
Sermons Preached in English Churches. Crown 8vo, 6s.
Twenty Sermons. Crown 8vo, 6s.
Tolerance. Two Lectures. Crown 8vo, 2s. 6d.

By the Venerable Archdeacon F. W. FARRAR, D.D., F.R.S., Archdeacon and Canon of Westminster.
The Messages of the Books. Being Discourses and Notes on the Books of the New Testament. 8vo, 14s.
The History of Interpretation. Being the Bampton Lectures, 1885. Demy 8vo, 16s.
The Bible Word-Book. A Glossary of Archaic Words and Phrases in the Authorised Version of the Bible and the Book of Common Prayer. By W. ALDIS WRIGHT, M.A., Fellow and Bursar of Trinity College, Cambridge. Second Edition, revised and enlarged. Crown 8vo, 7s. 6d.

MACMILLAN & CO., LONDON.

www.ingramcontent.com/pod-product-compliance
Lightning Source LLC
Chambersburg PA
CBHW022018240426
43667CB00042B/926